W9-AHA-330

ADVOCATES FOR ANIMALS

ADVOCATES FOR ANIMALS

An Inside Look at Some of the Extraordinary Efforts to End Animal Suffering

Lori B. Girshick
Foreword by Gene Baur

ROWMAN & LITTLEFIELD
Lanham • Boulder • New York • London

Published by Rowman & Littlefield
A wholly owned subsidiary of The Rowman & Littlefield Publishing Group,
Inc.
4501 Forbes Boulevard, Suite 200, Lanham, Maryland 20706
www.rowman.com

Unit A, Whitacre Mews, 26-34 Stannary Street, London SE11 4AB

Photo by Eric Brown, of the author engaged in educational outreach for
Homeless Animal Rescue Team (HART).

British Library Cataloguing in Publication Information Available

Library of Congress Cataloging-in-Publication Data

Names: Girshick, Lori B., author.
Title: Advocates for animals : an inside look at the extraordinary efforts to end animal suffering /
    Lori B. Girshick.
Lanham : Rowman & Littlefield, [2017] | Includes bibliographical references and index.
Identifiers: LCCN 2017002784 (print) | LCCN 2017021194 (ebook) | ISBN 9781442253209 (elec-
    tronic) | ISBN 9781442253193 (cloth : alk. paper)
Subjects: LCSH: Animal welfare—United States. | Animal rights—United States. | Animal rights
    activists—United States.
Classification: LCC HV4764 (ebook) | LCC HV4764 .G52 2017 (print) | DDC 179/.30973—dc23
    LC record available at https://lccn.loc.gov/2017002784

∞ ™ The paper used in this publication meets the minimum requirements of
American National Standard for Information Sciences Permanence of Paper
for Printed Library Materials, ANSI/NISO Z39.48-1992.

Printed in the United States of America

CONTENTS

FOREWORD

Working in the cause of animal protection exposes you to the best and worst of humanity. You come face to face with cruelty and callousness when people torture animals and subject them to gratuitous sadism. You also witness heroic courage and generosity as people risk their own safety and give of themselves to help others. The way we treat animals—or people, for that matter, who are powerless to do anything to help us—says a lot about our character. As Mahatma Gandhi said, you can judge the moral progress of a nation by how its animals are treated.

I am deeply grateful for the many thousands of volunteers and activists who give their time, energy, and resources to make a positive difference for animals, and to make our world a kinder place. I hope you will be moved by the examples in this book, and that you'll be inspired to become more active yourself. There is something everybody can do, both in their individual choices and by joining with others, to confront cruelty and promote compassion.

By recognizing the consequences of our actions and making thoughtful choices, we can each make a difference. Visit a sanctuary instead of a zoo; adopt an animal instead of buying one from a pet store or breeder; share literature and post information about animal issues online; use cruelty-free soaps and cosmetics; and choose to eat plants instead of animals. Small daily acts add up and can bring about big changes over time, so take heart from any positive thing you can do, no matter how small it may seem. It all matters.

Human beings are social animals, and we typically adopt the behaviors and habits of the people around us, which collectively, become cultural norms. It is not uncommon for cultures to normalize and defend attitudes and actions that are unjust or inhumane. When everybody is behaving the same way, we tend to assume that it is normal and appropriate, without thoughtful consideration. Throughout human history, and still today, cultural beliefs and norms have enabled prejudiced attitudes and discriminatory behaviors toward disenfranchised groups of people and animals. It is vitally important, and ultimately liberating, to reflect on systemic injustices and to pay attention to how our actions impact others.

When we treat others unjustly, there is a desire to look the other way, or to rationalize behavior when it conflicts with our humanity and requires that we ignore our empathy. Instead of thoughtfully questioning unfair societal norms, wherein our actions are misaligned with compassionate values and aspirations, it is common to deal with cognitive dissonance by distraction and rationalization. We may tell ourselves that our victims don't deserve better, or that our behavior fits into a natural order, or that it's always been this way. But the fact that certain behaviors and institutions have existed for thousands of years doesn't mean they should continue. If that were the case, slavery would still be legal and women would not be allowed to vote. Today, a growing number of people are beginning to examine and reevaluate our relationships with other animals.

I grew up eating meat, like my parents and everybody around me, without really thinking about it, and I assumed this was normal and healthy. But as I learned about factory farming, and realized it was possible to live well without consuming animal products, I decided to go vegan. I also learned that in some countries people eat cats and dogs, while in other countries they don't eat cows or pigs, which shows that the distinctions between the animals we eat, and those we don't, are arbitrary. All animals want to live and enjoy life, and if we can live well without causing unnecessary harm, why wouldn't we?

In developed countries like the United States, millions of cats, dogs, and other companion animals live in our homes as cherished members of our families. In this sense, we are a nation of animal lovers, and as I write this a Chihuahua named Pepe is sitting on my lap. But, at the same time, we exploit and slaughter billions of chickens, pigs, cows, and other animals for food. They comprise over 95 percent of the domesticated animals in the United States, yet their suffering is hidden from public view, and agribusiness wants to keep it that way. Millions of other animals suffer in laboratory research and for entertainment, and the lives of countless wild animals are threatened by human activity.

The human population is growing and expanding across the globe, disrupting increasingly scarce natural ecosystems and making it impossible for other species to survive. Scientists estimate that Earth is now losing species at a rate of between one hundred and one thousand times faster than normal, and they posit a new geological epoch called the "Anthropocene," which is characterized by human-caused global disturbances, including the loss of biodiversity and climate change.

It is often said that humans are rational animals, but it's more accurate to say we are rationalizing animals. Over the course of human history, we have been adept at rationalizing and justifying inhumane and irresponsible behavior, but the consequences of this approach are greater now than ever. Our technological advances have fueled massive human population growth with unprecedented impacts on our planet. We are killing off other species and threatening our own.

It is no longer acceptable to look the other way or to rationalize cruel and irresponsible behavior. For too long, when the topic of factory farming has come up, for example, people have said, "Don't tell me. I don't what to know. It's too upsetting," or they have asserted it is necessary to eat meat for adequate nutrition. But, when you look at empirical reality, these rationalizations fall apart. The good news is that we can learn, and we can evolve, and we can do better.

Cruelty to animals is bad for animals, and it's also bad for us. Can you imagine what it would be like to work in a slaughterhouse, killing animals, cutting their throats, one after another? I feel bad for both the animals and the people working in these horrific places. Such killing and violence is a blatant assault on our empathy and an affront to our humanity, and it has wide-ranging consequences, individually and collectively. Violence leads to more violence, and cruelty to animals often leads to cruelty to people. But just as cruelty can spread, so too can compassion.

The good news is that compassion feels better than cruelty, and it can become contagious. Our hearts are filled and our lives enriched when we see joy in others—whether a giggling child, a playful puppy, or a frolicking calf. We can create more of these happy experiences, and fewer of those where we want to turn away, by paying more attention to our daily actions and making choices that are aligned with compassionate values. Kindness to animals is good for animals, and it's also good for us.

Animal advocates are among those at the forefront of examining old habits and challenging exploitive patterns of conduct. We work to redefine our relationships with other animals, to prevent unnecessary suffering, and ultimately to create mutually beneficial relationships with our fellow earthlings. Like us, other animals have complex cognitive and emotional lives. They dream and have memories, and they develop lasting bonds and relationships. They grieve and experience a wide range of emotions, from sadness to joy. They are social creatures that learn from, and are affected by, others in their communities. The more we pay attention and understand other animals, the more we see how similar they are to us, and the more we understand how all our lives are inextricably linked.

—Gene Baur
President and Cofounder of Farm Sanctuary

ACKNOWLEDGMENTS

I have enormous gratitude for the participants who agreed to be part of this study. I was inspired by their dedication and their stories, and I learned so much from them. Because of them, I researched many topics I knew little about. Because of them, I learned how to do trap-neuter-return (TNR) and now devote much of my volunteer time to helping feral cats.

I want to thank my friends who checked in with me on the progress of the book and those who encouraged me at every step of the way. Thank you especially to my brother David, and friends Ayla, Karyn, Christi, Eric, Isabella, Juliette, and Patrick. I appreciate your support for my passion for animals, and for letting me talk endlessly about "the book, the book."

I have been influenced and inspired by many national activists, writers, and researchers, and by countless local activists. Over the years I have learned so much from the work of Ingrid Newkirk, Richard Oppenlander, Will Potter, Captain Paul Watson, Ric O'Barry, Henry Spira, Carl Safina, and Gay Bradshaw. I want to especially thank all the undercover investigators who endure and witness heartbreaking cruelty to expose the truth to stop this suffering.

My editor, Kathryn Knigge, contacted me at first about a very different book. When I told her I was no longer working in that area, I expected that was the end of our conversation. Instead, she asked me if there was a book I wanted to write instead. As I thought about this, I realized if I was to dedicate myself to writing another book, it had to be related to animals. I proposed one that allowed readers to hear the voices of those working to help animals and doing their part to end animal suffering. From an email conversation that could have gone nowhere, we arrived at an exciting project honoring animal advocates and exploring the reasons why this work to end suffering needs to be done. Thank you, Kathryn, for guiding me to this project, for answering my many questions, and for supporting me this past year and a half.

Melissa McNitt, my production editor, helped me craft the book to make it a better reading experience. I have enormous appreciation for her attention to detail and her responsiveness to my questions and my frequent tweaks. Thank you, Melissa, for your patience with me!

Special thanks to two colleagues at Chandler-Gilbert Community College, who helped me with the technical aspects of an online survey—Mary McGlasson and Linda Zehr. I am somewhat technically challenged, so this was new territory for me.

Last, but certainly not least, are my furry family members. As cats will do, mine loved lying on piles of paper that served as chapter organizing tools. Whether on the papers on the table, walking back and forth on the keyboard, demanding playtime by constant pawing at my papers, or resting on the desk shelf above my computer monitor, my kitties were ever present. Thanks to Maya, Maggie, Mickey, Nikki, Frida, and Fiona for distracting and centering me, for making me laugh and annoying the heck out of me, and for when you all curled up and napped, living in the present moment and showing complete acceptance. You six mean the world to me!

INTRODUCTION

. . . but there's so much value ascribed to the human story and no value to the animal story. And I think that we lose a lot . . . —Alka

As far as the world is concerned, I believe that there is going to have to be a paradigm shift regarding the earth and all human and nonhuman animals. The first part will be regarding nonhuman animals. They can no longer be considered property, but must be regarded as beings with feelings of pain, fear, comfort. We must let them live out their lives without interference from humans (for humans' convenience). I am speaking of wild animals. Obviously domesticated animals must have some interference from humans, as we have put them in such a position that many cannot fend for themselves nor would some want to. —Molly S.

I started rescuing around the year 2000, after we moved to North Carolina from Pennsylvania. I visited the Harnett County shelter and was shocked and saddened by how many animals were there. At that time there weren't many outsiders trying to help the shelter animals in this rural community. Most of the animals were killed. . . . I wrote letters, contacted the media, wrote letters to the editor, visited the shelter, and posted flyers around the county, put ads in the local newspaper for adoptions, etc., trying to get more attention for animals at the shelter. —Alison

Some people choose to spend their time and resources working to end animal suffering. They may be volunteers, or their paid jobs may be at an organization that assists animals. These people choose to engage with animals for many reasons—they say they love animals; they want to help the helpless; they might be outraged at human cruelty to nonhuman animals; they are concerned about sustainability; or they have any number of other compelling reasons from personal experience. They may see themselves as advocates, activists, protectors, or compassionate human beings. They give their time, money, and a myriad of other resources and skills. They want to both change the suffering of the one individual animal in front of them, as well as alter shelter policy, influence legal protections and rights, and shift the paradigm of thinking that animals are to be used by humans. Advocates for animals are a varied group, and whether working alone or in a national organization, they have undeniably become a powerful force in the efforts to end animal suffering.

Why do people even begin to spend their time on animals, and continue on for years, maybe even devoting their lives to animals? This introduction looks briefly at some of the pertinent societal context issues: popularity of companion animals, moral considerations, cultural attitudes, a sample range of animal exploitation issues found in our daily lives, legal approaches that help but don't solve all animal suffering, and a chapter overview of the book.

AMERICANS LOVE PETS

Americans are a pet-loving culture. According to a report by The Humane Society of the United States (HSUS) on pet ownership, an American Pet Products Association (APPA) survey estimates that in 2015–2016, 79.7 million American households, or 65 percent, had a pet. The study estimated Americans owned 163.6 million pet dogs and cats. Forty-four percent of the households had at least one dog (77.8 million dogs), and 35 percent of the households had at least one cat (85.8 million cats). Forty-two percent of households had more than one pet.[1]

The APPA also studies the domestic pet industry market, looking at spending on food, supplies, vet care, live animal purchases, grooming, and boarding. In 2015, $60.28 billion was spent on pets in the United

States. The estimate for 2016 is $62.75 billion. Most spending was on food and specialty health products, followed by vet care. The industry has witnessed growing spending on pets every year since record-keeping began in 1996.[2]

But we are not only sharing our households with cats and dogs. Birds, horses, fish, reptiles, ferrets, rabbits, hamsters, and other animals are in homes. According to Born Free USA, millions of wild animals, such as reptiles, primates, lions, tigers, wolves, bears, venomous snakes, alligators, and cougars, are in private possession. They report, for example, that between five thousand and seven thousand tigers are kept as pets in the United States, a number that exceeds those in the wild! Exotic birds are the most popular wildlife in homes, with estimates that at least 35 to 40 million birds are kept as pets.[3] The trade in wildlife is the third most profitable illegal trade in the world, and millions of these wild animals are confined in environments totally unsuitable for them in terms of their health, safety, and well-being. Regulations of health and safety for both humans and the wild animals are inconsistent, as laws vary from state to state.

ATTITUDES ABOUT ANIMALS

National polls reveal our attitudes about animals. Faunalytics's Animal Tracker studies provide a yearly look at the attitudes and behavior of U.S. adults toward animals. In year eight, published in April 2015, the organization found that 77 percent of U.S. adults believed protecting animals is very or somewhat important. Only 17 percent felt it was "not very" or "not at all" important to protect animals. The credibility of animal protection groups is also high; only veterinarians ranked higher. Furthermore, in looking at many different social movements (for example, workers' rights, environmentalism, immigration reform, and others) 70 percent gave a "favorable" opinion of animal protection; only workers' rights ranked higher.[4]

In terms of awareness, only one in eight said they heard animal rights or welfare discussed frequently (13 percent) in the past three months. Thirty percent reported discussion of rights or welfare "occasionally," and 32 percent said "rarely," while 25 percent said they did not hear about or discuss animal issues at all. This may relate to why 28 percent of these adults were not sure, or did not know, if laws were adequate for protecting animals. Most respondents thought laws were "adequate" for companion animals, endangered species, wildlife, and animals in zoos/aquariums or shelters. The only animal situations deemed "inadequate" in terms of current laws were horse and dog racing, animals in food production, animals in laboratories, and animals in circuses and zoos.[5]

A Gallup poll released in May 2015 showed that almost a third (32 percent) of Americans want animals to have the same rights as people, "to be free from harm and exploitation." This is an increase from 2008, when 25 percent thought this. Sixty-two percent responded that animals deserve some protection but could be used in certain cases to benefit humans. When looking at specific situations, Americans are very or somewhat concerned about animals in the circus (69 percent), animals in contests or sports (68 percent), and animals in research (67 percent). They are least concerned about pets (only 46 percent were very or somewhat concerned). Though still more than half of respondents, only 54 percent, were very or somewhat concerned about animals in factory farming.[6]

Gallup also released poll findings from May 2016 that showed 41 percent of Americans believe medical testing on animals is morally wrong—an increase from 26 percent in 2001. Sixty percent of Americans "view cloning of animals as morally wrong." Furthermore, 37 percent believe the buying and wearing of clothing made of animal fur is morally wrong.[7] These public opinion polls show a consistent trend of Americans viewing animals with more compassion on a range of issues.

MORAL CONSIDERATION

That the treatment of animals by humans merits moral consideration does not seem to be in debate. While our culture does look at different species of animals differently—such as those we might eat versus those we won't, or those we might hunt versus those who are companions—these are cultural ideas we learn. Pope Francis agrees we create these uses; his 2015 encyclical, *Laudato Si'*, or *Praised Be*, is notable for its frequent discussion of animals, and his assertion that all God's creation has intrinsic value separate from *any* use. The Pope, leader of the world's 1.2 billion Catholics, exhorted Catholics to not mistreat or cause harm to animals. "Dominion" over creation, as addressed in the Bible, did not mean "absolute dominion," but rather protection and care. Their inherent value should never lead to suffering, according to the Pope.

Pope Francis tweeted, "It is contrary to human dignity to cause animals to suffer or die needlessly." In *Laudato Si'*, he called for the recognition that "our indifference towards fellow creatures of this world sooner or later affects the treatment we mete out to other human beings."

Other major spiritual teachings similarly call for the end of animal suffering, and remind us of the responsibility humans have in their humane treatment. According to the organization Jewish Veg:

> Judaism teaches that we are forbidden to be cruel to animals and that we must treat them with compassion. Since animals are part of God's creation, people have special responsibilities to them. These concepts are summarized in the Hebrew phrase *tsa'ar ba'alei chayim*, the biblical mandate not to cause "pain to any living creature." While the Torah clearly indicates that people are to have "dominion over the fish of the sea, and over the fowl of the air, and over every living thing that creeps upon the earth" (Gen. 1:28), there was to be a basic relatedness, and people were to consider the rights of animals. Animals are also God's creatures, possessing sensitivity and the capacity for feeling pain; hence they must be protected and treated with compassion and justice. God made treaties and covenants with animals, just as with humans. [8]

These major religious ideas call for us to live our lives in harmony with animals, in an inter-relatedness that would not include exploitation and suffering.

This book is focused on people who have stepped up to do something about animal suffering. People do interpret their relationships to animals differently; for example, it isn't that the respondents to this study are all vegans (45 percent are vegans; 14 percent are vegetarians; 41 percent eat meat). As Gay Bradshaw (who is interviewed in this book) wrote in *Turning Points in Compassion*, "How we live and whom we eat comprises an individual contract with nature, the universe, and soul."[9] This contract changes over our lifetime and is interpreted differently given individual circumstances.

Two compelling campaigns recently started to challenge the ideas we have about animals. When Cecil, a beloved lion in Hwange National Park in north Zimbabwe, was lured outside park boundaries and murdered by recreational big-game hunter Walter Palmer in 2015, there was international outrage at the loss, the cruelty of Cecil's hunt (extending his death to forty hours), and challenge to the idea of trophy hunting generally. People all over the world questioned if it made sense to kill animals on the verge of extinction, or if hunting on ranches where animals are bred for this purpose was acceptable. One response was to remind people that other animals besides wild animals were equally deserving of consideration. The "I am Cecil" campaign showed photos of farmed animals, such as a pig or a cow, with the caption "I am Cecil," hence, equally meriting compassion and life (#IamCecil). These images circulated on the Internet.[10]

A second campaign challenging our ideas of compassion for all animals is the Go Vegan World campaign, originating in Ireland in 2016. Embarking on a public advertising campaign, the group has placed billboards in Ireland and England to raise awareness that compassion should be at the center of our treatment of all animals. Some examples of the billboards include a photo of a lamb with the caption "She has one precious life. Will your dinner take it?"; a photo of two pigs with the caption "Like us their lives matter to them."; a photo of a mouse with the caption: "They trust us. We betray them."; and a photo of a cow and her baby with the caption "Dairy takes babies from their mothers."[11]

Both of these campaigns exemplify the ideas of the Bible and the Torah, and the compassionate views of people of every religion and no religion. What is clear is that caring about animals is based on values related to suffering and compassion. This is no surprise, given how extensively our lives are intertwined with animals' lives.

ANIMALS IN OUR LIVES

Animals, whether by their actual physical presence or their use by humans, are suffused into daily life. Hardly a day goes by without an interaction or a mention in the news of some animal-related issue. The following demonstrate ways in which we hear about or interact with animals (specific legal issues are in the next section):

- An estimated 40,000 dogs, on average, are used in dogfighting in the United States every year, though the number ranges from a low of 16,000 to a high of 160,000.[12]
- Every year hundreds of dogs die in unattended, hot parked cars.[13]
- A report from the International Fund for Animal Welfare claims 1.7 million wildlife animal trophies have been exported across borders in the last ten years, with at least 200,000 of them endangered species. Hunters from the United States are the largest killers of these animals.[14]
- The sale of leather goods is predicted to hit $91.2 billion globally by 2018.[15]
- Over 70 percent of U.S. grain, and 80 percent of corn, is fed to farm animals.[16]
- It takes 2.5 pounds of grain and 518 gallons of water to produce one pound of chicken meat.[17]
- A salmonella outbreak in 2013, traced back to chickens, made six hundred people sick in twenty-nine states. Thirty-eight percent had to be hospitalized.[18]
- The Wildlife Services department of the U.S. Department of Agriculture killed more than 3.2 million animals (gray wolves, coyotes, black bears, mountain lions, bobcats, river otters, foxes, bald eagles, beavers, and prairie dogs) in 2015.[19]
- More than twenty pounds of bycatch (sharks, rays, starfish, red snapper, sea turtles, and others) are caught and killed for every pound of shrimp consumed.[20]
- It is estimated that more than 115 million animals worldwide are used in laboratory experiments every year. The most common include mice, fish, rats, rabbits, guinea pigs, hamsters, farm animals, birds, cats, dogs, mini-pigs, and nonhuman primates. The number is a dramatic undercount since many animals, such as reptiles, mice, birds, and rats bred for experimentation, are not included in the count.[21]
- An animal is killed in a shelter every 1.5 seconds.[22]
- Approximately 50 million animals are raised on fur farms and killed for their pelts. This number does not include rabbits, but it

is estimated that more than a billion rabbits are killed for their pelts every year.[23]

- Soring, the process used to achieve a horse's high-stepping prance, involves putting a caustic substance on the horse's legs and wrapping them in plastic so that the chemicals cook into the flesh. In 2014, 40 percent of horses in the Tennessee Walking Horse National Celebration were disqualified by the USDA inspectors due to this illegal and unethical practice.[24]

LEGAL AND POLICY CHANGES

There has also been a proliferation of legal actions—court cases, laws passed, individuals charged with crimes against animals, policies implemented by government, and industry practice changes—in the last year alone! Here are a few examples of these actions:

- Ringling Bros. and Barnum & Bailey Circus announced in 2015 that it would phase out all elephant acts by 2018. That timeline was pushed up, and the elephants went into retirement May 1, 2016. Questions remain as to the adequacy of the sanctuary these elephants were moved to.
- On July 1, 2016, a Texas law went into effect that bans the sale of shark fins. Approximately 73 million of the 100 million sharks killed each year for various shark products are killed for their fins.[25]
- A U.S. District Court ruled in August 2015 that Idaho's ag-gag law is unconstitutional, and violates the First and Fourteenth Amendments. The law was passed to prevent undercover investigations into factory farms to expose their cruel practices and show the public how the food industry actually operates. The Animal Legal Defense Fund is challenging a similar law in Utah on the same grounds.
- In June 2016, the U.S. Fish and Wildlife Service classified captive chimpanzees as Endangered (wild chimps already are so designated). This means the seven hundred chimps in research labs will no longer be experimented on and will be moved to sanctuaries, as one implication of the classification change.

- In March 2016, SeaWorld announced it would stop breeding captive orcas.
- The Toxic Substances Control Act passed Congress in May 2016, and has the potential to stop, or severely curtail, testing on animals.
- Perdue Farms announced in June 2016 that it will install windows in two hundred of six thousand existing poultry houses, and add straw bales, perches, and a little more space between birds. Perdue slaughtered 676 million chickens in 2015. We can only wait to see if these reforms will make a significant difference in the conditions chickens are subjected to, but they do seem to promise access to at least some normal chicken activity.[26]

As we can see, many decisions about animals are made at the national (or international) level, some impacting our environment, some related to industry practices, some related to state legislation. Other aspects impact us in our daily lives but are behind the scenes, such as the production of the food we eat, the backstage treatment of animals in entertainment we might engage in, or access to information that we might base our behaviors on. It is, without doubt, complex. Part of what makes animal use and abuse possible is not only what is hidden from us, but also what we culturally have learned to ignore.

CULTURAL FRAMING

In her 2011 book, *Why We Love Dogs, Eat Pigs, and Wear Cows*, psychologist Melanie Joy discusses the cultural attitudes about animals that form around mental classifications called schemas. These schemas involve whether an animal is seen as "prey, predator, pest, pet, or food. How we classify an animal, in turn, determines how we relate to it— whether we hunt it, flee from it, exterminate it, love it, or eat it."[27] The cultural belief system that conditions us to eat certain animals but not others she calls carnism. Further, Joy discusses that while it is true most people don't want animals to suffer, by virtue of eating some animals and using animals in entertainment, in clothing, and so forth—all of which cause suffering—we use psychic numbing to disconnect from the processes that allow us to engage in these practices. To continue eating meat, for example, we cannot be consciously aware that the "meat" was once a live, breathing, sentient creature with feelings and a family. Carnism is that system that allows us to disconnect, and which is supported by cultural values and norms.

Another relevant example of cultural framing was seen in Al Gore's analysis of global warming in *An Inconvenient Truth*. With the focus on fossil fuels as the leading culprit of global warming, citizens could change behaviors such as lightbulb choice, car efficiency, or electricity use. We could, without moral angst, focus on carbon dioxide emissions. What he did not include in his analysis is the role of animal agriculture in methane production, which contributes even more to global warming than carbon dioxide. Such an analysis would challenge our meat-eating behaviors (and along with it, factory farms and treatment of animals for human use), a much harder sell to the public.

The film *Cowspiracy* also showed the lack of naming animal agriculture (or the food industry) as a primary cause of climate change. The main reason: To not offend donors to leading national environmental organizations. The very organizations we trust to protect us from point-of-no-return climate harm are ignoring the major shift we need to make in the culture and the world. Animals and our relationship to them, including our use and abuse of them, must be front and center. Eating animals is the most exploitive use of animals, creating the most suffering. According to the United Nations, we raise, kill, and eat over 70 billion animals each year for food,[28] but the impacts of this food system—land used, rain forests destroyed, water depleted, diversion of food from people to animals to produce less protein outcome, and the like—these impacts are invisible to the average consumer.

CHAPTER OVERVIEW

According to Mary Brewster and Cassandra Reyes, in their book *Animal Cruelty: A Multidisciplinary Approach to Understanding*, animal advocates and activists are the most likely group "that influences public perceptions of the issue of animal cruelty, and with that, effects cultural and legislative change."[29] We will examine these extraordinary efforts in the following chapters. Each chapter discusses aspects of the study participants, their experiences and insights, followed by one issue highlight that relates to animals in our lives and the suffering that needs to be addressed. If the suffering was not compelling, people would not be trying to end it. It is my hope that readers will be more informed about the lives of animals, and will be motivated to become involved to help animals, joining those who already do.

Chapter 1 focuses on the demographics of the study participants, such as sex, age, income, education, and so forth. Two hundred and four people participated in an online survey, and over 70 percent agreed to a follow-up interview. The issue highlight in this chapter is feral cats and TNR (trap-neuter-return). We'll focus on the many issues surrounding outdoor cats, feral kittens, successful and unsuccessful programs dealing with ferals, and study participants' experiences with TNR.

Chapter 2 discusses the path to the volunteer work or job of the study participants. Why did they start to work for animals? What influenced them? Considerations include family influences, love for animals, impact of a pet, and more. The issue highlight is on factory farming (chickens, turkeys, pigs, and cows), ag-gag laws, and farmed animal sanctuaries.

Chapter 3 looks at what advocates actually do, what they call what they do, and how they see themselves in these efforts. The chapter covers their support networks, or lack of support. The issue highlights are pet overpopulation; breeders and puppy mills; spay/neuter efforts, benefits, and myths; and the No-Kill shelter movement.

Chapter 4 examines the top animal-related issues as identified by the study participants. We find that people not only care about a wide range of animal concerns, but they find different issues most compelling. This is followed by a focus on rescue organizations (cat, dog, and rabbit rescues and adoptions) and wildlife issues—trophy hunting, trapping, wildlife as pets, captivity in zoos and marine parks, and wildlife sanctuaries.

Chapter 5 discusses how study participants look at ending animal suffering in relation to other social justice issues, and where they find similarities between issues. This chapter highlights animal cruelty and covers a range of cruelties, such as Bureau of Land Management wild horse roundups, USDA Wildlife Services hunts, animal fighting, soring, circus animals, roadside zoos, horse-drawn carriages, puppy mills, hoarding, and cat declawing. I start the issue highlight by discussing Justice for Tiger.

Chapter 6 explores the personal impacts of volunteering or working to end animal suffering. I'll discuss the impact on study participants' lives: their careers and skills; meaning, purpose, and community; diet choices; and consumer patterns. The issue focus here is veganism. Levels of meat consumption, numbers of vegans and vegetarians, marketing appeals, the humane meat myth, growing availability of plant-based foods, and other issues are discussed.

Chapter 7 brings to light what participants are hoping to accomplish with their actions, and their ideas about how these goals can be met. These goals cover ending speciesism, education, ending suffering, overall compassion, shelter reform, and more. The issue focus is on animals and the environment, covering water and oceans, land and rain forests, pollution, waste, and greenhouse gases.

Concluding Comments reflect on these extraordinary efforts, and invite you to become part of these acts of compassion. The book is a journey into a range of animal concerns and many of the actions that can do something positive about them.

I

WHO WE ARE

I was pondering why I take care of my feral friends. It's something about making up for the poor treatment that they have received thus far by humans; for the unfair hand they have been dealt. I want to protect and show them the love they deserve. . . . They deserve love and care, and I'm going to give it to them. —Anni

We see a direct correlation of animal work within the community as it is linked to law enforcement and social work. As we rescue animals and do TNR, we connect with the public on many other social issues from hoarding to poverty to animal cruelty. —Eric

I realize after talking to people that there's always going to be cats at the shopping center as long as there's restaurants and as long as people feed them. It's just this transition period of having lived there for so long and then having nowhere to live, and they're building back up again. I think it will be OK, and I think there will be cats there again. . . . But I just have this feeling inside that developers are very greedy people; people are greedy and always want more. They always want more, they don't have enough gas stations, not enough stores, restaurants, not enough, not enough. When is enough enough? When do we realize? We're having black bear hunting now because a few bears came into neighborhoods, people were feeding them, some people were attacked, so now we're having bear hunting in October. And I want to put signs in people's homes, from the bear: "This used to be my home." —Judy McG

Who are these people who responded to my call for participation in a national survey about advocates for animals? Obviously they care about animals. But, what else about them? The following profile data is only about the 204 individuals who responded and filled out the online survey. Seventy-three percent then participated in a survey follow-up. Of those, 55 percent did the follow-up by email, 22 percent had a conversation with me over Skype, 14 percent met with me in person, and 9 percent spoke with me on the phone. The verbal interviews were recorded and transcribed by me.

Honestly, I wish I could have spoken to every individual in the study. Our conversations were fun, informative, high-spirited, and passionate. I learned what people cared about and how their activities impacted their lives. I validated the work they were doing and felt inspired in my own work. As mentioned in the Acknowledgments, I was so moved by the passion and commitment of people doing trap-neuter-return (TNR) and feeding feral cat colonies that I became involved in this work myself. I did not fully understand the issues of outdoor cats before these interviews and before researching ferals online, and a whole world was opened up to me.

This was not a random survey of all people involved in animal work, but a reflection of individuals who heard of the study from friends or at their workplace, or saw a posting on social media or organization websites. I contacted many national organizations that forwarded information to staff and volunteers. These organizations included: The Humane Society of the United States (HSUS), Compassion Over Killing, Vegetarian Resource Group, Animal Legal Defense Fund, American Anti-Vivisection Society, Farm Sanctuary, People for the Ethical Treatment of Animals (PETA), Greenpeace, Direct Action Everywhere, Doris Day Animal Foundation, Our Hen House, Vegan Outreach, Sea Shepherd Conservation Society, In Defense of Animals, Mercy for Animals, and The Bunny Alliance.

More of these 204 individuals live in the Southwest (71) than in any other region. That is a function of my living in Arizona, my personal contacts in area organizations, my networking in the Phoenix area, and sending emails directly to rescue organizations in Arizona. Forty respondents live in the Southeast, and twenty in the Northeast. Twenty-nine come from the West, one from Hawaii, and twelve live in the Midwest. Nineteen did not indicate which state they live in. Twelve people live outside the United States, in Canada (six), England (two), the Philippines (one), Israel (one), Ireland (one), and Scotland (one). This surely shows the power of the Internet, since I did not do any targeted outreach outside of the United States. That respondents are scattered across the country is no surprise since animals are everywhere, and the needs of animals have to be addressed everywhere.

A whopping 87 percent of respondents are female and 13 percent male. Anecdotally, we know there are many more women who step up to volunteer for animals than men, but there are no national statistics to support this. We also do not know if men are more likely to do certain kinds of tasks for animals than women are. But we are confident that most volunteers in organizations addressing needs of animals are women.

The majority of participants are in the thirty-to-fifty-nine age range (139 people, or 68 percent). The next largest category is people sixty or older (45 people, or 22 percent). This might reflect the time people have in their retirement to dedicate to animals, or that many people choose to continue volunteering into their older years. There were three people under age eighteen, and only fifteen between ages nineteen and twenty-nine. Attending college or demands of early career development might influence this small number. Two individuals declined to state their age.

This is a highly educated group of people. If you count some college (thirty-four), college graduate (sixty-seven), trade or technical school (four), associate degrees (seven), master's-level degrees (forty-five), PhDs (fifteen), some graduate school (five), and JDs (two), 88 percent of the respondents are accounted for. Eighteen were high school graduates, two had GEDs, two did not complete high school, and three were still attending high school.

Given the very high education levels, we found household income very evenly spread through the income categories. This might be partly due to the lower-paying staff salaries of people working in nonprofit animal-related organizations, or the fact that in retirement, people's earnings generally drop. This could also reflect the lower incomes women still receive in professional careers. Household income revealed: less than or equal to $24,999 (18 percent); $25,000 to $49,999 (22 percent); $50,000 to $74,999 (22 percent); $75,000 to $124,999 (25 percent); $125,000 or more (13 percent); and two gave no answer.

Ninety-three percent of respondents had one or more companion animals at home. While this number may not be a surprise, the range of animals is extraordinary. The most common pets are cats (127 people). This was closely followed by 121 people sharing their homes with dogs. The next most common animals at home were fish (13), rabbits (10), chickens (10), birds (9), and goats (8). Other animals found in these homes included gerbils, guinea pigs, lizards, snakes, pigs, ducks, turkeys, peacocks, rats, mice, turtles, tortoise, hermit crabs, frogs, sheep, a cow, guinea fowl, horses, and feral cats fed outside the home.

In looking at how many years people have been involved in animal work at the time of filling out the survey, the majority have been at this for over five years. Thirty-two percent were just starting out, involved for five years or less (only fourteen people were advocates for a year or less; fifty-two have been working or volunteering between two and five years).

One hundred and thirty-two individuals (65 percent) showed enormous commitment. Forty-four people had been involved in animal work for six to ten years; forty-five people had significant time in, between eleven and twenty years; and for forty-three people, animal work is their life passion, having been involved twenty-one years or more. There were six respondents where this data is missing. We can see this time commitment further reflected in the fact that thirty-five people (17 percent) founded or cofounded a rescue, sanctuary, or animal-related business or organization.

The typical study respondent is a female, over thirty, who graduated college, with household income over $50,000. She has multiple companion animals at home, and she has been working or volunteering with animals for over ten years.

Study participants were asked if I could refer to them by their first names, and most agreed to this. In cases of similar names, a last initial is used. A few high-profile people also agreed to the use of their last names. A few individuals chose their own pseudonyms, and any name that begins with "F" is an assigned pseudonym by me.

ISSUE FOCUS: FERAL CATS AND TNR

Cats are considered feral when they are not socialized to human inter-action; usually people cannot get very close to them, and petting these untamed cats is rare indeed. Generally, they will never become lap cats or be happy indoors. Stray cats, on the other hand, have been socialized to people and have lived in a home as a pet. These cats may have lost their homes by being dumped by their owners, or perhaps they were outside and got lost. While they can become quite fearful of humans over time spent outside, for strays there is the possibility of them once again becoming house cats.

There isn't complete consensus about the health of outdoor living for cats. Clearly there are the dangers of larger predators (including cruel humans), vehicles, and untreated medical problems. However, research on over one hundred thousand stray and feral cats in spay/neuter clinics in six states shows that "less than 1 percent of those cats needed to be euthanized due to debilitating conditions, trauma, or infectious diseases."[1] Also cited in this report, a 2008 study found that only 4.3 percent of rabies cases were found in cat pets and ferals.[2] Even when looking at feline leukemia (FeLV) and feline immunodeficiency virus (FIV) in ferals and outdoor pet cats, low rates of these diseases were found.[3]

Ferals and strays live outdoors. While their overall health does not differ significantly from indoor pets, there is another major problem—they are not being spayed and neutered. While estimates vary widely about the number of feral cats (sometimes referred to as community cats), the usual range is thirty to forty *million* in the United States. Studies have shown that only about 2 percent of ferals are spayed or neutered. It is sobering to realize that 80 percent of kittens born each year are from outdoor feral cats.[4]

This fact shows, without any doubt, how important it is to spay and neuter ferals if we want to address cat overpopulation. The primary way to successfully accomplish this is to trap the cats. This is referred to as trap-neuter-return, or TNR. When the cats are spayed/neutered at the clinic, their left ear is cut at the tip (called "ear tipping") while they are still under anesthesia so that the same cat won't be trapped again. Julie tells us of her experience:

*I moved into a condo in Phoenix, which had a large stray dog and cat
population; dogs running free, new kittens in the sewer/alley/trash-
can/my backyard. I tried to talk with neighbors about fixing/tagging/
containing the dogs, and researching what to do about the cats. We
ended up socializing, trapping, fixing, and adopting a cat, my boyfriend adopted three, and neighbors adopted two from that place. I
then moved to North Phoenix—and I still have no idea where these
cats came from, but feral cats began appearing. I went to a TNR class
through Arizona Humane Society, and connected with a neighbor
who fostered kittens for the HSUS, and she was instrumental in getting several kittens from the colony accepted to the humane society.
We TNRed the rest and now manage a colony of approximately thirteen to fifteen ferals. For two years now, we have had no kittens!*

Another interesting fact is that 10 to 12 percent of the population
feeds feral cats.[5] Most feeding is done by people independent of affilia-
tion with any organization. Bernice, living outside of Boston, tells us
how she got involved with ferals and the success she had:

*I have always loved animals, but it wasn't until I moved into my
present apartment (about thirty years ago) that I became actively
involved with feeding and trapping feral cats. One morning I noticed
cats jumping over a fence and into our dumpster looking for food. I
started putting food along the fence very early in the morning. (The
cats were gone before most tenants were up.) A few weeks later I
received a notice from the management to stop feeding the cats, or I
would be evicted. Having no intention of abandoning them, I began
to look for a new feeding place off our property.*

*The owner of a construction company on the other side of the
fence told me the cats were living there among the truck equipment,
etc. He was sympathetic to my situation, offering me a safe area to
feed the cats.*

*The cats thrived and multiplied. I called Animal Control for ad-
vice. She told me about local organizations, and a wonderful vet that
helps trap, spay/neuter, foster, and shelter feral cats. I bought my
own trap and soon inherited another colony of a nearby complex (the
person who was feeding them moved). Throughout several years and
with the help of these wonderful organizations, the two colonies were
pretty much cleared. I am currently feeding two cats that haven't yet
been trapped.*

Bernice ran into hostility from the apartment complex management, and this does happen. However, public opinion differs significantly from management opinion. In a 2007 study commissioned by Alley Cat Allies with Harris Interactive, 81 percent of respondents said that it is better to leave a cat outside than to trap and kill it.[6] When respondents were asked if an outdoor cat that only had two years to live should be euthanized or left alone, 72 percent said leave the cat where it is.[7]

Outdoor Kittens

Many other individuals in this study took leadership in responding to the needs of feral cats and their kittens. If discovered young enough (by twelve weeks, or possibly as late as sixteen weeks), being born outdoors can be overcome in terms of cat socialization. Socializing these feral kittens requires intensive attention. The kittens need to feel safe, so placement in a crate, preferably off the floor so they can see around the space, and speaking to them in soft tones without loud music or television, really helps lower stress. They need to be handled and held by people to get them used to interaction with humans. Alley Cat Allies even suggests, "For very young kittens, a soothing technique is to wrap a ticking clock in a towel—it reminds them of their momma's heartbeat."[8]

If kittens are found while they are nursing and the momma cat cannot be found, kittens will need to be bottle-fed. Food is another incentive for kittens to make positive associations with people. Kittens three to four weeks old are ready to play with toys, and this will help them become more comfortable with being indoors with people. Once kittens are comfortable sleeping in a lap, or purr with people, they are ready for introductions to other people, dogs, and other household cats.[9] Most TNR programs, and individuals who trap, will turn over the socialized trapped kittens to rescue organizations for adoptions into the community, and the transition from feral kitten to indoor pet can be made. Others are finding homes for these kittens on their own.

Jodie does TNR as part of the Marion County, Oregon, trapping program. When a mom has kittens, you don't want to take the kittens away too soon, if they can stay together. Also, in one case, Jodie said:

I am feeding in traps currently, but am waiting for the momma cat to bring out her kittens to the feeding station before I try to trap her. We have had two FeLV-positive cats show up in my colonies, so I am careful. I want the kittens to be feeding on their own before I trap mom, in case she is positive. I have had a few new cats show up in my colony in the last couple weeks, and if I can figure out which station they are eating at, I will trap them as well.

The level of commitment to the well-being of these feral cats is astounding. Nina and her husband are doing TNR in their neighborhood "on our own dime and time," along with tabling, fostering, petition-signing, fund-raising, and rescue work. JoAnn R. volunteers with Animal Guardian Network, and feeds a feral colony on her own. She is feeding one hundred to 150 feral cats, many spayed or neutered by another neighbor. She writes:

Two neighbors and I started taking care of the homeless kittens in our neighborhood about three years ago. The first year I provided food only. The next year I got involved in feeding the kitties as well as providing food. This past year I took over much of the feeding and provided all of the food, as my two neighbors lost a good portion of their income. The last six months I am the only one left—one neighbor moved out of state and the other is currently out of state until September. Most of the kitties know my car and come out to hurry me along to get the food in their bowls.

Helen G. and her husband, Tom, have been active in TNR and rehoming kittens for seven years on their own. They have helped over 150 kittens through their efforts. Helen G. writes that after they trap the cats and kittens, "we have them fixed and shots given, treat them if ill, then if not tamable return them to their living areas. If tamable or if kittens, we take them in using tri-level cages, tame them, and get them used to other cats and dogs, then find good homes for them where they will be indoor only."

In another example, Homeless Animal Rescue Team (HART) does extensive trapping and networking in the East Valley of Phoenix, Arizona. Eric, a cofounder with his wife, Jacey, told me:

We started animal rescue in response to becoming involved in TNR in an industrial area. After successfully sterilizing a colony and estab-

lishing a feeding station, we rescued a set of kittens. This awakened us to the need of TNR in our area, and we decided to become involved. The involvement grew and blossomed into wanting to network with as many people as possible in order to TNR as many cats as we could, and save as many kittens and tame, free-roaming cats as possible. Our desire to make a difference culminated with us incorporating our new hobby into a legitimate charity and 501(c)(3). . . . In addition to our TNR efforts, we currently feed eight feral colonies nightly (approximately one hundred cats, all sterilized); we foster cats and kittens (up to fifteen at a time); and we do our own fundraising and media outreaches.

Sandy B. stands as a powerful example of what one person can do. She organized a TNR program in her neighborhood that her homeowners' association (HOA) supports. To gain this support she had to attend meetings and educate community members on the statistics about cat reproduction. One pair of cats can end up producing hundreds of cats over a period of years if they and their litters are not spayed and neutered. It got people's attention when they realized how out of control the problem could become.

Sandy B. established a partnership with a local rescue group, Desert Paws, which takes virtually all the kittens the TNR group traps for adoption. The neighborhood TNR group also raises money for Desert Paws, and fosters for them. They started in 2014 and trapped thirty-four cats and had them spayed or neutered. Eighty percent of the cats have been adopted; many of them were kittens. The HOA pays for the spaying and neutering. Sandy B. feels it would be great if other HOAs and organizations could follow their model since it has been so effective. There are five or six feeding stations throughout the community, with small numbers of cats at each, plus some people feed on their back patios. But the outcome has been fewer cats (now spayed and neutered) living outdoors, cats living safely in homes, and a potential nuisance problem avoided. Once male cats are neutered, they rarely spray urine, roam less, and fight less. Diseases that could be spread through mating are reduced.

Unsuccessful Alternatives to TNR

For many decades, trap-and-kill policies were common for outdoor cat populations. However, not only is this highly questionable in terms of the ethics of killing otherwise healthy animals, it is also expensive. According to the Foundation for Homeless Cats website, The Humane Society of the United States estimates that municipal shelters are killing over four hundred cats per hour at a cost of $2 billion per year.[10]

Furthermore, and extremely important, killing outdoor cats is not a solution to the homeless cat population. Due to the "vacuum effect," when an area of feral cats empties, other cats move in to join those who avoided trapping. Cats are attracted to areas where there is shelter and food, and they may reoccupy areas. Males are attracted to unspayed females, and female cats tend to have larger litters in colonies under stress (hence populating the colonies just emptied out).

The trap-and-relocation approach to the feral population is expensive, and usually not successful. Often the "relocation" is to a shelter for euthanasia. Virtually 100 percent of feral cats brought to a shelter will be killed because they are considered unadoptable.[11] Some shelters won't accept feral cats for euthanasia at all, or they charge more for euthanasia than spay/neuter.

These killings are usually unpopular with the public since they want shelters to save animal lives, not destroy them.[12] Furthermore, those cats that are released usually find their way back to the area where they had been living, as they bond to where they had been originally dumped or were born. Large-scale relocation attempts also don't address the fundamental problem—spaying and neutering to prevent cat births. Judy McG shared the experience of relocating ferals in a "barn cat program" in Florida:

> We put two cats in a really nice thoroughbred stable. However, they were kept in a tack room and there were no windows, so the cats couldn't see out. Even though it was a very nice place, and they kept them in there two or three weeks, and fed them in there, the minute they let the cats out, they were gone. They couldn't see outside, they couldn't acclimate to their surroundings, so you have to be really picky about where they go.

Michelle L., who is affiliated with the Spay/Neuter Hotline, a program of the Animal Defense League of Arizona (ADLA), was involved in a rare successful relocation at her house when a woman had to relocate her five feral cats:

> It was a big project, because for two months [the cats] were in cages on my property. We had to, twice a day, go into the cages, clean their litter boxes, feed and water them. It was a lot of work. We did release them and they've stuck around, we've been fortunate with that. . . . They don't let me pet them, and they're not terrified of me, but they don't come up to me. They are around me but I've never touched them.

A legal consideration for removal is that some locales have passed laws making removal illegal. In Arizona, for example, relocation is considered animal abandonment. Arizona law states that cats are free roaming. These free-roaming cats are not a local animal control responsibility, but a "property management issue." Back in 2002, Maricopa County and its Board of Commissioners passed a resolution that declared TNR as the official means to address feral (or free-roaming) cats in Maricopa County, Arizona. [13]

Another unsuccessful approach has been feeding bans. Enforcement of these bans is difficult, and most people who feed continue to do so because they feel compassion for the cats. Cats may move closer to homes or restaurants, but not totally leave an area. According to a HSUS report, this only results in "more nuisance complaint calls, greater public concern for the cats' welfare, and underground feeding by residents." [14] They may be more of a nuisance, but they rarely will leave. Bans just don't work, and they don't prevent unwanted kittens. Another related consideration is that you need to feed in order to trap and spay/neuter. Once cats are used to being fed in a certain area, it is easier to use food to lure them into a trap. Bans make trapping harder, if not impossible.

TNR Success

The trend today, based on public support, financial considerations, and successfully addressing the problem at the root, is TNR. Success has been substantiated by the amount of local and state legislative support, national and local organizational program support, the commitment of individual volunteers, and, most tellingly, cats *not* reproducing because they have been spayed or neutered. Volunteers not only trap, transport cats to spay/neuter clinics, and provide aftercare, but also establish feeding stations where they leave food and water daily for the altered cat colonies.

While TNR is becoming more and more popular as established protocol, that does not mean it is accepted by all property managers or neighbors. People are constantly negotiating where they can feed, and usually the cost of feeding falls on individuals and not organizations. For example, Michelle L. in Arizona shares:

> You end up with a feral colony, you end up getting them fixed, and you end up feeding them for the rest of their lives because what are you going to do? . . . Right now I supply food for one lady who is in Tempe, and I share the feeding schedule with another one in Chandler. And that Chandler one I've been doing for fifteen years . . . Think about it. They're here all year round. Every strip mall; everything that has a restaurant; you see them at gas stations. I see them everywhere now that I'm aware of it.

But Michelle L.'s efforts aren't without risk:

> I've had feral cats poisoned I don't know how many times. I've been accosted I don't know how many times feeding feral cats. . . . One place they were super nice and wanted to help me, and the other: "Get out of here! We don't want the feral cats, they bug us, they're in our yard, they're hurting small children." . . . I don't know why these people can't get it. Just because I volunteer with this organization doesn't mean I get [services] for free. I pay the normal price . . . . One time, I TNRed thirty-one cats in this neighborhood—spent countless weekends doing this—just to be accosted by people in the neighborhood. "I fixed them, you're not going to have any more kittens. What's your problem? I didn't bring them here."

Judy McG lives in a Florida community where catch-and-kill is the primary method of dealing with feral cats. In the early 2000s, she started to TNR and feed sixty to seventy cats that were living around an old shopping center and in the woods behind it. Judy McG told me they were living in "sewers, drainage pipes, empty buildings, bushes, anywhere they could find shelter." The shopping center was due to be demolished, and work started in 2014.

> *The construction supervisor was not nice and told me that they would be tearing down the woods and more or less said, "Too bad," when I explained that this was the only home these cats had known. We had put several cold-weather shelters in the area because there were some very cold days here, and when we asked if we could remove them because they had roped off the area, we were told "No," and they destroyed or threw them away. Also there were reports of workers being nasty to the cats and the supervisor himself throwing rocks at them.*

Judy McG considered writing the company that employed these workmen, but instead looked up the developer in Atlanta. She emailed him this letter:

> *I wish I could touch your heart in hope that you will understand and help the cats and kittens of the P— H— Shopping Center.*
>
> *For years, people have dumped domestic house cats behind the shopping center and in the wooded areas around it. Albeit harsh, this is now home for these beautiful, affectionate, terrified, and distressed pets that are unprepared to live in the wild.*
>
> *Demolition has begun on the site and I am terribly afraid these discarded pets will get crushed as heavy equipment moves in and buildings collapse. The cats have no other refuge and no place to flee. Now that the property is fenced off, those of us who bring them food and water can only watch from afar with desperation and broken hearts.*
>
> *As temperatures plummeted, I recently put out six bins near a storefront where kittens and a mother cat live with the hope of keeping them warm if they can escape through the fence. Their building is due to be demolished very soon.*
>
> *Many kind people who have shopped at the center and seen the plight of the cats could not, in good conscience, turn their backs on them. They have helped these animals over the years by providing the food and shelter with the hope of eventually trapping them, having them cared for by a vet, and finding a new home with a family for them. Not unlike the other caretakers, I have saved thirty-four of these animals over the years . . . But it is never enough.*

I am ashamed to say that our local Humane Society has done nothing to save the cats or aid in the situation. Conversely, they have been known to sweep through the area at the request of local officials to exterminate the cats. Any that are captured are euthanized.

I know that you (and your contractors) are not intentionally trying to harm any animals. I am appealing to your compassion in this regard. Would it be possible [to] set up a food and water station for shelter in a designated area away from your site, so that we could perhaps lure the cats away?

Without public awareness and the opportunity for all of us to intervene at what could be a turning point, this problem will continue well beyond the commissioning of your new shopping center. Please allow me and the other community volunteers who care for these cats to work with you in a positive and productive way to alter this outcome.

With your leadership and support we can exemplify Gandhi's quote, "The greatness of a nation can be judged by the way its animals are treated."

In response, this man sent the advocates a check for $1,000 for TNR in a nearby location. Judy McG and others were able to trap and rehome many of the cats. The new shopping center was built. Twenty cats still live scattered in the area, people are still feeding them, and attempts to trap and spay/neuter continue.

Community Networking

An example of another level of community organizing is The Foundation for Homeless Cats, a 501(c)(3) founded by Carla Jewell in 2008. Carla was already doing TNR on her own, and helping elderly people with cats. There was no feral group coordination, and Carla decided to fill this gap. On the website, the organization's mission statement reads:

> The goal of The Foundation for Homeless Cats is to educate community leaders and residents of Maricopa County, Arizona, on implementing an economically feasible method for humanely reducing the population of stray and free-roaming cats, thus easing neighborhood tensions, fostering compassion, and to see abuse diminished and laws enforced. [15]

The Foundation for Homeless Cats also sponsors the meet-up group Phoenix Feral Friends (PFF). PFF has over four hundred colony cat caregivers and trapping members through the greater Phoenix area. The members share resources and information, assist with trapping, help coordinate filling in at feeding stations when someone goes on vacation, and give advice on cat issues such as injuries or illness. This provides an invaluable networking resource for those working with feral cats.

Carla feeds fourteen cat colonies, with permission at all sites, including at two fast-food restaurants and in industrial areas. Back in 2003, when Carla started feeding, she hid her activities, but now the approach is to feed only with permission of business owners and landowners. Carla also works with the Maricopa County Animal Care & Control to release ferals that have been turned over to the shelter back to their home areas. Otherwise, these cats would surely be killed.

Greater education about feral cats has helped change public opinion to favor TNR and enabled people to see outdoor cats as nonthreatening. Previous efforts to "eliminate" these cats have proven unsuccessful, and we now have a better handle on why that is. Furthermore, people are realizing that ferals are no more sick or diseased than cats in homes.

Information, along with the valiant efforts of dedicated volunteers across the country, has resulted in greater compassion toward ferals, who will always be with us. Information has also enhanced public health and safety. Greater cat well-being is possible with TNR. The work continues, since the vast majority of outdoor cats are still not spayed or neutered. This must be attempted, since TNR *is* the key to cat overpopulation. Remember, there are an estimated thirty to forty million feral cats, and only 2 percent are spayed or neutered. We need more people to step up and involve themselves in TNR.

Chapter 2 explores the paths people took to get involved in work on behalf of animals. The issue focus is on factory farming, and we'll also look at several of the sanctuaries that study respondents started or volunteer at.

2

PATHS TO ACTION

A very special dog came into my life. She became a therapy dog, and working with her opened my eyes to the healing power of animals. When she passed away, I knew I had to "pay forward" what she taught me. I began by going back to college (in my forties) to become a veterinary technician. In clinic at college we cared for beagles released from a medical research breeding facility. We examined, vaccinated, neutered, trained, and then worked to get them adopted. At the end of the session, a few had still not found homes. I volunteered to foster two of them. Once adopted, I decided fostering was great, and searched for some shelter or group to foster for. In my search I came across info about puppy mills, joined a specific mill dog rescue, eventually got on the board of directors, started a group with friends focusing on mills in Pennsylvania (Amish), then started my own rescue in New England, expanding from mill dogs to all special-needs dogs. I worked as a dog day-care tech, which led to study of dog speak (understanding the way they communicate with others and us). Eventually I became a vegan, and designed a senior pet care and hospice program. Short version! But, it all started with a "free puppy" sign in my neighborhood, and the dog that changed my life! Her name was Pepper. —Deborah F.

I grew up on the Gulf Coast. I was raised with a deep respect for all animals and a love for the water. On April 20, 2010, my heart broke watching the news of the Deepwater Horizon oil spill. That was my backyard growing up. My family still lives there, and I would speak to my dad daily on what he and the community were doing to protect the wildlife from the oil that was continuing to make its mark. I was angry. . . . A few months later I met someone who was involved in Sea Shepherd, and immediately I recognized the name as one of the organizations that was (and is) active in the Gulf. Within a few days I filled out my application to become an Onshore Volunteer. I am now the chapter co-coordinator for the Minneapolis chapter of Sea Shepherd Conservation Society. I am proud to volunteer with an organization that is taking direct action in changing the fate of our oceans and its residents. —Melissa

It was piece by piece, as I witnessed and learned things. My reasons grew and grew . . . It is not charity for me; this is self-defense as well. I can't live without birds in the sky and fish in the oceans. I can't live without bees, worms, microorganisms in the soil, and biodiversity. When 70 to 80 percent of ocean animals are either extinct or threatened, when aquifers are being depleted primarily because of animal agriculture, when it takes fifty-five acres of rain forest for one hamburger . . . when I know full well what goes on in farms and zoos and with vivisection and in research labs and breeding facilities and circuses and fur farms and so on—and I know, too, about speciesism and how some bodies are worth more than others—it affects me as a deaf female, as well as other people. It's not charity to fight back. — Scout

The reasons people become involved in animal work are varied, but most people do refer to their love for animals as key. Still, the motivator for action may be due to family upbringing, or because of having more time at retirement. There may have been an "aha" moment, or a special pet. It may be politically motivated, a spiritual connection, or philosophically based. Liz B.'s "aha" moment came when she read about her local SPCA in Pennsylvania helping survivors of domestic violence who could not take their animals to abuse shelters. She started to foster animals in that program, which she did for more than ten years.

INFLUENCES AT A YOUNG AGE

Some of the study participants were brought up in vegetarian households (such as Unny, Lilia, and Meghan). Meghan's mother was passionate about animal rights, and they attended national animal rights conferences together. Today, Meghan volunteers with Farm Sanctuary and Mercy for Animals (MFA). Lilia's parents instilled a deep respect for animals and nature. She writes:

> I got involved in forest defense in my early twenties in Tasmania (Australia), and quickly came to understand how defense of forests was also a defense of the wild animals that lived in them, as well as a resistance to land use practices that see forests cleared for grazing farmed animals. My forest defense work ultimately led to me to get a job with Sea Shepherd in Australia, and then I moved to the United States, where I continued to work for Sea Shepherd.

While she has a different household experience, Jasmine M. also works to help animals:

> I grew up at a dressage and show-jumping barn, and have always loved animals. When I was twelve we moved to New Mexico, near the Navajo reservation. Dogs on the rez have a very hard life, and there is a huge need for s/n [spay/neuter] and relocation. I have fostered upward of seventy dogs and puppies in the two-and-a-half years I've been with Blackhat Humane [Society].

Nadia's father was a screenwriter and novelist. He wrote *Bichu the Jaguar*, for example. As a kid, Nadia spent time on the MGM set for *Clarence the Cross-Eyed Lion* and the spin-off TV series *Daktari*. Nadia recounts:

> I was about twelve years old, and at Christmas my father had ramped up a script for my Christmas present. I opened it up and there it was, the story of Clarence, the cross-eyed lion. And I went with him to the set whenever he went there. And I was a kid, and they kept me quiet by putting me in the infirmary with all the baby lions and elephants, and the baby ostriches and baby pythons and cheetahs.

While Nadia grew up with captive wildlife, she doesn't believe it's right anymore. Later in life she founded Golden Bone Rescue for dogs. She says, "I grew up with a lot of compassion in my family, and my plea to everyone in the world is teach this to your children, because my parents did and it was the greatest service they could ever have done for me in my life."

Many individuals in the study showed concerns for animals very early in life. Mikayla became a vegetarian at age ten. The family had a dog named Buddy and, for Mikayla, "[i]t suddenly hit me that eating a pig or cow was almost the exact same thing as eating dog, or basically like another human being." For her bat mitzvah, she "started volunteering at an animal rescue organization that set up inside PetSmart on Saturdays" and continued for two years. In high school she chose to write a research paper on the leather industry, which, in her view, "disgusts me." Now in college, Mikayla is majoring in Vet Science.

Amanda writes about a common path for those who start to care about animals early in life:

> I started helping animals when I was a young kid, and my grandma had a feral cat colony living under her porch. We helped get the animals spayed and neutered and adopted the kittens out to wonderful forever homes. I was inspired to dedicate my life toward working for animal rights when I first learned how cows were slaughtered for food when I was twelve. I immediately became vegetarian, and have been so ever since, and I started writing letters to PETA [People for the Ethical Treatment of Animals] for information at that young age. I have been actively involved with many organizations over the years, volunteering for animal shelters, starting student groups, interning for animal rights attorneys and organizations, and am now living my dream of working for PETA.

Daryl has a similar story. She "released the frogs due for dissection in the sixth grade." She stopped eating hamburgers at age ten, and stopped all meat at age fourteen. She told me, "My first job, age seven, was sweeping up hair in a grooming shop. I later became a zookeeper because I thought taking care of animals was a noble cause—wrong! I *hate* seeing wildlife in captivity now." Daryl is a lifelong animal activist.

Lindsay is an example of many kids who bring home strays or injured animals. She became a vegetarian young. She writes, "I believe that all kids make the connections to animals that I did, but it's something we lose when growing up in a society so disconnected from our food system." Once she learned about the mistreatment of animals in the egg and dairy industries, she went vegan. Furthermore, "I then started to perform investigations on my own into various animal facilities, and then eventually started working for PETA. I now work for MFA." At Mercy for Animals, Lindsay recruits and trains undercover investigators.

Many volunteers and staff advocating for animals started at an early age. Julia, for example, got a job in high school at a roadside zoo for apes. She didn't know at the time that it was not a "great place." She realized over time that there were practices she was uncomfortable with. However, this led her to the work field she went into—as a primatologist. She worked seven years with PETA as a primatologist, and now she consults with the organization, as well as does consulting work with chimpanzee sanctuaries.

Joanne "never could say no to a homeless animal." She started at age eight or nine, bringing home stray kittens and cats, then stray dogs. Farm animals, baby birds—she loved them all. She joined the Physicians Committee for Responsible Medicine "to stop animal testing and the use of animals in medical schools and in the U.S. Department of Defense. I am currently a volunteer at the Humane Society of Southern Arizona."

Robin commented that "every experience I had was one step up, helping me build knowledge and become a better advocate and activist." She started volunteering in a vet's office at age thirteen, then worked as a vet assistant throughout college and afterward. Then she went into wildlife rehab and shelter work. From there she went to work at PETA. She had become a vegan in college and learned about many issues, such as vivisection. She felt her time at PETA "was amazing, and allowed me to do so much more—to help more animals, reach and educate more people, and make a bigger difference."

IMPACT OF A PET

Our connections to our pets often motivate us to do more for animals. This was true for many in the study. For example, Leah is a rabbit advocate with the national Rabbit Advocacy Network:

> *I was an omnivore before sharing my life and home with an animal that is used for livestock/meat, fur, and testing. That animal happens*

to be a rabbit. Once I realized how badly they are exploited for so many things I became sad and angry. I also realized that if I would not eat my rabbit, or any rabbit, why would I eat cow, pig, or chicken?

I grew up with cats and dogs, and it wasn't until rabbits came into my life that [I made] the connection between food animals and pet animals [as] no different. I fell in love with this little rabbit just like I did cats and dogs. But I know that people eat them; it broke my heart. So I started using cruelty-free products in my home—cosmetics, cleaning products—and gave up all meat.

Josie found a stray dog, and was surprised at how few options there were for him. She kept him, and later cofounded Help A Dog Smile, fostering and placing hundreds of dogs for adoption. She's also a vegan activist.

Mike's eyes were opened to animal cruelty in factory farming when his dog, Curly, died. He learned how dogs were eaten in other countries, and the similarities between that and the cows, pigs, and chickens on his dinner plate. He went vegetarian, then vegan, and started working as an undercover investigator for PETA.

When Amber lost her dog—her best friend—to cancer, she started volunteering to give back. She volunteers with the Humane Society of Southern Arizona, Arizona Cactus Corgi Rescue, and Tucson's Cause for Canines. She "discovered a deep passion for rescuing dogs that helped me feel whole and find meaning." She's done it all—shelter work, home visits for potential adopters, fostering dogs, transporting dogs, working with special-needs dogs, and adoption events.

Laurie and her boyfriend adopted a dog, Oliver, from a local pound:

I knew he was special, but I didn't know how he was going to change the course of my life until the following year, when I was laid off from the insurance agency I worked for ten years, my relationship ended, and I found myself having to find a new direction/purpose. Oliver drew so many people into my life, and gave me this platform to talk about shelter animals and their worth. With all the new time I had on my hands out of work, and Oliver's severe separation anxiety, I looked for a way to get more involved in the community and at the same time to help Oliver overcome his fears. Oliver and I started volunteering for the HSSA [Humane Society of Southern Arizona]. First [I was] at the thrift store and a kitten/cat foster, and then [we] went on to become a certified therapy/comfort dog team, which we still enjoy doing together!

In 2012, after spearheading a fundraiser to raise money for and build dog beds for all the kennels at Pima Animal Care Center (PACC), I was asked to join a group of four other women to form a board and open our own animal shelter. After a year of hard work, we [the Pima Paws for Life animal shelter] opened our doors in January 2014. We have a contract with PACC (where I adopted Oliver from) to pull and treat their URI (upper respiratory infection) dogs/cats, and in the year and a half that we've been open, have saved over 500 lives.

I owe the last five years of my involvement in animal rescue/advocacy to my little dog Oliver, who himself has touched countless lives, and I've been told has saved a few too! He has also been an ambassador for the Shelter Pet Project (a national rescue/adoption campaign), and came full circle last year, being voted Pima County's poster dog, gracing PACC's dog licensing campaign poster.

Cats, of course, also motivate many individuals. After Sandy B. learned her cat had feline leukemia, she adopted others that were special needs. She started to volunteer at a cat rescue, Save the Cats Arizona, and later deepened her commitment by starting a trap-neuter-return (TNR) program in her community.

Dolores started with one feral cat, and soon after got involved with TNR, fostering, and working with organizations in First Nations communities in Canada. Now she coordinates Stray Cats About Town.

Daya recounts her experience living in Alaska:

I fed strays when I came across them, and eventually one walked into my apartment in college and wouldn't walk out. She became my life's most constant companion for the next seventeen years. One winter I noticed a bunch of feral cats were living under a restaurant in Glennallen, Alaska, and trying to subsist out of the dumpster. It gets -40 degrees there, it's no place for a cat. I got a small grant from the ASPCA [American Society for the Prevention of Cruelty to Animals] to trap them, sterilize them, and rehabilitate them. I went vegan when I read Temple Grandin's book Animals Make Us Human, *which is about all the improvements that have been made in the animal-ag industry. I read the section about dairy and eggs and thought, "This is an improvement?! I don't want any part of this!" So I decided to become vegan.*

When Sheila was nineteen, someone killed her cat in her yard. She was devastated and furious. The incident "set me on my path to helping animals in need and trying to teach people about the importance of treating animals with respect and caring for them properly." She volunteered with Cat Haven and Save Our Strays in Baton Rouge before retirement.

Bill founded a group called Protect All Living Species (PALS) to end rattlesnake roundups around the country, but primarily focused on Whigham, Georgia. Bill had property in Georgia with a large population of gopher tortoises, which coexist with the eastern diamondback rattlesnake (EDR). He became a licensed wildlife rehabilitator in 2005, and his first animal was a gopher tortoise. This experience increased his interest in the gopher tortoise, and he learned about the relationships between the tortoises and the EDR. He learned about the history of rattlesnake roundups, and that the eastern diamondback was in danger of becoming extinct. The gopher tortoise he rehabilitated from its wound (a shot in the carapace by a .22-caliber rifle) motivated him to create the best possible environment for the gopher tortoises and rattlesnakes on his property, and led him to become an activist to try to end the roundups still occurring in Georgia. PALS is also involved in efforts to have the EDR listed under the Endangered Species Act as a threatened species.

BELIEF SYSTEMS

For many people, philosophical, spiritual, or religious beliefs have motivated their involvement in ending animal suffering. Charles, a staff member of Vegetarian Resource Group, writes that "doing the least harm possible, change through nonviolence, [and] not believing in killing people led [me] to being vegetarian and vegan" over thirty years ago. Dove respects all animal species. She stated, "I believe that human, domestic, and wildlife animals are linked, inextricably, in the chain of life. We survive or perish, together."

True species equality matters to Desirée, a volunteer with Furever Friends Rescue:

> *As a secular humanist, I don't see a hierarchy of importance for all living creatures. Everything on this planet should be equally considered and allowed to live naturally. Humans have encroached on habitats and then get upset when animals "fight back"—such as mountain lions and coyotes appearing in backyards. It's ridiculous to believe that humans can just bulldoze their way across this planet and not be sensible about our cohabitators.*

For others, religious beliefs about treatment of animals is key. Alessa, volunteering with the Humane Society of Southern Arizona, wrote on her survey:

> *I feel animals are God's creatures, as we humans are. However, we are bestowed with capacities and abilities to create, emote, and communicate at a more sophisticated level than animals. Consequently, with these advanced capacities, there is an expectation of humans' caretaking role toward these more vulnerable creatures. It is my belief that God created human beings to be animals' stewards.*

Richard, a member of Jewish Veg (named International Jewish Vegetarian Society at the time he joined), found a Biblical justification for how humans should treat animals:

> *Since [becoming vegetarian in 1978], I have learned much about vegetarianism's connections to health, nutrition, ecology, resource usage, hunger, and the treatment of animals. I also started investigating connections between vegetarianism and Judaism. I learned that the first Biblical dietary law (Genesis 1:29) was strictly vegetarian, and I became convinced that important Jewish mandates to preserve our health, be kind to animals, protect the environment, conserve resources, share with hungry people, and seek and pursue peace, all pointed to vegetarianism as the best diet for Jews (and everyone else) today. To get this message to a wider audience I wrote a book,* Judaism and Vegetarianism, *which was published in 1982. (A second, expanded edition was published in 1988.)*

DOCUMENTARIES, BOOKS, AND SOCIAL MEDIA

Education in the form of documentaries, podcasts, books, and literature about animal welfare influences many people to volunteer or to go vegan. Elizabeth K., a volunteer with Animal Rights Hawai'i, says, "I have always felt particularly close to animals. After seeing *Meet Your Meat* and *Earthlings*, I felt compelled to go vegan and help educate others about animals' current plight. Volunteering seemed a natural way to contribute."

Steve writes about one particular documentary that influenced the course of his life:

> *I had been vegan and slightly active for several years when I watched a movie featuring Britches, who was rescued from a [University of California] Riverside experiment. I had read about Britches ten years earlier, but I had never seen video of him. Seeing him immediately after his rescue was jarring, and it forced me to reflect on my efforts for the animals over that decade. I felt like my efforts had not been enough, so I became a more steady activist. After meeting some of Vegan Outreach's activists, I decided to focus my limited time on the 99 percent of animals who are killed for food products. I started leafleting, and I helped turn Central Florida Veg Fest and Central Florida Earth Day into huge community events where thousands of people explore vegan food. I had an opportunity to volunteer more intensively with Vegan Outreach during the summer of 2011, and at the end of that tour I left my old life behind and became a full-time activist.*

For Jeanette, a volunteer with Viva! and Animal Justice Project, both in the United Kingdom, watching a documentary about dairy, where many cows are fully conscious while hanging upside down for slaughter, led to her becoming vegetarian. She became a passionate defender of animals.

Connecting with animals through stories is a powerful motivator for many. Helen, who lives in Canada, says:

> *What motivated me to specifically start volunteering at Vegan Haven was reading the stories of all the pigs at Pigs Peace Sanctuary. After spending one night in tears reading all the beautiful stories about the beings rescued at the sanctuary, I knew I wanted to start volunteering. Another turning point I can remember is watching this video by*

the Toronto Pig Save. Even though I had seen graphic footage and many other videos of animals before, that specific video really touched me. I think that seeing into the eyes of individual pigs reached into my soul and moved me to do more than just live my life as a vegan.

TURNING POINTS

For some, there has been a turning point. For example, Molly S., who has loved animals since childhood, had several jobs that changed her life:

I worked in a pet store when I was eighteen, and somehow knew there was something wrong with it. I worked for several veterinarians in my twenties and saw some horrible abuse. Then, around 1977, I went to work as an animal caretaker for [an animal research center] in Seattle, Washington. It was horrific. I saw the monkeys with electrodes sticking out of their heads. They were terrified of humans. I saw the chair where they strapped them down. I saw the rats, mice, monkeys, goats, rabbits, and pigs, and the small cages they were kept in. I never saw the actual experiments, but every morning when I came in there would be some animals gone. I tried to make their lives as good as I could, but it didn't help. I can tell you of several incidents about a rabbit with a broken leg, a monkey with a prolapsed rectum, a goat they let die. I almost killed myself I was so depressed. And PETA didn't exist yet. I couldn't take them home or set them free. We were in the middle of a big city and there were hundreds. When [the researchers] said they were bringing in cats and dogs, I couldn't stand it. They got them from the local animal control. I just walked out one day. It still haunts me. In 1989 I read Animal Liberation *by Peter Singer, and it changed my life. I threw myself into AR [animal rights] actions and became first a vegetarian, and then a vegan.*

Molly S. is in the process of starting her own cat rescue organization.
For Ryan, now a PETA employee, it was the slaughterhouse smell:

The first moment I remember feeling genuinely moved by the issue was while I was on a road trip in college. As I drove through Amarillo, Texas, I passed about 40 straight miles of factory farms and slaughterhouses. I was driving a convertible, and the sights and smells of industrial agriculture were nauseating. Upon returning to my hometown in Virginia, I began watching undercover investigations and videos like Meet Your Meat *on the PETA website, and requested a Vegetarian Starter Kit.*

International experiences also influence people to volunteer or work for animals. Anne still lives abroad:

I have always been an animal lover, but didn't realize how animals are treated. I moved to Indonesia in 1995. The animal cruelty is in your face. Chickens tied up by their legs hanging upside down on a motorcycle. Cows crammed into trucks. It was enough for me to go veg. The United States does a good job of hiding the animal abuse from people. I worked at an animal shelter in Indonesia for years. I now live in the Philippines, and volunteer for an organization called Compassion and Responsibility for Animals (CARA). I also leaflet for PETA here, and I sign every petition that comes my way.

Molly F. has volunteered all over the world, with a wildlife focus:

I've always been an animal lover, with a particular interest in the illegal wildlife trade. After college, I started on the path to be a zookeeper. But the more I went along, the more I disagreed with so many aspects of captivity. I became involved with Animals Asia and volunteered at its sanctuary in China. That got me interested in international animal welfare, and since then I've worked and volunteered, mostly with wildlife, both nationally and internationally (including AAP Primadomus in Spain, the Lilongwe Wildlife Center in Malawi, and the Detroit Zoo's Center for Zoo Animal Welfare . . . as well as various domestic animal shelters). From there I found the course I'm currently completing at the University of Edinburgh: MSc in Applied Animal Behaviour and Welfare.

Alicia has a master's degree in history and presently works for PETA doing Latino outreach. While an undergraduate she lived in Spain. Her studies turned out to be connected to animal issues in ways she had not expected:

Living in Spain, I learned a lot about Latin America and challenges faced by indigenous people in the twentieth century. I learned a lot

*about labor issues in Latin American coffee plantations and banana
plantations. My work was on post-civil war in Guatemala. And in
2005 or 2006, I went to Chiapas, Mexico, and did some work with the
Zapatista movement. People there were talking about how the animal
agriculture industry affects the environment, and has a really direct
impact on how people relied heavily on their natural surroundings,
and that was what prompted me toward going vegan.*

LOVE FOR ANIMALS

Virtually everyone in the study mentioned, "I have always loved animals," or, as Janet, who volunteers with Save Our Strays Mississippi, said, "I love animals and feel a sacred duty to protect and save them from all harm and destruction."

Rita "would take them all in if I could." Rita saw neighbors shoot dogs running loose (in Missouri), helped with puppy mill rescues, and is outraged when people poison or shoot feral cats. Today Rita does TNR with Animal Legal Defense Fund in Arizona.

Liz T., involved daily with animals while working at the Humane Society for Southern Arizona, feels she is "the most emotionally satisfied in my career than ever."

LeAnn, volunteering at Wildhorse Ranch Rescue in Arizona, echoes what many feel in their involvement with animal welfare: "Helping animals is just a way of life for me. It is part of who I am." This compassion is very powerful—and common among people who want to end animal suffering.

ANIMAL SUFFERING

Alexis volunteers at Wildlife Haven Rehabilitation Centre in Manitoba, Canada. She makes a very poignant comment: "People, so complex and rational and intelligent, and we are the only species to inflict pain on others for reasons outside of survival."

Many, many individuals become involved in animal work because of the suffering humans cause. Elizabeth S. had already been vegetarian, and then vegan, for decades when, "[i]n 2002 a horrific case of animal abuse disturbed me so much that I decided I wanted to become more active in working for animals. That case still haunts me and is often my motivation." She volunteered for animal organizations after college, but then "I heard an interview with Lesli Bisgould, whom I consider to be Canada's preeminent animal rights lawyer, and was so impressed that I decided to do a law degree to work in animal rights law."

A veterinary technician, Nicole reflects on the many changes she has made to end suffering:

> Sixteen years ago, I was chosen to "pet the killer whale" at SeaWorld Orlando. It was that moment that I knew I could not stand by or silent any more. Over the past six years I have volunteered with Sea Shepherd Conservation Society. . . . In my youth I had raised my own cows, pigs, and chickens for slaughter. Now I lead a vegan lifestyle. My first job was at Busch Gardens [and] at a time that they had dolphins. This gave me access to SeaWorld. I now speak out against cetaceans in captivity.

For Izabela, her activism started with learning about dolphins and small whales slaughtered annually in Taiji, Japan. Michelle L. first learned about animal suffering in a letter from PETA describing the laboratory research on two beagles, and of "the great bond [the dogs had] with each other for comfort after having horrible tests and broken bones, all in the name of research." And Jamie C., volunteering with Poplar Spring Animal Sanctuary, says what so many of those in this study could state: "Once I learned of the suffering of animals, I could no longer participate by eating or wearing animals, or supporting using them for entertainment."

ISSUE FOCUS: FACTORY FARMING

There is no getting around it: Producing food from farmed animals for human consumption creates horrific suffering. The animals cannot be treated as individual sentient beings with their own lives, desires, personalities, and relationships. They must be seen as commodities, as objects, as subordinate to people. The farmed animal industry is institutionalized as part of the economy, with connections to other industries such as feed, pharmaceuticals, transportation, farm machinery, and bank loans, which are, of course, all geared for profit. The government subsidizes parts of this industry, lobbyists work for favorable federal legislation and weak regulation, and a powerful marketing arm prepares the public to accept animal suffering (or keep it invisible), to socialize us that animal protein, milk, and dairy are healthy. Since we eat animal products throughout each and every day, animals as products are assumed to be a fact of life. We are talking about over nine billion animals raised and slaughtered annually in the United States. More than seventy billion animals are slaughtered each year globally, which excludes the trillions of fish and other aquatic life killed.[1]

People who volunteer or work to end animal suffering of farmed animals are primarily at farm sanctuaries caring for animals, or they may be involved in rescuing farm animals that will then live at sanctuaries. Some people work as undercover investigators to expose cruelty and unhealthy practices during the animals' miserable lives or at slaughter. Others are involved in education, perhaps tabling or leafleting about factory farming. Many work to expose the connections between factory farming (which includes farmed fish) and environmental degradation, such as poisoning of water, soil, and air, and very significantly, the connection to climate change. Factory farming, so integral to American life, is also a source of moral contradiction and physical destruction.

Rebecca F. volunteers at CJ Acres Animal Rescue Farm in Florida. Sometimes she helps feed the animals, and other times she is "cleaning stalls and pastures, brushing horses, giving sheep haircuts, [doing] lawn care, filling mud holes for the pigs, giving animals hay, etc. CJ Acres is the place where I can live my dreams. When the day is done you feel exhausted, but at the same time you feel more incredible than you ever have before."

Jamie C. was motivated to volunteer for animals because she had learned of their suffering. She's a regular volunteer at Poplar Spring Animal Sanctuary in Maryland, driving over an hour each way to get there from her home.

> *We clean the areas of the goats, sheep, pigs, horses, cows, and fowl (chickens, turkeys, a peacock, and a guinea hen). Since the sanctuary is 400 acres, with half of it wooded, sometimes we don't see the cows who like to sleep in the woods. I consider these animals an extension of the animals with whom I share my condo. I love them dearly! I have gotten to know their very distinct personalities and have some very special relationships.*

She also helps at all Poplar Spring's fund-raising events. In addition to the sanctuary volunteering, Jamie C. is a vegan coach for new vegans, does public speaking about animal abuse, environmental, and health issues, and she has film screenings in her home to educate people about veganism and the animal food industry.

Ruth started as a volunteer at Poplar Spring Animal Sanctuary, and then took a paid position. She wrote in her follow-up interview:

> I have been a paid staff member for five-and-a-half years. I work two to three days a week, depending on time of year. I volunteered for nine months prior to being hired. I take care of the chickens, turkeys, a few other types of birds, and one feisty bunny. Duties include feeding, medicating, cleaning barns and bowls, supervising volunteers, and talking to visitors who come to my area of the sanctuary during tours and events. The latter two involve teaching people about animal behavior, animal husbandry, making people see everyone as individuals with unique personalities, discussing their stories, etc.

Several of the study participants were so moved by the plight of farmed animals that they started farm sanctuaries, and have devoted their lives to farm animals.

Following a brief discussion of ag-gag laws, which attempt to prevent the dissemination of the truth about animal cruelty and suffering on factory farms, along with health violations, worker mistreatment, and food safety, some information about farmed animals and the brief stories of those who care for them is provided.

Ag-Gag Laws

Ag-gag laws are basically a corporate and state reaction to the outpouring of negative publicity and response to animal agriculture after an undercover investigation is publicized. These laws criminalize the making of secret videos, audio recordings, or photographs that document what is really going on in factory farms. Some of the legislation includes criminalizing "misrepresentation" by an applicant who applies for the job in order to engage in an undercover investigation. These investigations document the abusive practices used on animals—now commodities in a factory—and how animals suffer without anesthesia in "standard practices" of botched slaughter, castration, dehorning, and so forth, as well as the cruel acts of frustrated employees who are under pressure to move scared animals weighing hundreds of pounds, who beat or cause pain to the animals to keep their jobs, and the cries of animals tortured for fun by sadistic employees plunging screwdrivers into their eyes or ramming objects up their rectums.

The first ag-gag law was passed in Kansas in 1990, and then in 1991, Montana and North Dakota followed. The next bill was not passed until 2012 in Iowa. Other states passed bills after that, but in 2015 a federal district court ruled that Idaho's ag-gag law was unconstitutional. A wide range of civil liberties are violated by ag-gag laws, such as freedom of the press and free speech. These laws hinder the public's right to know about food safety, labor violations, and protections for animals. The Animal Legal Defense Fund, one of the plaintiffs in the Idaho case, says it clearly on its website: "Factory farms want to keep their cruel practices hidden from the public."[2]

There is little doubt among animal activists that these laws are unconstitutional, and that eventually all of them will be off the books. Not only that, but the public *wants* to have these abusive practices exposed. Research conducted in 2012 by Lake Research Partners for the ASPCA found 71 percent of Americans support undercover investigative efforts by animal welfare organizations to expose animal abuse on industrial farms, including 54 percent who *strongly* support the efforts. Accordingly, almost two-thirds (64 percent) of Americans oppose making undercover investigations of animal abuse on industrial farms illegal, with half of all Americans *strongly* opposing legislative efforts to criminalize industrial farm investigations, commonly referred to as "ag-gag" legislation.

The nationwide survey also reveals that 94 percent of Americans feel it is important (81 percent feel it is *"extremely important"*) to have measures in place to ensure that food coming from farm animals is safe for people to eat, and 94 percent agree that animals raised for food on farms deserve to be free from abuse and cruelty.[3]

Chickens and Turkeys

Hundreds of millions of these sociable birds live miserable, tortured lives in overcrowded barns (up to three billion in the United States are slaughtered each year). They rarely see sunlight or feel grass under their feet in their short lifetimes. They live in filth and cannot escape the ammonia from their manure, causing "ammonia burn" caustic eye disease. Illnesses such as gastrointestinal diseases, blood diseases, and especially respiratory infections are common. Furthermore, broiler chickens are forced to gain weight so quickly that they suffer from lameness, and often cannot move at all as their bodies are too heavy for their legs. [4]

Chickens and turkeys are debeaked without anesthesia; in this process a blade cuts through the beak tissue causing intense pain. Farmers do this to minimize fighting caused by severe overcrowding. Debeaking leads to difficulty eating and preening. Turkeys are also de-toed without anesthesia, which results in difficulty walking. The unhealthy environments these birds are raised in also contributes to infections with salmonella, listeria, and campylobacter bacteria, as well as avian influenza viruses. It is no surprise that poultry is the leading cause of food poisoning in humans.

Between six and twelve weeks of age, chickens are brutally gathered and transported for slaughter (between twelve and twenty-six weeks for turkeys). No U.S. law oversees the treatment of these farmed animals, so they are treated as the "unfeeling" objects they are viewed as by the industry. After they are hung upside-down on conveyor belts, they are electrically stunned. This stunning only paralyzes their muscles; they are fully conscious and feeling when their throats are cut (though often their throats are missed), and then they are plunged into the scald tanks to remove their feathers (sometimes still alive).

Approximately 95 percent of eggs come from chickens in battery cages, where the living space is the size of a sheet of paper. The chickens are so crammed that they cannot spread their wings. This fact has become common knowledge to the point that pressure put on the egg industry has resulted in some agreements for "cage-free" hens. Many corporations have agreed to phase out battery cages over the next decade (some sooner, some later, and some have not set timelines). [5]

Hens in cage-free environments are now less than 10 percent of the total, according to the U.S. Department of Agriculture. But even as more and more hens are transitioned to these environments, the animal agriculture industry still has problems that may be insurmountable. For example, the air quality of closed barns, with constantly moving, crowded chickens, will be more problematic for workers and chickens.

The chickens also won't be separated from their waste, as they were with battery cages, resulting in more ammonia buildup and possible feces on eggs. Because attacks and cannibalism increase due to stressful, crowded conditions, debeaking will continue, but more deaths will no doubt result. While there may be added windows and perches for some natural preening behaviors, it will be the rare hen in a factory farm that will ever set foot outdoors—even with cage-free going into effect.[6]

Robert Grillo founded Free from Harm in 2009. Robert chose to focus on chickens because they are 99 percent of all animals used for food in the United States. According to the website, most of Free from Harm's chickens are rescued from poultry markets and kill shelters in the Chicago metropolitan area.[7] Robert told me:

> I began to adopt chickens about six years ago and that was a real eye-opening experience as you can imagine for someone who had never known a chicken before and all of a sudden has a flock of chicks and starts to raise them into adulthood. My intention at the time was not necessarily what it is now. I wasn't sure what to think or what to expect. And I learned very quickly, as I bonded with them and they with me, that they became members of our family.

In its short time in existence, Free from Harm has had a huge impact. Robert writes:

> In 2014, Free from Harm reached six million web users through a variety of awareness building campaigns. . . . We already believe that harming animals when we could easily avoid it is wrong. It's the reason why we condemn dog fighting and horse slaughter and the news story of a kitten being tortured by someone. If it is wrong to harm animals unnecessarily and gratuitously just for some pleasure we obtain from it in these cases, then it logically follows that it is wrong to do the same for reasons of pleasing our taste buds. One case cannot be wrong while the others are okay. We just need to apply what we already claim to believe to four species we have traditionally excluded: chickens, turkeys, pigs, and cows.

Karen Davis has been at the forefront of poultry advocacy. She writes on her website, "My work is United Poultry Concerns, the nonprofit organization I founded in 1990 that addresses the treatment of domes-

tic fowl in food production, science, education, entertainment, and human companionship situations, and promotes the compassionate and respectful treatment of domestic fowl and a vegan diet and lifestyle."[8]
She wrote on her survey why she became an activist:

> I have always cared about animals and I have always hated animal suffering, especially human-inflicted animal suffering. I have a life-long affinity for birds. An essay that had a profound effect on me was Tolstoy's essay "The First Step" (toward becoming a truly nonviolent person), which I read in the early 1970s. His description of the animals in a Moscow slaughterhouse woke me to the meaning of "meat." I became a vegetarian immediately, and subsequently went vegan on learning about eggs and dairy. I didn't have to be converted from believing that eating animal products was necessary. I just had to learn about how animals in food production are treated.

Her turning point was in 1985, when she found a crippled and abandoned chicken from the meat industry. Karen named her Viva, "a valuable being, somebody worth fighting for. She was not 'just a chicken.' Viva was a chicken, a member of Earth's community, a dignified being with a claim to justice, compassion, and a life equal to anyone else's."
Lori W. volunteers with Animal Place Rescue Ranch in Vacaville, California. She described Animal Place this way:

> We have 600 acres in Grass Valley and sixty acres in Vacaville. Our sixty-acre facility in Vacaville is called our Rescue Ranch. That's where we take all of our rescues, and that's when we decide at that point whether we can adopt them out or whether they will stay at the sanctuary. We have some goats at Rescue Ranch that we're going to adopt out. We have mostly chickens there, but at the permanent sanctuary in Grass Valley, we have about 300 animals, a mixture of all farmed animals there.

Lori W. started her animal volunteering with dog rescue, and was a vegetarian. She got "into" the local food movement and from there realized she:

> could no longer support even local farms for animal products. I became a vegan six years ago, and wanted to be more active for farm animals. I became trained as a volunteer at Animal Place Farm Sanc-

tuary, and volunteered doing animal care in Grass Valley. Later, I
began helping with large-scale chicken rescues from factory farms
and small-scale rescue from pasture-based and backyard opera-
tions. . . . I've been trained in chicken health care, and help during
and after rescues. I also help in finding forever homes for the rescued
hens and roosters. I do advocacy work with Animal Place as well
with their tabling and "brave the cage" events.

The large-scale chicken rescues Animal Place has been doing for the
past three years are primarily from one factory farmer in the Central
Valley. Egg-laying chickens are kept in battery cages, and factory farmers typically replace their flocks every eighteen months, when egg production begins to decrease. The chickens are in terrible shape, often
near death, from the conditions in the sheds, the ammonia, the lack of
sunlight, and so forth. In California, these hens are not used for dog
food or fertilizer, so they are, essentially, trashed. If not rescued, they'd
be gassed or buried alive or disposed of in some way—thousands of
chickens every eighteen months. Lori W. tells me:

> *What we're doing is we're saving [the factory farmer] the trouble for*
> *2,000 of his hens. We're saving him the trouble of his workers going*
> *in, pulling them out of the cage, and gassing them, so he saves on gas*
> *and labor. We can only handle about 2,000 at a time, so we go down*
> *every couple months. It takes about a month of really intensive care*
> *to get them back to health, and then we adopt them out to pre-*
> *screened homes. The homes we adopt them out to . . . we don't mind*
> *if they use [the chickens] for eggs as long as they're going to keep*
> *them their entire lifespan, and we check out their predator control,*
> *and we have a talk with them. We have them fill out a form and we*
> *call them twice, and we meet them when they come get the chicken.*
> *Up to the last minute, if we don't have a good feeling about them, we*
> *won't let them adopt.*

Animal Place also has adoption partnerships with the Sonoma SPCA,
the Stockton SPCA, and Santa Cruz SPCA. They'll take some of the
chickens and do community workshops for people who want to have
backyard chickens, and they encourage people to adopt rather than get
them from hatcheries.

Of course, many of these rescued chickens are euthanized because
of their ill health. While the chickens that survive and are given new

lives with people who aren't harming them is everything to those individual chickens, in no way do these rescues stop the factory farms from *their* continued use and abuse of thousands and millions of chickens. Other organizations and volunteers address that aspect of the farmed animal industry, either calling for cage-free farming and improved conditions, or through veganism and an end to eating animals altogether. Cage-free does not mean cruelty-free, as chickens would still be debeaked, overcrowded, exposed to ammonia burn, and generally live indoors.

Pigs

According to The Pig Preserve website, "The various breeds of farm pigs have been removed from the fields and woods [and] crammed by the millions into gigantic concrete and steel enclosures, deprived of fresh air and sunshine, genetically engineered to quickly produce lean meat, fed manufactured feeds laced with hormones and antibiotics and slaughtered in numbers that approach two million pigs each and every week."[9] Their miserable lives in the factory farms last only six to eight months. Since they are farmed for meat, pigs are bred to be five times larger than their natural weight. Because of this, they suffer from hoof abscesses and leg joint problems. Arthritis is a constant problem for pigs in farm sanctuaries.

Pigs are highly intelligent—equal to dogs, or perhaps even smarter. They are playful and mischievous. It goes without saying that the severe confinement they endure, separation from their families, and overcrowding, are all frustrating and crazy-making. They are denied their rutting behaviors and a natural existence. According to David Jackson and Gary Marx, writing for the *Chicago Tribune*, thirty-eight states exempt farm practices from animal cruelty laws. No anesthesia is used for piglet castration, or for tail, teeth, and ear clipping. As pointed out in their article, "Whipped, Kicked, Beaten: Illinois Workers Describe Abuse of Hogs," quoting law professor Joan Schaffner, "If you were to do the same thing to your cat or dog, it would clearly be criminal." Standard practice with sickly or runt piglets is to take them by the back legs and smash their heads onto the floor or wall.[10]

Compassion Over Killing (COK) reported on one of its undercover investigations at an Iowa pig-breeding factory (Hawkeye Sow Centers). According to the website:

> [T]he daily miseries forced upon pigs that our investigator witnessed and painstakingly caught on camera in December 2011 represent pork industry norms. Cruel, yet standard practices include immobilizing breeding pigs in barren metal crates barely wider than their bodies. These smart and social animals are so intensively confined, they can't even turn around and they're treated like mere piglet-producing machines. Artificially inseminated, they spend months inside a narrow gestation crate during pregnancy and are then moved to an equally restrictive farrowing crate where they'll give birth and nurse their young through metal bars. After a few weeks, their piglets will be taken away and the process will start all over again. Gestation crates are so cruel, they're already banned in the European Union (effective 2013) and are being phased out in eight U.S. states.[11]

Furthermore,

> As is industry norm, piglets are routinely mutilated—workers cut off their tails and rip out the males' genitals—without any painkillers. These painful procedures are performed directly in front of their mothers who, unable to help the screaming piglets, repeatedly grunt in obvious distress. The severed testicles and tails are left on the floor of the sows' crates.[12]

The slaughterhouse experience for pigs is nothing short of horrific. Another undercover 2015 COK investigation at Hormel in Minnesota revealed these findings:

> This facility is one of five in the United States operating under a USDA pilot program, known as "HIMP," that allows for high-speed slaughter and reduced government oversight. That means this facility operates at faster line speeds than almost any other facility in the United States: approximately 1,300 pigs are killed each hour, their meat to be sold as SPAM or other Hormel pork products.

The excessive slaughter line speed forces workers to take inhumane shortcuts that lead to extreme suffering for millions of pigs. It also jeopardizes food safety for consumers. Animals were being beaten, shocked, dragged, and improperly stunned—all out of view of the few government inspectors.[13]

The investigator saw downer pigs, those unable to walk to the kill floor. Pigs "covered in feces or pus-filled abscesses" were slaughtered with USDA approval. The investigator saw "improper stunning and slaughter, potentially leading to some animals entering the scalding tank while still alive." This is common treatment in the pig industry.[14]

The massive flooding in North Carolina by Hurricane Matthew in October 2016 showed the environmental challenges presented by open pits (or lagoons) of fecal waste, which overflowed into the ocean, contaminating groundwater along the way. Several thousand hogs drowned, along with several million chickens and turkeys. The world's largest hog-processing plant (thirty thousand animals daily) is located in North Carolina, and the number of hog factory farms and lagoons is staggering. Improvements had been made after Hurricane Floyd in 1999 (such as moving lagoons to higher ground), but some elements of factory farming will never be free of negative consequences to animals, people, or the environment.[15]

Farm animal sanctuaries end up with pigs rescued from slaughter, but also with pigs that started out as pets. Potbellied pigs are wild animals, and were never supposed to be living in homes and kept as pets. When people realize this, they dump them. According to The Pig Preserve, they might be brought to county shelters to be killed, or dumped in parks or the desert where they are attacked by dogs or shot by ranchers or authorities. Yet pigs are highly intelligent, clean, friendly, social animals; they love to be with other pigs and enjoy belly rubs by people.[16]

Cofounded by Mary Schanz and her husband Ben, Ironwood Pig Sanctuary, outside of Tucson, Arizona, "provides a permanent home in a safe, nurturing environment for abandoned, abused, neglected or unwanted potbellied pigs from both the Phoenix and Tucson areas."[17] They now house about six hundred pigs. Mary's story shows a wide-ranging dedication to animals:

We moved to Arizona in 1988, and not long after that I got involved in many land-use issues and petitioning here in Tucson. I also got involved in many environmental issues that led to my interest in doing bat surveys and protection. . . . I ran across some people who were collecting signatures to ban leghold traps on public lands in AZ.

*This began my real involvement in animal issues. I became very
involved with this issue and worked on it until the final win to ban
the traps in 1994. During this effort, I became very involved in animal rights issues and became a board member of Voices for Animals
in Tucson. Later, [that group] joined forces with other groups and
became a statewide animal rights organization called Animal Defense
League of Arizona. During this time Ben and I retired and had made
some trips to Costa Rica and became involved with a wildlife rescue
there. We went there in 1998 for two months to run the wildlife
rescue while the founders were away.*

*At the end of 1998 I was reaching the end of my line with the
animal rights movement because I was always angry and frustrated.
There are so many, many issues, and I was beginning to drown in
despair. I saw an article in the* Arizona Daily Star *about a woman in
the Picture Rocks area in need of help with her pigs in a pig rescue.
My animal rights organization had received some phone calls that
her animals were suffering. Ben and I decided to contact her and visit
her to see if we could get involved and give her a hand. That was the
beginning of our involvement with pigs. I needed to be involved with
helping animals, but needed a break from the movement. Ben and I
became very involved as volunteers, and over the next two years saw
that there was a huge need for another and larger sanctuary for
needy pigs. In the fall of 2000 we bought land, and in the spring of
2001 we took in our first pigs.*

Richard Hoyle, owner and director of The Pig Preserve in Tennessee,
shared this story:

*My wife conned me into getting her a potbellied pig as a pet in the
late 1980s. Shortly thereafter we got a companion pig for the first
pig. [We] became vegetarians and began rescuing potbellied pigs
locally on an acre and a half. Soon [we] purchased and started a
seventeen-acre sanctuary in Northern Virginia, mainly for miniature
pigs. [We] expanded to take in farm pigs and became vegan.*

*[We] decided we wanted to allow our pigs to live as natural a life
as we could provide for them. When I retired for the second time
(from fire and rescue), we purchased one hundred acres of pristine
wilderness in the mountains of Tennessee, where we now provide
sanctuary space to around 135 potbellied pigs, feral pigs, and farm
pigs. Our pigs live confinement-free, chemical-free lives, with special
feed milled for them each week and the freedom to live life on their*

*own terms. We have potbellied pigs who are over twenty years old
and farm pigs who are over sixteen years old.*

Richard's is a mom-and-pop sanctuary; he and his wife, along with his
stepson, are the only workers. They have no volunteers, partly due to
the remote location. Richard also just doesn't have time to train volunteers who might come once a month or so. He further explains, "Here
our pigs are spread out over one hundred acres . . . as are their barns
and living shelters. We cater to the lifestyle of the pigs rather than to
the ease of operation of the sanctuary. As an example . . . We feed at
nine different locations, plus we use the feeding time as an opportunity
to physically see and do a hands-on check of every one of the 135 pigs
on the sanctuary."

Cows

A case can be made that dairy cows suffer more than cows raised for
meat, if you consider the many different types of indignities and the
length of time they suffer in their longer lives. Most people don't connect milk production with pregnancy, but the sad truth is that cows
must be continually made pregnant artificially, and their babies taken
from them, so humans can drink the milk they produce. They are essentially raped for pregnancy. They are fed hormones and chemicals to
produce more milk than they naturally would. Their udders swell so
enormously that many cows do not have a normal gait and are often
lame, and they suffer from painful mastitis (udder infections). The average dairy cow produces for industry ten times more than she normally
would to feed a calf. If they weren't a unit of production subjected to
unnatural measures, they might live up to twenty years. But most dairy
cows are slaughtered after two or three years.[18]

Perhaps the most painful aspect of the dairy cow's life is the forceful
separation from her calf shortly after birth. Mothers will bellow for their
babies for days. These calves will either become dairy cows themselves
or, like all the males, will become veal or be sent to feedlots to be
fattened for slaughter. Both feedlot cows and dairy cows are fed an
unnatural diet of grains and animal by-products. This increases the
likelihood of diseases such as mad cow disease. Cows are naturally
foragers and should be eating vegetation.

Tail docking is another painful practice—removing most of a cow's tail by using a rubber band to force the tail to fall off—and uses no anesthesia. The cows lose the ability to swat flies, and this practice is purely for the convenience of the factory farmer, who believes this will reduce tail biting and also keep the area cleaner.

Tara Lohan, senior editor at AlterNet, also reports that while small farms have dramatically decreased, large farms with a herd size of over one hundred have increased 94 percent. In California, for example, there are dairies with over ten thousand cows, and the San Joaquin Valley area has 2.5 million dairy cows.[19]

Cows raised for meat have much shorter life spans—after six months grazing on pasture, they are sent to a feedlot, which is usually a dirt lot with thousands of other cows. They often stand endlessly in their own waste. The goal of the feedlot is to fatten them up in the shortest amount of time. They are fed a corn-based concoction, but since grass is the species-appropriate diet for cattle, this unnatural diet can make them sick. It includes antibiotics, and often inedible matter. The cows will be sent to slaughter when they are between fourteen and sixteen months old. Most feedlots and slaughterhouses are in just four states (Nebraska, Iowa, Kansas, and Texas), so cattle can be shipped long distances.[20]

Before the feedlot experience, cows have experienced great pain from having their horns burned out, castration, and branding—all without anesthesia. The pain can be chronic. The slaughter experience is horrifying, as a 1,200-pound cow may not be successfully stunned by the bolt gun before she is hoisted up and shackled by one leg, then has her throat slit so she can "bleed out" on the kill floor.[21]

FARMED ANIMAL SANCTUARIES

Susie C. has worked at Farm Sanctuary for fifteen years. She oversees the three farm sanctuaries (located in Orland, in Northern California; Acton, in Southern California; and Watkins Glen, in New York). She began "because I always loved animals and did not realize the [abusive] treatment of farm animals. It started with dogs and cats, anti-fur, and then led to farm animal advocacy. Working with farmed animals is what made me go into this work—really seeing who they are in a setting where they were no longer frightened."

In her job, Susie C. is in constant communication with the farm managers, creates the budgets, prioritizes projects, and trains managers on issues such as pasture rotation and medical care. Their medical care needs are intense. She told me, "Because of who these animals are, they have really serious medical issues that we have to deal with." The goal is for these animals to have a high quality of life and live long, comfortable lives.

Sandra Higgins is the founder and director of Eden Farmed Animal Sanctuary in Ireland, and founded Matilda's Promise Animal Rights & Vegan Education Centre as well as the Compassion Foundation of Ireland. Furthermore, she recently founded Go Vegan World, a global marketing campaign to encourage people to go vegan. When asked about her influences to do the work she does, she replied:

> One of the most significant catalysts for me was a visit to a goat dairy. Until that moment I did not know that mothers are separated from their children so that humans [can] consume dairy. Neither was I aware that males are killed at birth. That was the turning point at which I became vegan.

She speaks of the impact of the animals on her efforts on their behalf:

> Eden grew organically around the needs of the residents, beginning with the first sheep who arrived here, rescued because they were born into families of triplets whose mothers could not feed them. Thereafter the first chickens arrived at Eden; they were rescued from a petting farm. I formed a deep connection with these first residents and they opened my eyes to their sentience as well as their cognitive capacities and their emotional and social lives.
>
> I formed a very deep bond with one particular hen, Matilda. Matilda was a most engaging character, full of life and intelligence, with such a friendly, inquisitive personality. She used to come in the kitchen window and sit on a chair beside me as I prepared lunch. She knew which drawer I kept the bread in and would hover at it until I gave her a slice. She melted the hearts of everyone, even people who said they did not like animals. The night she died I promised her that I would spend the rest of my life telling the world about the nature

and character of the people we harm when we are not vegan. In her memory, I founded Matilda's Promise, to honour my promise to her.

My activism is deeply informed by the histories and experiences of the lives I care for at Eden. Yes, some of them arrive at Eden badly traumatised from abuse and neglect. But for the most part their suffering comes from the simple fact that they are bred for human use. I have learned that not even the best sanctuary care in the world can undo this damage. This is why I founded Matilda's Promise Animal Rights & Vegan Education Centre: to promote the abolition of all animal use.

John N. grew up on a farm and had a dream to start a sanctuary:

My veganism and concern for animals stems from my faith, as a calling to steward and care for creation. [My calling] started in high school, which led to vegetarianism and activism, which finally led to veganism about eight years ago. I am a believer in direct action, and so support Sea Shepherd both financially and by volunteering as a chapter coordinator for Baltimore/Washington, DC region. Having grown up on a family farm, I achieved a mission milestone by starting a sanctuary for farm animals about a year ago: Peaceful Fields Sanctuary in Winchester, Virginia. The land itself was purchased at the end of 2013.

John N. and his wife cofounded Peaceful Fields, which is thriving. Their animals come to them through government or organization abuse raids, through surrender by individuals, through rescue networks, and through advertisements. For John, the hard work of sanctuary farm life "is our mission and we wouldn't have it any other way."

The pathways to animal advocacy are many, but all demonstrate a deep commitment to the recognition that animals should not suffer. Whether volunteering to foster dogs on occasion, giving time to global wildlife protection, working to end animal testing, or even committing your life to running an animal sanctuary, actions by individuals impact the lives of animals far beyond what any laws touch. In fact, it certainly can be argued that laws protect and *allow* abuse of farmed animals by accepting "industry standard practice" as a justification for most of the factory farming practices. While legislation *is* needed, what turns the reality around for animals, in any circumstance of human use, are the attitudes and beliefs about their rights, and who controls their very lives and the quality of those lives. People who work with and for animals are not of one mind on this, but more often than not they do believe all animals should live according to their species' needs and desires. This is a challenge to the dominant paradigm about the relationship between humans and animals. What is striking about the individuals in these pages is that they are acting on their beliefs, and truly demonstrating what this different relationship looks like.

In the next chapter, we will examine what people actually do for animals, what they call what they do, and if they are supported by friends and family in their actions. We will then focus on the issue of cat and dog overpopulation, breeders and puppy mills, dog show impacts, spay/neuter benefits and myths, and the philosophy and implementation of the No-Kill Movement for cats and dogs.

3

WHAT WE DO

The TNR and rescue my husband and I have done in our neighbor-hood (which is a low-income, minority-majority area, with insufficient resources and animal control) has been on our own dime and time, so that's where so much of our time has gone. I have leafleted for Vegan Outreach; volunteered for BARC (in Baltimore, Maryland) to help with events by tabling; we fostered a dog for a local rescue called MJ's Sanctuary; I have sold handmade jewelry to benefit a sanctuary (Poplar Spring) and a rescue (Small Angels Rescue). I get alerts to send letters and emails for all kinds of groups. —Nina

I learned how many pets were killed at our local animal control facility in the local newspaper. They challenged someone to form a friends group, and I did. I wanted to change that number. Their biggest problem was promotion, so we photograph, promote, and have changed that number by about half. We still have a long ways to go. We act as middlemen between rescues and the shelter. We pro-mote spay and neuter as a means to keep pets out of the shelter. — Carol

Puppycide is the murder of dogs by police. . . . Most of these animals are on their own property, many inside their homes. Some are with their caregivers on leashes and under the caregivers' control. Many are killed in front of pleading family members and children. Most are killed for no reason. I advocate on this issue, handing out a business card with the information for dog lovers. —Sybil

ACTION OVERVIEW

Individuals engaged in addressing animal suffering are usually involved in multiple issues. It is rarely *just* about trying to stop animal testing or *just* being concerned about horse/mule protection. For example, ending puppy mills is often connected to rescue/adoption work. When asked to check the issues they were currently involved in, the top ten involvements mentioned were: rescue/adoptions; spay/neuter; vegetarianism/veganism; ending factory farms; sanctuary work; ending animal testing; ending puppy mills; protecting whales, dolphins, sharks, and sea life; protecting animals used for fur; and ending production of foie gras. But there were many other issues important to these study participants, such as anti-vivisection, anti-hunting work, declawing, the pet trade, horse/mule protection, and so forth.

Of the 204 people in the study, 153 (75 percent) said they volunteered with one or more organizations. Thirty-eight (19 percent) worked in a paid position at an animal-related organization. Fifteen people both volunteered and were paid, usually at different organizations. The organizations with paid staff that had a national presence included: Vegetarian Resource Group, Vegan Outreach, Our Hen House, The Humane Society of the United States (HSUS), Compassion Over Killing, Sea Shepherd, People for the Ethical Treatment of Animals (PETA), Pet Club, Farm Sanctuary, Jewish Veg, Mercy for Animals, Free from Harm, United Poultry Concerns, and PetSmart Charities. Regional or local organizations included: Hillsborough Animal Health Foundation, Poplar Spring Animal Sanctuary, The Kerulos Center, Compassionate Action for Animals, Furever Friends Rescue, A Whole Lotta Love, and Let the Animals Live, which is in Israel.

Fifty-eight people, who might volunteer or do paid work in animal-related organizations, also took actions on their own, independently. Feeding feral colonies and doing trap-neuter-return (TNR) is often done outside of organizations, by individuals. Signing online petitions, networking online, and managing meet-up groups are easily done by individuals. Donating and fund-raising, fostering, independent rescue and transport, writing about animal issues, organizing film showings, attending events and protests, promoting veganism in numerous ways, and engaging in artwork to raise awareness or donate to organizations—all are ways in which these people worked for animals.

Overall, the most common actions people were engaged in were (in order from most popular): donating money; letter writing or petition signing; fostering; adoption counseling/animal care while in an adoption center; investigation of animal abuse/cruelty; feral TNR; feeding feral colonies; and leafleting about vegetarianism/veganism. But, these individuals were engaged in a huge range of activity, including: organizing VegFests in their cities; updating websites; public speaking; running rescues they founded; sanctuary accreditation; and starting a vegan spirituality group.

While online petitions and Internet networking were mentioned frequently, participation in meet-up groups was not as big a factor as I expected. The most common meet-ups mentioned were vegetarian/vegan-related, and these were often eating out or potluck-related, as opposed to advocacy or activism. Meet-ups related to feral cat work was the next most common. Then there were individual mentions related to, for instance, a vegan athlete group, a dog hiking group, Direct Action Everywhere, Team Humane League, and individual organizations.

While most people in the study were not involved in meet-ups, many belonged to national or regional organizations. Usually membership was to keep informed about current information on the issues. The most popular organizations for this group of animal advocates and activists included (in order from most mentioned): The Humane Society of the United States, Farm Sanctuary, PETA, the American Society for the Prevention of Cruelty to Animals (ASPCA), World Wildlife Fund, Animal Legal Defense Fund, and Defenders of Wildlife. Fifty other organizations had mentions, ranging from the Physicians Committee for Responsible Medicine to the Sierra Club to the Factory Farming Awareness Coalition. Sea Shepherd Conservation Society, The Humane League, and Best Friends Animal Society had many mentions as well.

TERMS: ADVOCATE AND ACTIVIST

A survey question asked how people thought of themselves: as an animal activist, as an animal advocate, or other. Respondents could check more than one answer. Seventy percent said they considered themselves to be an animal advocate. Fifty-two percent called themselves an animal activist. Twenty-eight percent checked both advocate and activist. The "other" category was quite large. Here are many, but not all, of the responses: animal supporter, spiritual vegan, anti-speciesist, animal rescuer, animal liberation activist, vegan activist, decent human being, lover, good neighbor, caregiver, guardian, and voice for the voiceless.

I also asked respondents what they called what they do. Their options were: animal rights, animal welfare, animal protection, animal activism, animal advocacy, and other (check all that apply). Fifty-three percent called what they did animal advocacy, and 49 percent called it animal welfare. Forty-three percent called it animal rights, and 35 percent called it animal activism. Another 42 percent identified the work as animal protection. Other labels for the work included: rescue, ending animal exploitation, comfort giving, vegan outreach or advocacy, animal liberation, wildlife self-determination, love and caring, education, spiritual veganism, neighborhood activism, lifetime care, giving voice, sanctuary, and anti-speciesism.

I was interested in how study participants viewed the difference between the terms advocate and activist. I have found that words and labels matter in terms of self-identity, behavior, and framing work for social change. I asked this question of many in my follow-up interviews: Are advocate and activist the same in meaning, or is there a fundamental difference? While most people saw them as differing somewhat, several saw them as quite different. Most people thought they resonated with the public differently, so their use of the term often depended on context. While everyone pretty much saw themselves as an advocate, many did not see themselves as activists.

Most people were in agreement that advocates spoke up for animals. As Kathleen K., an organizer for the Fargo/Moorhead Vegetarians & Vegans meet-up group, says, "Advocate has the root word 'voc'— voice—so by being a voice for those that don't have the voice, people can understand." Activists took direct actions, such as "organizing or taking part in demonstrations, rescuing animals, writing articles, volunteering for animal charities, setting up petitions, leafleting, etc.," according to Jeanette, active in the United Kingdom with Viva! and Animal Justice Project. To Steve, working with Vegan Outreach, activism is "about broad social and cultural changes." Kathy S., a cofounder of Save the Cats Arizona, told me:

In the strict sense of the word, an advocate is someone being very vocal about it, and speaking to people. When we have people come into Petco, we're always educating them on don't declaw, the danger of leaving your pet outside, those kinds of things. An activist is somebody, to me, who is actually going out and physically doing something; maybe who's a rescuer who goes out and traps the cats.

Jamie C., who considers herself an animal activist and volunteers with Poplar Spring Animal Sanctuary, had this to say:

I think of an advocate as someone who speaks out for something when given an opportunity. An activist takes it a bit further by doing things publically to gain attention for a cause. I never miss an opportunity to speak out for farmed animals in any conversation, or to mention I am vegan and why. I also write letters of protest when needed, or letters to the editor in the paper, and have luckily had several published. I have done many protests in my time—against companies supporting animal torture, like circuses, and egg-producing facilities, and especially on Fur Free Friday, to protest the use of fur. I have leafleted to the public on why people should consider a compassionate vegan lifestyle.

Kim Meagher, founder of Wildhorse Ranch Rescue, gives specific examples of how she has been both an advocate and an activist:

I feel an animal activist is someone who actively handles animals and rescues animals, is part of an animal rescue organization that physically does those things, like Wildhorse Ranch Rescue. I was also an advocate when I was the American Horse Defense Fund representative for Arizona. We didn't do any hands-on anything. All we did was go to Capitol Hill and lobby on behalf of animals. To me, that's an advocate.

Sandra Higgins, founder of Eden Farmed Animal Sanctuary as well as Matilda's Promise Animal Rights & Vegan Education Centre in Ireland, writes in a follow-up note about social change:

Yes, I think there are important differences. I see the word activist as a stronger word. Advocates speak out on behalf of other animals but activists have the intention and motivation to bring about social change for other animals. My activism is about changing how we think of, feel about, and interact with other animals in a very radical way. For example, I use the personal stories, histories, and characters of the residents of Eden in a way that very deliberately invites my audience to connect in a radically different way to farmed animals. Their stories are told in such a way that the listener and viewer is forced to confront the myth that other animals are different, unequal, and that our use of them is harmless to them. I hope that I tell their stories in ways that do not simply present them as our victims, but that also confront the viewer or reader with the magnificence of their individuality, and the power and purpose of their lives, that we also desecrate by our use. I see vegan education as a very powerful form of activism.

Several people, such as Esther, who educates her fellow therapists about animal issues and also does animal-related artwork, say that the term "advocate" is safer for the public. "Advocate is more appealing to the public, more accessible. People can be turned off by the term activist," she tells me.

Helen K., volunteering at Vegan Haven, uses both terms. She says:

There is a difference; each has a different connotation. Advocate doesn't sound as threatening. Activist shuts people down and makes them defensive. Depending on who I'm talking to, I use different words. I was a public affairs advocate for Planned Parenthood. Advocate was the word we used, and I was always aware of the word. Advocate leads people to say, "Tell me, what do you do?" The media has covered activists as violent. There are negative views of the PETA activist. That's the first thing they think of. Animal advocate seems to lead to more of a conversation.

Jack of Vegan Outreach agreed with this "palatability," even though the words have overlap. He suggests that "people don't feel culpable if they can marginalize us as being too extreme. . . . People want to think of us as a little bit crazy so they don't have to change their diet."

The context in which the words are used matters. For example, Hope, staff for United Poultry Concerns and founder of Compassionate Living in Sonoma County, California, told me in our phone interview:

I do use the terms interchangeably, depending on my audience. If I'm talking to a friend of my mother's, and she's introducing me, and I'm trying to explain what I do, then I may use the word advocate. I'm an animal advocate, or I work in animal protection. Because the word activist can be kind of charged, it can maybe have more of an impression of fists in the air, or being angry, or who knows what kind of stereotypes people have in their minds. So, if my audience is a little more conservative—if I'm trying to sound a little more professional maybe—I might use the term advocate.

Will Tuttle, author and educator, doesn't want to turn people off, "like if I say I'm an animal rights activist to someone who's just maybe a mainstream person and they're already defensive. If I say, maybe, I'm an advocate for animals, perhaps that's less threatening and they'll feel like, yeah, I'm an advocate for animals too. If we're going to use labels, we might as well use labels that get the job done. We want to open the door to better understanding to help the animals. But I think activist is a good word because it is important for us to be active."

This factor was mentioned by many people: Keeping the conversation going by using the word "advocate," because of activist stereotypes. As Alicia, Latino outreach manager for PETA, said, "If I'm talking to a mainstream reporter, I will probably say animal advocate, just because animal activist sounds a little scary; when you think 'activist,' you think of someone in the street yelling and screaming, ruining your day."

JoAnn R., a volunteer with Animal Guardian Network, is an example of someone who sees her actions encompassing both terms. "I used to think of myself only as an advocate, by signing petitions, volunteering, providing information. But I have now become more of an activist, by protesting, leafleting, having online 'discussions' with the county attorney regarding his views as animals being property, and his failure to uphold the law that animal abuse is a felony."

Others do not embrace the "activist" label. Here is what Amber, volunteering with dogs at three different rescues, shared:

I see an activist as someone who is very politically active—picketing organizations that sell fur or use animals in testing, writing their congress member regularly, definitely a vegetarian, refuses to wear leather. . . . I am none of those things. I eat meat, though I try to be picky about choosing meat raised more humanely. I love my soft leather purse. I mostly choose animal-cruelty free beauty products, but not always. I see myself as an animal advocate because I support dogs and help them get adopted, be safe and healthy, and find great forever homes. I will go so far as to share a Facebook post about the importance of spaying and neutering your pets or about not walking your dog on hot pavement, but that's about as political and righteous as I get. I will stop traffic to rescue a dog, though, and I had one day, in a South Tucson completely Spanish-speaking barrio, where I went ape-shit over a pit bull someone left tied to a fence in the full sun with no water and no way to lie down. That was about the closest I got to calling myself an activist.

SPECIFIC ACTIVITIES

As has already been indicated (for example, in discussing TNR in chapter 1), these advocates and activists do a wide range of activities. This next section will look more closely at other examples of what people who care about animals do. Some of the activities, specifically fostering and rescue work, will be discussed in coming chapters. We'll see the endless possibilities for involvement.

Vernon, for example, is the one paid employee with the American Sanctuary Association (ASA). He processes applications from sanctuaries for ASA accreditation, and also helps find sanctuary placements for animals. He writes, "These requests can come from individuals, state wildlife agencies, laboratories, zoos, etc., and we place all species of animals, except dogs and domestic cats. . . .This is a nationwide placement service—we may, for example, place a bear in California with a sanctuary in Colorado."

Leah is active in South Carolina with the national Rabbit Advocacy Network. She says, "We are primarily online, but we have also had planned physical protests at Whole Foods. That is our main target right now. We are trying to focus on one store at a time, getting rid of all rabbit meat in stores, but we also advocate for no angora fur and medical testing, plus adopt, don't shop."

Marine Life

Several people spoke about their dedication to ocean life, specifically with Sea Shepherd Conservation Society (SSCS). Melanie is the group's media and communications director:

I oversee all media and communications for SS in North America. I have ultimate responsibility for the content on the website, social media, media relations, archives, TV and video production, assisting with celebrity relations, etc. I have a team of three staff and two freelancers who report to me. I also direct and work with our media crews on campaign.

Melissa is a volunteer Sea Shepherd chapter coordinator in the Twin Cities. She tells me:

What our chapter looks like is mostly outreach stuff, educating people here in the Twin Cities about ocean wildlife conservation and what we can do here. Most people think of Minneapolis as the "middle of nowhere," and the fact is the Mississippi starts in Minnesota, and everything that we do here directly affects the Gulf of Mexico, and in turn, the oceans. So that's what we really try to focus on, to make people aware of.

John N., in addition to founding Peaceful Fields Sanctuary, is a coordinator of the Sea Shepherd Baltimore/Washington, DC chapter. He says, "It has been great to organize and attend events to talk to the public about the marine conservation work performed by Sea Shepherd, and to help raise funds to make the campaigns possible."

Lilia is an outreach manager for Sea Shepherd (as well as a volunteer with Wolf Patrol), working mostly on fund-raising, managing social media pages and the website, and creating outreach materials.

Writers and Artists

Will Tuttle, who wrote *The World Peace Diet*, feels the book and the facilitator training workshops he leads create change. "I think we all basically plant seeds, and when we plant seeds in other people they obviously can plant seeds in other people, too," he said. Writing is a very powerful tool, which Will attests to. "I've met many hundreds of people over the last ten years . . . who have directly gone vegan because of the book."

Another writer, Richard Schwartz, said, "I frequently speak to groups and contribute articles, letters to editors, and comments to articles online, promoting vegetarianism, veganism, animal rights, and related issues. I have over 200 articles and twenty-five podcasts of my talks and interviews at www.JewishVeg.com/schwartz and I am the author of three editions of the book *Judaism and Vegetarianism.*"

Other involved individuals are artists. Dana's business is animal paintings, mostly of sanctuary animals. She donates 10 percent of her proceeds to three local sanctuaries. She and her husband also walk dogs every weekend for a local shelter.

Isabella takes pictures of all the cats at two animal shelters around Berkeley, California, so they can be posted on social media for adoption. She is also working on a major photography project where she photographs landscapes that include all kinds of farms—farm animals that are in sanctuaries, on feedlots, and at dairy farms. Her work will be exhibited with a goal of provoking viewers to reflect on animals as individuals, on farm life, and on how we use animals. Isabella is also involved with Direct Action Everywhere and the vegan community in the Berkeley area.

International Work

A few people in the study are involved in international animal advocacy. Jessika A., for example, has volunteered since 2009 for nongovernmental organizations (NGOs) in Asia. She's volunteered in Kathmandu working with street dogs, and consulted with Help Animals India focusing on stopping the industrial dairy industry. At the time of our interview, she was in a master's program in biostatistics. She already holds a master's degree in nonprofit management, and is positioning herself for a career in animal-related public policy work. As she said, "This is my life's work."

Molly F. is dedicated to global wildlife and also volunteers with Animals Asia, an organization that focuses on the biofarming of bears in China and Vietnam. Due to her goal of working with wildlife rescue and rehabilitation, she has gained experience all over the world (China, Spain, Malawi, the United States). Like Jessika A., when we spoke, Molly F. was in a master's program in Applied Animal Behavior and Welfare in Edinburgh, to enhance her work.

Undercover Investigation and Monitoring

Others work in undercover investigations. Meghan, for example, volunteers with Mercy for Animals in Atlanta, Georgia. She told me,

> I've definitely just done some random kinds of undercover investigations that they've required in the past, like going to different areas and taking photographs and sending e-mails, and that doesn't really require a lot of time. But then, last year, I coordinated and ran the Mercy for Animals booth at VegFest, as well as at the Pride festival.

Lindsay, who at one time was a PETA undercover investigator, now works with Mercy for Animals. "I train the undercover investigators. Recruiting is how I spend most of my time. So, talking, finding individuals who are able to go in to work in factory farming, slaughter plants, hatcheries, dairies, any industry where animals are used." Lindsay's undercover career started when she was young. "I started doing my own investigations in high school and college, just really small things in animal agriculture and pet stores. I had my little camera and would take pictures and send them to the authorities."

Mike W. works for Compassion Over Killing as the investigations manager. "I recruit the investigators and manage them in the field; I manage all current investigations, help with the case breaks, media, law enforcement, all aspects." Previously he had been an undercover investigator for PETA and The Humane Society of the United States.

Elaine has a history working in slaughterhouses in England, and learned all she could to understand how to make slaughter as humane as possible. This became increasingly impossible as numbers grew and different companies took over the industry. She then assisted animal rights organizations, providing film and still pictures. She writes:

> What I do is provide information. [For] the pig plant I monitor, I give information to both Viva! and Animal Aid [animal rights groups in England]; if they think there is a breach of welfare code then I pursue with reporting it. The type of welfare breach I have gone ahead and reported has been 'death of pigs in transit,' 'death in lairage,' leaking of waste pipes (blood rushes), stacking of lorries exceeding the waiting time—and a long running reporting of environmental breaches (excessive smell).

Laws and Regulations

Others are working on the legal end. Farrah, an attorney with a national animal rights organization, explains her work:

> *I generate litigation that targets the worst abuses to the largest number of animals. So the idea is to get the litigation going—that's one model—or we partner with others, or we get a pro bono firm, or we hire local counsel, or sometimes we'll do the initial work on the case and then we pitch it to a law firm and they put their money into it. Just depends on the situation. But the common thread is, how do we use existing law to target the worst abuses for the largest number of animals—the institutionalized stuff?*

Amanda, who works as the company liaison for PETA's Beauty Without Bunnies cruelty-free certification program, describes her work this way:

> *I regularly negotiate with companies to end tests on animals for cosmetics, personal care, and household products, and to remove animal ingredients from their products. I also work on regulatory issues surrounding tests on animals, including international regulations (European Union, China, etc.) and changing laws in the United States. I absolutely love my job and am so grateful to be helping animals every day. I should also mention that I went to law school in order to have the credentials to back up my passion for animal rights, so I'm a lawyer by trade, and working for PETA is my dream job.*

Vegan Education

For some people, vegan education and outreach is where they put their energy. Jack cofounded Vegan Outreach in 1993, and has been paid staff since 2004. Part of his job is to maintain www.veganhealth.org, a vegan nutrition information site. Alka, a senior laboratory oversight specialist with PETA, also volunteers time every weekend to stock the vegan starter kits at locations throughout Washington, DC. She tables and leaflets for PETA, Mercy for Animals, and Compassion Over Killing at the many events in the DC area. Kathleen K. has helped start several vegetarian/vegan groups in North Dakota—Fargo/Moorhead Veg, Bismarck Veg, Grand City Veg, and Keiferman Veg. And, Jeanette has helped with "Vegan Roadshows . . . where they offer free vegan food tastings, cooking demos, talks, advice, and so on."

The individuals in this study are truly remarkable in the experience they bring to animal care, and the time, money, and energy they devote to the well-being of animals. Heather had been an officer with Chesapeake Animal Control in Virginia for three years before accepting her job at PETA in the Community Animal Project division. She writes:

> *This means that on a daily basis I go into both the local community, as well as travelling to North Carolina, to try and help owners with their animals through education, vet care, and basic care. Though a lot of our work deals with dogs and cats, I also work with birds, reptiles, livestock, exotics, and wildlife. Basically, if something is breathing and not human, I get to play with them. Our division supplies dog houses, straw, and transport for vets, or spay/neuter services, food, collars, flea medication, education, and euthanasia.*

SUPPORT FOR THE WORK

The advocates in this study felt they were overwhelmingly supported by friends and family. Ninety-four percent claimed support, and only 6 percent said they were not supported. I asked, "How was this support shown?" Many people talked about how their families, in particular, but also friends, participated with them.

For example, Jodie feeds feral colonies, and she said, "My family supports me. When I cannot feed my animals, they help feed. They stand behind me in what I do most of the time."

Nancy, who cofounded Furever Friends, a cat and dog rescue, wrote, "[O]ver the last five-plus years, my family and I have fostered over two hundred cats and kittens through various rescue organizations. They are supportive and committed to helping these marginalized pets become happy and healthy family members."

Alessa volunteers weekly with her twelve-year-old daughter at the local humane society. Amber's husband often helps with rescue and fostering. Furthermore, Amber says, "[M]y mother, two neighbors, two friends, and my ex-husband also help rescue, foster, or transport when asked." Some family members show support through donations, such as

Mary's and Nicole S.'s. Denise's family attends demonstrations with her. Joanne's husband, Joe, "picks up more of the household chores."

Laurie's network shows their support in many ways:

> with kind words of encouragement, by volunteering at the shelter, by adopting and referring friends and family to adopt, by donating money and in-kind goods, and something as simple as sharing my stories and posts via social media, which does work to find dogs and cats homes.

Many referred to the support for their beliefs and values. Sometimes support is gradual. For instance, Daya, who does rescue on her own, says that her family originally was not supportive and made fun of her. But, "now my partner is vegan and some friends have become vegan and those that haven't are now more open-minded about it." Bernice talks about a mixed response: "Most of my friends and family understand my love for animals and are supportive. A few don't fully understand when I put concerns for animals ahead of my own interests and needs."

Cat, who is involved in TNR, started Mildcats at Arizona State University, and founded an intervention program for children who abuse animals, has had this experience as well. She wrote, "[M]any of [my friends] think I go too far in my beliefs regarding animals, and the money I spend of my own sometimes, but my real friends understand that is who I am."

Many families are proud of the animal advocacy. Melissa J. has this to say about her father:

> As children we were always involved in volunteering. It was my dad who instilled the respect for the water and the animals in it. He is part of the Coastal Conservation and has worked with numerous organizations that are involved in the protection of ocean wildlife. When I told him that I had decided to volunteer with SSCS [Sea Shepherd], his response was "I'm so proud of you for making a difference."

Steve, with Vegan Outreach, echoes this sentiment about his family and friends: "My family understands that working for the animals is what matters the most to me. I connect most with others who are passionate about making the world a better place and reducing suffering, so most of my friends are enthusiastic about the work I am doing."

Support does not always mean others follow the same volunteering or vegan diets. Charlee, who is an office manager at Compassion Over Killing and a volunteer with Poplar Spring Animal Sanctuary, explains:

> My friends are very supportive and understand why I do what I do even if they live differently. My boyfriend also supports me, but finds it harder to cope sometimes, as we live together. He can feel insulted by some of my words or actions, although I never mean them to come off as condescending. My family is very supportive and is open to listening, however not open to change. Originally they were worried for me and thought this was a phase. Now they realize how passionate I am and know that I am doing this for the greater good.

Hope shares something similar. "My family is very supportive. They are proud of me and the work I do, however, they have made no changes in their diets or lifestyles, which is disappointing. But it could be worse. They have never been disrespectful or negative about my work. They are sympathetic and understanding."

Many respondents have influenced others due to their animal work, especially family members. For example, Ryan, PETA's director of International Youth Outreach, writes:

> Since I began working on animal rights issues, my friends and family have become increasingly sympathetic. My sister has gone vegetarian, and my brother has also gone back and forth, cutting out meat for months at a time. My parents continue to eat meat in their daily lives, but when eating with me, they eat vegan, out of respect. As a side note, I have also recently become a father, and my wife and I are raising our daughter vegan.

Another typical comment is from Elizabeth K.'s experience: "My friends have expressed their support multiple times and credited me [with] causing them to reduce their own intake of animal products."

Jessica B., a volunteer with Animal Advocates of Arizona and PETA, relates a common process of influence:

> In the beginning it wasn't easy. I was very angry about the suffering of animals on factory farms, animals used for entertainment, and in

laboratories. I didn't know how to talk effectively about how passion-
ate I was about this. My anger and aggression turned the people
around me off. Once I learned how to talk to people better I had a lot
more support. My family is proud of the work I do for animals and
has even joined me on certain things. I've had family and friends go
veg/vegan, and most of them have stopped going to circuses and
aquariums. My sister stopped buying clothing that contained fur
(trim) and my mom joins me at fur and circus protests.

Diana, senior youth marketing coordinator for peta2, writes about boy-
friends cutting down on meat intake, parents who will plan vegan dishes
at holiday meals, and friends participating in vegetarian potlucks. Sarah
M., who helps with adoption events and is a dog walker with the Animal
Care League, says even though her mother and stepfather probably
won't become vegans, they do ask many questions about veganism and
"honestly seem proud of me."

However, the comments of indifference are also numerous. Anni,
who feeds feral colonies, has heard, "They can take care of themselves"
and "Why are you wasting your time?" Rachel reported, "[Family mem-
bers] give me lip service but consider me to have less value since I do
not have a suitable career." Andrea's friends and family "think I'm crazy
for thinking that all living beings are equal and deserve equal rights to
life." Mike C., who advocates for animals through music, looks at the
issue of support from friends and family in the larger context: "It's
imbedded into their culture that animals are here to be eaten or to be
viewed as a source of food."

Belief systems are crucial when it comes to the treatment of animals.
For example, Desirée, a volunteer with Furever Friends, says, "[M]ost
of my family believes animals are on a lower hierarchy and aren't supposed to be treated with dignity." Melonie is also at Furever Friends. In
her experience, even though she feels support, "I do not see them
[family] making any personal changes in their lives in regard to animals.
They would rather just not know and continue doing what they are
doing." In Lynne's case, "Many of my friends and family members are
frequent hunters and don't believe the same things I do." Lynne volunteers with Sea Shepherd.

A few people mentioned a change in relationships because of their
pro-animal work. Gay Bradshaw, who founded The Kerulos Center,
writes, "At one point in my life, I ended friendships with those who do

not support animal social justice." Melanie, volunteering with Sea Shepherd, "had a rift with my scientist sister over it in the past." Sandra Higgins aligned her social life with her values: "I do not socialize where other animals are being exploited, and I do not remain in the company of people who are eating other animals; therefore opportunities to meet with family and friends are less than prior to my activist life."

For many animal advocates and activists, most of their friends are similarly involved. Isabella says, "My parents do not oppose my work; my siblings are indifferent or hostile. I have surrounded myself with others who advocate for animals."

Mike W. has "geared my life to only include friends and family who are supportive. Those who were not I no longer am in contact with."

This is a common refrain. From pet groomer Molly S.: "I only have friends that are like-minded"; from Save the Cats Arizona volunteer Sandy B.: "All my friends love animals. If they didn't, they wouldn't be my friends"; and from Carla, founder of The Foundation for Homeless Cats: "Everyone knows that if they hang with me, they're going to have to help me with the cats in some way." All show that concern and action for animals are at the center of their lives.

ISSUE FOCUS: OVERPOPULATION, SPAY/NEUTER, AND THE NO-KILL MOVEMENT

When asked to list their top three animal-related concerns, about one-fourth of the study participants listed spay/neuter, making it the most frequently mentioned concern. Most advocates realize spay/neuter is the number one solution to cat and dog overpopulation, as well as being healthier for them compared to not being altered. Spay/neuter is also the top step (of many) in the No-Kill Movement.

For cats, the overpopulation issue is primarily a problem of unspayed or unneutered *outdoor* cats (most cat guardians spay or neuter their cats). This is why the focus on TNR is so important. For dogs, overpopulation is primarily a problem of breeders—breeders who deliberately increase the number of dogs through farmed litters to sell in business. Connected to this is the marketing idea that purebred dogs are desirable dogs, and shelter or rescue dogs are substandard. Hence, rescue dogs are killed by the millions, while purebred dogs are purpose-fully bred to fill the demand for puppies.

Breeders and Puppy Mills

There is a societal preference for purebred dogs; people think they are healthy, special, and they are seen as a status symbol. A Westminster Kennel Club or Crufts dog show winner becomes the dog breed standard for the next ten-plus years. However, breeding is only about looks: It doesn't tell anything genetically about temperament, health, or training. The dog show judges are merely using their own likes and dislikes when they express preference for short or long noses, different ear types, or different body builds.

These preferences have serious outcomes. Breeders will immediately begin to breed traits to achieve certain "looks," to take advantage of the marketing that follows the winners. Televised dog shows, dog auctions, dog breed magazines, websites, and availability of types of dogs globally create the "in" type of dog. The business model in the breed industry, which is, of course, to sell dogs, depends upon dog auctions, dog shows, Internet advertising and sales, and pet stores to push breeds. This business model *needs* rescue and shelter dogs to be seen as undesirable, since money is not made off them.

Puppy mills exist to fill the demand for certain types of dogs created by dog shows. Puppy mills produce large numbers of puppies at low cost, to maximize profit, by breeding females repeatedly. The puppies are kept in cages, possibly without medical care, exercise, and socialization. These mills, or farms, are found all over the world, and puppies are even transported from country to country. According to HSUS, there are an estimated ten thousand licensed and unlicensed puppy mills in the United States alone.[1] Whether bred at a puppy mill, by a small-scale hobby breeder, or by a large-scale breed farm, genetic illness has often occurred—breathing problems, hip problems, seizures, skulls that are too small, and other disorders. Unsuspecting dog lovers have too often brought their purebred dog home only to spend hundreds and thousands of dollars on medical bills for illnesses and disabilities that were *caused* by breeders.

According to Kim Kavin, in her 2016 book, *The Dog Merchants*:

Supply is not exceeding demand. Americans want about eight million dogs a year as new pets, while only about four million dogs are entering the shelters. Americans kill about two million of those shelter dogs each year while US dog lovers get their new pets from other sources. If just half the Americans already getting a dog went the shelter route, then statistically speaking, every cage of US animal control facilities could be emptied.[2]

Unfortunately, "a solid third of America's dog-buying citizens believe that the best way to get a pooch is to buy a purebred."[3] In fact, according to a 2015–16 American Pet Products Association survey, 34 percent of the respondents purchased their dogs from a breeder (up from 32 percent in 2012–13).[4] The respondents believe shelter or rescue dogs are unpredictable and have unknown, negative backgrounds. Fund-raising ads for nonprofits usually have very sad-looking animals, which can solidify the idea that these animals are not healthy. Ironically, so many of these dogs are not only healthy, but they have already been socialized and lived with families. They are not the unhealthy and fearful dogs you might actually find in a pet store or on a website connected to a puppy mill or small-scale backyard breeder.

Another irony is that a quarter of the dogs in U.S. shelters are purebreds.[5] They may have been owner-surrendered after a Disney movie or fast-food ad made a breed popular, for any number of reasons. Sadly, puppies can even be killed if they aren't the "popular" color seen in movies or ads. Another disconnect is that rescue organizations themselves sometimes buy purebreds at dog auctions. They may feel they are taking the dog out of the system, but they are encouraging more breeding of that type of dog for the money.

An additional negative of purebred mania is breed-specific legislation (BSL). Once there are widespread ideas attached to breeds, these can lead to universal negative ideas about the breeds—not just the desirable outcomes for increased sales.

No breed is genetically more aggressive than another—these are largely taught and trained behaviors. Pit bulls have the highest dog kill rate in shelters, and many BSL laws relate to pit bulls, forbidding them from being owned within city limits. Yet, pit bull is not even a breed! It is "a commonly used term to describe an athletic-looking class of terrier that includes the American Staffordshire terrier, American pit bull terrier, Staffordshire bull terrier, and mixes of those breeds. There are over twenty-five breeds of dogs who are routinely mistaken for pit bulls."[6] This misnomer is a manifestation of the very idea of "breeds," when the focus should be more on health, socialization, and personality of individual dogs.

Looking at the Numbers

PETA reports that about seventy thousand puppies and kittens are born each day in the United States. Some of these animals are born to pets whose caretakers want them to have litters, some are born to breeders whose business it is to sell the animals, and most are born outdoors to unsterilized feral cats and strays.[7] Clearly, this results in cat and dog overpopulation—caused primarily because humans domesticated these animals and "their reproduction is no longer regulated by predators or habitat." Altering cats has become a human responsibility.[8]

According to the website of the Spay-Neuter Assistance Program (SNAP), almost three million cats and dogs are killed annually in shelters across the United States. While it can be debated as to the "we don't have any room for these animals" rationale for killing versus what efforts and programs are being used to get the cats and dogs adopted, there is no debate as to the fertility of unsterilized animals. A fertile dog can have two litters a year, with six to ten puppies. A fertile cat can have three litters per year, each with four to six kittens. The numbers are sobering: In seven years, one unspayed female dog and her offspring can produce 508 puppies. Similarly, in seven years, one unspayed mother cat and her kittens can produce up to 4,948 kittens.[9] Tragically, unwanted puppies and kittens are often disposed of—drowned or abandoned, or turned over to shelters where they are killed.

In 2015, PETA set a record for its low- and no-cost mobile spay/neuter clinics, sterilizing 11,929 animals. According to the website, this included 6,765 cats (409 were ferals) and 5,159 dogs. The article further reports that more than 122,000 dogs, cats, and rabbits have been spayed and neutered since the program began in 2001. "Using national estimates, that means PETA has prevented the births of some 1,506,652 puppies and kittens who would have added to—and suffered from—the homeless-animal problem."[10] Still, we need the dedicated effort of more organizations and individuals to address the tens of millions of unsterilized animals.

The Benefits to Spay/Neuter

Spaying can take place at two months of age (or at two pounds for kittens); neutering is safe at eight weeks as well. Spay/neuter is the only 100 percent effective method of population control for cats and dogs. Not only that, but there are numerous benefits (health, behavior, saving vet visits) for the animals.

In fact, there isn't one negative impact to sterilizing cats and dogs. In terms of health, spaying female cats and dogs eliminates the possibility of uterine or ovarian cancer, and reduces the threat of mammary cancer. Female cats spayed before their first heat experience tend to be healthiest. Males who are neutered eliminate their risk of testicular cancer. Urine-marking (or spraying) by cats and dogs dramatically decreases with spay/neuter. Also important, the roaming of females in heat and of male cats seeking them stops. Fighting over females stops. Altered cats and dogs tend to be calmer, stay closer to home, and are more likely to show affection. Because fighting is decreased, cats and dogs are not returning home with wounds and abscesses that require vet care (and vet bills).[11]

Myths and Facts about Spay/Neuter

There are many myths about spaying and neutering. For example, it is a myth that a cat or dog should have at least one litter before being spayed. But this just gets us more puppies and kittens, and, in fact, the female will be healthier if she does not have a litter. Spaying reduces the risks of cancers and tumors.

Some people are afraid their cat or dog will change its personality, but any slight changes are in the direction of better behavior. Dogs will still be protective—this is not connected to sex hormones. Furthermore, pets won't feel "less of a male," since animals don't have these identity concepts. Males might be around you more, as they roam less and fight less.[12]

There is a myth that cats and dogs get fat because of being altered. Weight gain is related to the food they are fed and lack of exercise, not to being spayed or neutered. Some people think that the offspring of their pets will be just like the parent, but there is no guarantee of this. Others are determined to only have a purebred pet, but "at least one out of four pets brought to animal shelters around the country" are purebred.[13] We don't have to keep breeding.

Another myth is that it is too expensive to have the surgery done. Every region of the United States has low-cost clinics, spay/neuter services, and sometimes, free vouchers. If you factor in the many costs of raising puppies and kittens, including food and shots, vet visits and training, as well as paying for animal control shelters and euthanasia, spaying and neutering is less expensive.[14]

Spay/Neuter of Outdoor Cats (Ferals and Strays)

Six to eight million cats and dogs enter shelters each year, and three— or possibly up to four—million are killed. Spay/neuter is, without doubt, a major strategy of reducing these kill statistics.

Ferals and strays are severely impacted by being fertile. As outdoor cats, they keep reproducing until volunteers or organizations find them (keep in mind only about 2 percent of outdoor cats are altered). But the numbers in the millions shows what a daunting task this is. As discussed in chapter 1, if we really want to get a handle on cat overpopulation, TNR programs are the number one approach. We need to have an all-out effort to trap these outdoor cats, so whole communities can get a handle on outdoor cat overpopulation. The same holds true for dogs running loose, particularly in rural areas. This can be done.

Rabbits

Spay/neuter regarding rabbits is quite similar to cats and dogs. According to Tranquility Trail Animal Sanctuary:

> [t]he neutering/spaying of rabbits is of utmost importance. Altered rabbits are healthier and live longer than unaltered rabbits. The risk of reproductive cancers (ovarian, uterine, mammarian) for an un-spayed female rabbit is virtually eliminated by spaying your female rabbit. Your neutered male rabbit will live longer as well, given that he won't be tempted to fight with other animals (rabbits, cats, etc.) due to his sexual aggression. Uterine adenocarcinoma is a malignant cancer that can affect female rabbits over two years of age. The best prevention for this disease is to remove the reproductive organs (ovaries and uterus) in a surgical procedure commonly called a spay. The procedure can be performed in females over four months of age. Spaying a rabbit also prevents pregnancy and can help control some

aggressive behavior. Male rabbits can also develop disease of the reproductive organs (the testicles) but with much less frequency than females. However, some male rabbits have a tendency to become aggressive in their "adolescent" years (8–18 months of age) and can also start spraying urine outside the toilet area to mark their territory. Surgical removal of the testicles, called castration, can control these behaviors if it is done before the behavior occurs or shortly thereafter.[15]

Pigs

When considering pigs, the August 2016 newsletter of Ironwood Pig Sanctuary looked at spay/neuter in terms of the health of the pigs, and also to address the problem of abandoned and unwanted pigs. The organization neuters and spays its sanctuary pigs as soon as possible, and there is a waiting list based on age, weight (many pigs arrive overweight and have to be put on a diet), and general health. As with other animals, neutering males reduces aggression, so staff and other pigs will be safer. Male pigs have a fairly quick recovery time from their less complicated surgery. Spaying females is more costly and more invasive. Recovery time is longer. Ironwood staff report that some older pigs need intravenous fluids after surgery, and they need to keep the incisions clean and dry for three weeks. Spaying and neutering is a constant with these sanctuary pigs, with over fifty waiting for their turn.

The No-Kill Movement

The No-Kill Movement recognizes sterilization as one aspect of a broad approach to saving animals' lives and reducing suffering. According to the No Kill Advocacy Center, "no kill" means "an end to the killing of all non-irremediably suffering animals."[16] This definition applies to all animals, not only domestic, and the suffering refers to "not being able to live without severe, unremitting pain even with prompt, necessary, and comprehensive veterinary care."

Best Friends Animal Society in Utah has taken a lead in helping more organizations in the country become no-kill shelters through education, programming, and funding. The society espouses "[n]o-kill organizations euthanize animals who are suffering irremediably. They do not kill healthy or adoptable animals and label it 'euthanasia' to make it more palatable."[17]

There are a few key ways to make a difference and actually reach the goal of "no kill." One, as discussed, is spay/neuter. We must reduce the number of cats and dogs, period, which will lessen the numbers in shelters and rescues. Promoting pet adoption from shelters and rescue organizations (which so many of the study participants volunteer and work in) is another.

But as PETA points out on its website, the problem must be stopped at its source. So, in addition to spay/neuter, it is essential that these sterilization programs be low-cost or free. We need to lobby for laws that stop breeders, phony "rescues," and businesses that supply pet shops. The pet trade by definition wants more animals, not less. PETA is concerned that a focus on kill numbers without a corresponding focus on root causes can cause animal suffering—animals turned away from shelters that later die on the streets, for example.[18] So, as discussed in the section on breeders and puppy mills, we need to stop the pet trade and the ideas that purebred animals are more desirable than those in rescues or shelters.

Best Friends agrees. Its nationwide programming addresses "shutting down puppy mills, fighting breed-discriminatory legislation, and keeping community cats [ferals] safe and out of shelters."[19] For example, Best Friends is working to end killing of cats and dogs in the state of Utah by 2019. The focus is on spay/neuter and increasing adoptions. Other programming in Los Angeles has a goal of reaching no-kill status by 2017. They have already reduced their numbers by 66 percent since 2012.[20]

The Humane Society of Southern Arizona (HSSA) has begun a shift to be a no-kill shelter. The society found it did need to go from an open-access shelter to managed intakes. Since HSSA now keeps every animal for however long it takes to adopt him or her out, the animals must do well in a shelter environment. HSSA also transfers pets in from other areas of southern Arizona, helping those shelters decrease their euthanasia rates.[21] While this is very good, there must always be a place for animals to go so that owners don't dump them or kill them. Open access shelters are still needed at this point.

What pulls this all together is the "No Kill Equation," developed by Nathan Winograd. While Winograd wasn't the first to think about no kill, the "equation" is a comprehensive program that can lead to great success if all components are followed. The list of components includes:

1. Feral Cat TNR Program
2. High-Volume, Low-Cost Spay/Neuter
3. Proactive Redemptions
4. Foster Care
5. Comprehensive Adoption Programs
6. Pet Retention
7. Medical and Behavior Rehabilitation
8. Public Relations/Community Involvement
9. Volunteers
10. Rescue Groups
11. A Compassionate, Hard Working Director[22]

Arianna Pittman, writing for One Green Planet, discusses several ways that communities are working to reach the no-kill goals. Moving animals to locations they have a better chance of adoption helps. One area might have too many small dogs while another has too few. Transporting them can increase their likelihood of being adopted. Another step is bringing animals out to meet potential adopters, perhaps offering a dog-walking lunch break at a workplace, where employees walk shelter dogs. Helping people out who come to surrender their pet is yet another idea. Perhaps they can be matched with a pet food pantry, a low-cost veterinarian, or get help with finding housing where pets are accepted. Ending BSL, promoting spay/neuter, and changing the public perception of shelter animals all are part of the no-kill approach.[23]

The individuals in this study working with cats and dogs—and other animals who find themselves in local shelters to a lesser extent—are involved in various aspects of the No Kill Equation. Their advocacy is guided by their compassion for animals and their desire to see an end to suffering. Laws are needed, but we see that laws by themselves are insufficient. Prioritizing community resources to address this people-created problem of cat and dog overpopulation works. We need more of it.

Next, we turn to the top issues of concern to study participants, and an issue focus of animal rescue—dog and cat organizations and adoptions, and wildlife issues and sanctuaries.

4

IDENTIFIED TOP ISSUES

So, after the [Humane Society of Southern Arizona] shelter closes for the day after six o'clock, we spend an hour one-on-one with a cat. It's not the kittens, it's the older, depressed cats that aren't adjusting to the shelter life. We spend an hour with them and we write a note in their chart about how they're doing so the next person that gets them, or if they go to an offsite location like a PetSmart, those adoptions counselors can read their files. —Lisa McQ

If you look at a chimpanzee in Uganda, versus a chimpanzee in Cameroon, the groups have cultural differences based on what they do. It's not genetic, it's not innate. It has to do with social learning. It's sad to see a chimpanzee in captivity that's been raised alone, or with one other chimpanzee, because they've been deprived of having a community, having a culture. And they suffer from that. —Julia

In the listing of your top three issues, you said "psychological well-being, prevention of psychological trauma and oppression, and human cultural change to becoming animal." What did you mean by that last one? —the researcher
    It is to say, basically, my belief is we have to divest ourselves from what we call civilization and shape ourselves to animal cultures. . . . There's a lot of wanting to have the cake and eat it, and the reality is that animals can't have their modesty, dignity, and freedom if we pursue the life we have, and that means forsaking human privilege. —Gay

Engaged and aware individuals often have difficulty narrowing down their personal top concerns; these study participants were no different. On the survey I asked them to list their top three concerns related to animals. When you care passionately about animal well-being, this is a tough task to rank the most important concerns—there are, unfortunately, so many. As an open-ended question, I also found that an answer could be applied to many different areas. Is "farm animals" the same as "veganism" or "dairy"? Is "animal psychological well-being" the same as "animals in captivity" and "animal experimentation"? To discuss the responses, I grouped the replies in broad categories.

Five categories of top concerns stood out (in order of frequency mentioned): issues with cats and dogs; the exploitation of animals for human use; animal abuse and cruelty; wildlife and oceans; and a very broad culture category. Even with these categories there is overlap, since, for example, dog racing can be under entertainment (exploitation category) or considered in the cats and dogs category. Keeping this in mind, we still want to get a handle on the issues people are passionate about, and feel they need to act on to end or resolve. I created certain categories, but these could be analyzed a bit differently by someone else.

Dog and cat issues span a wide range of topics, but form a large pool of key concern for these study participants. Forty-nine people specifically listed spay/neuter, and two listed TNR. Sixteen mentioned no-kill/euthanasia. Feral cats, homeless cats, and homeless dogs were mentioned by thirteen people. Three listed the need for low-cost veterinarian services. Finding homes and rescue/adoption was in the top three for fourteen people.

Seven people were concerned with lack of education on pet health. Mentioned by a few each (thirteen total) were: lack of lifetime commitment to domestic pets, vaccinations, poor nutrition of pet foods, people not adopting older cats and dogs, and people buying pets instead of adopting from shelters. Twenty-nine individuals listed puppy mills and breeders as a specific top three concern. Sixteen mentioned shelter overpopulation, and shelters and strays as a problem, and seven felt shelter reform was badly needed. Five people mentioned breed-specific legislation as problematic, particularly the misconceptions of pit bulls. Two people mentioned police shooting of companion animals (puppycide) as a top concern for them.

Concerns about the exploitation of animals for human use is a huge category, including use as food, entertainment, for experimentation/ testing, hunting, trapping, trade, and animals used in clothing or personal care products. Several people stated this simply as "all animal use." Eighty-seven people specifically mentioned animals used for food. The breakdown: used for food (twenty); farm animals (sixteen); factory farming (forty-eight); dairy (two); and chickens (one). Sixteen people listed veganism in their top three concerns; one listed vegetarianism; and two people stated alternatives to animal consumption. One person mentioned the ag-gag laws that prevent undercover investigations into factory farming. If you add all these food-related concerns, more than half of the study participants (107) shared a top concern about animals used for food. This is not especially surprising, since the animal agriculture industry creates untold suffering for animals, and most people, including meat-eaters, are aware of this to some extent. After all, we eat food all day long, every day, and hence indirectly are interacting with food animals every day.

Animals used in entertainment (zoos, circuses, aquariums/marine parks) was mentioned by eighteen people. Seven listed animal captivity; dog-, cock-, and bullfighting was listed by twelve people as a top concern; primates were specifically mentioned once; and two people listed animal psychological well-being.

Forty people counted animal experimentation, or vivisection and animal testing, in their top three concerns. Eleven individuals listed hunting, trapping, trade, or fishing, and one specifically wrote about the use of dogs in hunting. Eleven people felt the use of animals for fur, clothing, leather, or by-products in personal care items ranked in their top three issues of concern. These areas reflect the speciesist idea that humans have a right to use animals in any way we want, and treat them as objects or commodities.

Animal abuse/cruelty was listed specifically by sixty-nine people as one of their top three concerns. The need for harsher penalties was mentioned ten times in the top three. Fourteen people mentioned animal abandonment. Also listed were: stronger law enforcement response; better laws to protect; Justice for Tiger (see chapter 5 for a full discussion); hoarding; tail/ear docking; and declawing. In this abuse/ cruelty category, we mostly find issues relating to actions by individuals that could be mediated by laws and law enforcement. Issues discussed in the exploitation for human use category could certainly be considered cruelty as well, but these tend to be practices widely experienced throughout our culture (food and entertainment, for example).

Concern for wildlife conservation, ecosystem destruction, or biodiversity was mentioned by thirteen people. Habitat loss or destruction was listed by fourteen people, and endangered species by two. Mentioned once each were primates as pets, great apes, and elephant rescue. Seven individuals were concerned with horses—breeding, Bureau of Land Management roundups, and slaughter. Biodiversity loss in the oceans, overfishing, and protecting sea life (whales, dolphins, seals, sea turtles, sharks) were mentioned by ten people. Global problems that are often connected to oceans, but affect us all, were also listed in the top three by a few people: plastics, pollution, and global warming.

Individual reflection on cultural views was seen in many ways. Speciesism—the belief in a system in which humans are superior to nonhuman animals (and hence the lack of animal equality)—was listed by six people. Other cultural ideas were: animal rights (five); lack of compassion (four); need human culture change (two); human complacency (two); animals as property (two); liberating animals from humans (one); government and media support the status quo (one); domestication (one); better, more effective animal activism (one); and recognition of the fact that humans are animals (one). This category is especially meaningful because these ideas create the context for all other behaviors, practices, and policies in the culture.

Examining this "top three" listing of concerns demonstrates where people are inclined to put their time, energy, and resources, as well as what they will support others doing. Some study participants are directly addressing one or more of their "top three" concerns in their work or by volunteering. Others might not have the opportunity to do so directly, but they care deeply about the particular issue. They tend to be a well-informed group on animal issues, and have multiple issues they care about and would like to see changed.

Next we turn to the rescue/adoption work people in the study are doing with cats, dogs, and rabbits—the expression of their passionate ideas and concerns translated into everyday action. Following this, we will look at the compelling issues related to wildlife and how desperately we need to "rescue" wildlife.

ISSUE FOCUS: RESCUE AND ADOPTION OF CATS, DOGS, AND RABBITS

Rescue work occurs in every small town and large city in America because compassionate people do not want to see animals suffer. There are countless reasons why companion animals end up homeless, but overall it is a problem of people—people breeding, abandoning, abusing, or acting irresponsibly toward their pets. These animals then end up, if lucky, treated for illness, spayed or neutered, fed, sheltered, and possibly placed in new homes through the efforts of volunteers. As we see by the numbers below, this is millions of cats and dogs. If you recall, from chapter 1, outdoor cats fare even less well. Thanks to trap-neuter-return (TNR) activists, many ferals and strays will be helped or even taken off the streets, but tens of millions of others will live outdoors dependent on colony feeders.

The Numbers

According to the American Society for the Prevention of Cruelty to Animals (ASPCA) website, there are approximately 13,600 community animal shelters nationwide.[1] The American Humane Association breaks this number into shelters with physical facilities (5,000 to 6,000), and rescue groups (approximately 8,000), which usually don't have physical facilities but rely on fostering situations (temporary housing in individual homes).[2] Petfinder, an online site that advertises adoptable pets to potential adoptees, listed 303,088 adoptable pets from 12,909 adoption groups on August 15, 2016.[3]

The ASPCA reports these national statistics (numbers vary by state and locality):

- Of the approximately 7.6 million companion animals who enter shelters nationwide every year, approximately 3.9 million are dogs and 3.4 million are cats.
- Each year, approximately 2.7 million animals are euthanized (1.2 million dogs and 1.4 million cats).
- Approximately 2.7 million shelter animals are adopted each year (1.4 million dogs and 1.3 million cats).

- About 649,000 animals who enter shelters as strays are returned to their owners (542,000 dogs and 100,000 cats).
- Of the dogs entering shelters, approximately 35 percent are adopted, 31 percent are euthanized, and 26 percent of dogs who came in as strays are returned to their owners.
- Of the cats entering shelters, approximately 37 percent are adopted, 41 percent are euthanized, and less than 5 percent of cats who come in as strays are returned to their owners.
- About twice as many animals enter shelters as strays, compared to the number that are relinquished by their owners.[4]

The number one reason both dogs and cats are relinquished to shelters is that their place of residence does not allow pets (dogs: 29 percent; cats: 21 percent). This is particularly important because 72 percent of renters have pets. The Humane Society of the United States (HSUS) reports that the rental industry went "pet-friendly," and allowed pets in the 1990s to attract and keep tenants by implementing extra deposits, fees, and sometimes monthly pet rents. Some offered amenities such as dog parks, valet walking services, and grooming spas. However, there are still problems: breed and weight restrictions, requirements for cat declawing, limiting the number of pets, and bans on kittens and puppies, or on senior pets.[5]

As we have seen, there are over ten thousand rescue and shelter organizations across the country. In my county (Maricopa County, Arizona) alone, there are easily one hundred organizations that deal with dogs, cats, rabbits, birds, wildlife, and reptiles, and many spay/neuter clinics, TNR groups, pet food assistance organizations, pet loss groups, and other animal services. Thousands of people across the country volunteer for, or work at, these types of organizations. County shelters generally accept any surrendered animal (along with a surrender fee), plus animal control officers pick up stray animals. These animals will be vaccinated, given rabies shots, and spayed or neutered before they are adopted out. However, as already discussed, government shelters are also responsible for the greatest number of deaths of animals, with very high kill rates. This is where the No-Kill Movement is working—to reduce these killings to near zero for any animal not suffering irremediably. According to HSUS, 80 percent of euthanized animals in shelters were healthy, and could have been adopted out.[6]

One example of rescue organization networking is seen in Maricopa County, Arizona, where the county shelter also has the New Hope program, saving thousands of cats and dogs as they are transferred to rescue organizations. According to the fiscal year 2015 (FY15) annual report,

> The New Hope program has always been an essential part in the day-to-day efforts at Maricopa County Animal Care and Control. Being a part of a community dedicated to saving the lives of animals is what makes animal welfare work. MCACC's New Hope partners include nearly one hundred rescue groups and animal welfare organizations. Per rescue group requests, MCACC transfers animals into their care from our shelters, while ensuring the pet a home and opening up space and resources for MCACC to care for other animals. In FY15 11,550 animals were transferred to New Hope organizations.[7]

In addition to participating in New Hope, Nancy, a cofounder of Furever Friends Rescue, explained to me how the Phoenix Animal Care Coalition, PACC 911, works:

> It is a consortium of probably one hundred-plus different rescues here in the valley. . . . PACC was instrumental in getting Maddie's Fund projects here. [**Note:** Maddie's Fund provides leadership and program funds to help eight million rescue and shelter dogs and cats annually.] PACC and the county ended up being the fiduciary for Maddie's, in order to disperse the funds to the different organizations that decided to participate in the adoption days. [What PACC tries] to do is set up offsite events for all the organizations that work for them. So, for those organizations that are foster-based only, having PACC put together these events is huge for a lot of these folks. [PACC has] an emergency medical fund that every organization has access to. Your criteria for using the emergency medical fund is attending at least three offsite adoptions events each year.

Kathy S., a cofounder of Save the Cats Arizona, has a story worth sharing. Save the Cats started out as a sanctuary for feral and stray cats being "removed" from a local nature preserve, then added cats from a hoarding situation, and evolved to adoption and outreach. She tells me:

> When I came across the efforts of a gentleman feeding and rescuing cats from a nature preserve, I felt very drawn to the cause. Many of

these cats had been abandoned by their owners, left to fend for them-
selves in a difficult environment. I hated to think of anyone once
having a loving home, and then finding themselves out on the street,
confused, and not knowing how to get just the basics in life—food
and water—let alone love and affection. Many had been abused (for
example, shot with BB guns). Some had never experienced a loving
home, were afraid of people, and were essentially forgotten altogeth-
er.

I became more and more drawn to helping the cats in the nature
preserve, and as time went on I learned a tremendous amount about
feeding cat colonies, how to trap using various methods, TNR, foster-
ing, adoptions, feral and socialized cat behavior, and feline medical
issues. I was at the preserve at least twice a week for at least two
years. When city government decided the cats must go, I led a small
group of concerned citizens to negotiate on behalf of the cats. One
thing led to another and before I knew it I was working with a
handful of people to start a cat sanctuary.

After needing to get eighty cats out of the nature preserve in a very
short time span (and accomplishing that), the group learned about a
desperate situation of sixty cats living in a trailer with a hoarder. Kathy
S. continues:

The original focus [was] on the feral cats at the preserve, getting
them set up so they had a home for life, and then here comes this. We
were so geared toward ferals. And then we get this whole different
group that came from an indoor environment, had never been out-
doors in their lives, very adoptable, but we had never dealt with that
kind of situation before. It's interesting: Ever since the beginning, it's
been rush, rush, rush. We've got an emergency! In the next two
weeks, we have to get eighty cats out of the preserve to safety, and the
sanctuary set up. And setting up the processes to get that right. Then
it was: Oh, my gosh, now we have to get sixty cats out of this trailer,
and never [having] dealt with that before. We have to quickly get
them out of the trailer. We have five days to do that. And then all the
spay and neuter, and we weren't prepared for that. Then it was all
the adoption stuff, and getting that all set up . . . we finally have that
working.

Rescue organizations rarely have their own facilities, and instead
depend on volunteer foster homes (fosters). Fosters are used for cats

and dogs needing medical attention, animals under assessment, and those who need quarantine; kittens and puppies who are waiting to reach their age and weight requirement for spaying/neutering; older animals that are unadoptable and need a place to live out their days; animals needing a break from kennel life if they are in a PetSmart or Petco adoption center; and cats and dogs that are rotating to different adoption venues. People power is essential to getting the rescue work done. Tracyene volunteers with Wags Rescue in Pennsylvania:

> I foster dogs for Wags. There isn't a Wags central location that I go to. I do pick my dogs up from the shelter, where I meet other fosters; take my fosters to the vet, where I occasionally run into other fosters; and take my foster dog to the transport location, where everyone whose dog is being adopted or moved up north brings their dog, so they can be loaded onto the transport van.

Kitty fosters in her own rescue, Tailless Cat Rescue in North Carolina. In her case, she has her hand in every duty:

> I keep all the records, build and maintain the website, foster most of the cats, transport to and from vet visits, process applications and arrange adoptions, and work adoption fairs. I do have a volunteer who helps with Facebook and media promotion, and another volunteer who helps with adoption fairs and occasionally helps with transport. Mine is the only full-time foster home, although I have a couple of people who will foster short term.

Nadia, a cofounder of Golden Bone Rescue & Rehab, talks about this foster-based rescue. Working all over the state of Arizona to take in senior dogs whose owners are going into a care facility or have died, she is "constantly managing foster homes." Golden Bone also specializes "in animals that have either emotional trauma or are very timid animals." The group works with behavior specialists and their volunteers to try to help senior dogs recover, and they work hard on special placement.

Libbi adopted a dog that came from a puppy mill rescue, which opened up a new world of involvement for her with local rescue organizations.

> I was asked by the rescue I adopted [my pet] from if I could meet another potential adopter that lived in my neighborhood to see if we

could help with the socialization of a dog she wanted to adopt. After helping out with that, I realized that I wanted to be involved. It grew from there into emergency fostering for that rescue, then fostering for other rescues, and then pulling animals from shelters, and transporting animals for rescues. I find my niche at this time is as a mentor for new fosters and new adopters, helping them get their new family member set to their household routine.

Jasmine M. volunteers as the Blackhat Humane Society's vice president on the Navajo Reservation in New Mexico. All Blackhat animals are in foster homes. She writes:

We do have quite a few animals on our forty acres. In addition to our six permanent dogs, we always have one to fifteen foster dogs (at most three of the fosters will be adult dogs. The rest will be litters of pups). We also have two cats in the house and one in the barn. Our farm animals include four horses, eight goats, several rescued rabbits, and quite a few chickens. . . . We have more than a dozen people who sometimes or always have fosters with us.

Another rescue, Wildhorse Ranch Rescue, has its HavasuPups program in Arizona, on the Havasupai Reservation. Kim Meagher, founder of the rescue, says the program runs about every quarter:

It all depends on money, because it runs us $2,500 to $5,000 each time. People are shocked by that, but what they don't realize is that includes bringing those animals out, getting them the health care they need, [and] transportation. We've got trucks and trailers, and we're getting eight miles to the gallon. It's a six-and-a-half-hour drive from here [Gilbert, Arizona]. Now that we're bringing out horses, it's a lot more expensive. So we try to go in every quarter, but if we don't have five grand, we don't go.

We have a crew of about eight to twelve. They stay the weekend; sometimes an entire week. The villagers have a place where our people stay. Glendale Air flies all of our gear in for free, 'cause we take food and medicine and crates. And then they fly all the puppies and kitties out for free. We haven't flown a horse out yet, they have to walk.

Animals that Wildhorse brings back usually have a rehabilitation period, and then they can be adopted out.

Rachel is one of the rare individuals who takes in sick cats that won't be adopted; these cats have many needs, yet they can live comfortably in someone's house. Usually fostering is short-term, and most likely the rescue is paying for food and medical care. Not so with Rachel.

> *All day long, I tend to sick cats who could not get adopted because of health reasons due to their abuse and neglect. I wipe noses and butts. I clean litter pans, clean up undigested food, give medicine and special food. I give love to the unloved so they can have the happiest lives possible, and a piece of me dies every time one of them passes on. I make sure the food supplies and litter supplies are delivered before they run out, and I make sure everyone gets along without any yelling or tension. This is a twenty-four-hour a day, 365-days-out-of-the-year job. There are no vacations or days off. I am financed through my husband, and no one else. I am at the end now, no more can be taken in. I have to be able to outlive them and not leave the burden of their needs to my family when I go. I probably have enough years left to live as long as my youngest cat. I have adopted out many, and hope the people did right by them. There are constantly more that need help.*

I asked Rachel where these cats came from. Some came from TNR situations from individuals. Some came from a few of her local rescue organizations, some came from neighbors who knew she would care for them. A year after our interview I emailed Rachel to see how she was doing. A few of her fourteen- and fifteen-year-olds had recently died. Rachel said, "They had a life they never would have had, and I loved them so much. I would do it all over again in a heartbeat because they gave me so much more than I could ever give them. I cared for them and they paid me back with snuggles—sometimes snotty, but always wonderful."

Sometimes fostering isn't for those organizations that lack a facility, but to give cats and dogs a break from kennel life in a county shelter. Rosanne, for example, usually fosters cats for the Pima County animal shelter. Then she got a call from a local group. They were afraid two of their cats—bonded seniors—would not do well at county. "So we've got them, and they're still with us. But, they were this close to death. They wouldn't have survived another forty-eight hours, I don't think." Animals need volunteers for this kind of consideration as well.

Rescues often have an adoption outlet at a PetSmart, Pet Club, or Petco, where the store might have kennels and some sort of adoption center, and the rescue provides volunteers to clean the kennels and work as adoption counselors. Animals in temporary kennels or pens are also brought in on weekends by some rescue organizations, along with rescue volunteers, so that the public can see these fostered animals and they can hopefully be adopted in a good match. PetSmart Charities helped adopt out 282,000 cats and 206,000 dogs in 2015 through partnering with 3,000 animal welfare organizations in the United States and Canada.[8] The Petco Foundation claims it finds homes for more than 400,000 pets every year through its Think Adoption First program.[9] Many organizations also sponsor large adoption events, perhaps in a large outdoor park or indoor venue, where rescues bring their animals for adoption, as well as provide information and business tabling. These are often festivals or holiday events that draw large crowds.

Sandy B. is active in a TNR program in her homeowners' association. They've partnered with a local rescue, Desert Paws, that has an adoption center in a PetSmart. "Whenever we trap kittens, [Desert Paws] takes them. We try to reciprocate by helping them foster, they put all our kittens through their adoption program, but we try to raise money for them, too." Here we see a successful model that really helps communities and cats—socialized outdoor cats are placed in homes, thus ensuring they're being cared for, and neighborhoods control their feral populations.

Amber volunteers with Arizona Cactus Corgi Rescue, Tucson's Cause for Canines, and the Humane Society of Southern Arizona (HSSA). Her weekly commitment is with HSSA. "I volunteer weekly for three to five hours a week, probably forty-two weeks of the year. Primarily I do offsite dog adoptions. Sometimes there are large events, but most weeks I am at a local PetSmart location."

Jamie L. volunteers with Help A Dog Smile, a foster-based rescue. "I do adoption events every single weekend, and the thing, every weekend, that surprises the heck out of me: We're inside a PetSmart, and people don't even realize what is happening at county. A hundred a day—literally a hundred a day—are being put down, and they're shocked."

Volunteers often start with one task and get increasingly involved. Shelley, for example, told me, "I started with cleaning cages at a Pet-

Smart once a week. I wanted to do more, so I began volunteering at a shelter. I eventually became the cat coordinator and volunteer instructor. The shelter stopped taking in cats, and then I started my own rescue [Kiss for Kittens]."

Leaps and Bounds Rabbit Rescue, in California, holds Saturday adoption events. Amy started helping out at weekly adoption events, learning about bunnies through hands-on experience. She's run some adoption events on her own over the years, and now she handles the inventory of the bunny care products. Two Saturdays a month she takes products to Petco.

To help animals be adoptable, they must receive good care and attention while in a shelter or adoption center. Vida, who volunteers with the Humane Society of Southern Arizona, gives a good idea of what's involved:

> I usually have a foster dog, with short breaks between fosters (to recover from letting them go). I also volunteer in [the] animal hospital on Sunday afternoons, socializing with the animals there and walking the ones that need to/can walk, cleaning their kennels, changing their bedding, hand feeding the ones that need it, petting them, playing with the ones that can play, etc.

ISSUE FOCUS: WILDLIFE

The reports are sobering. The World Wildlife Fund published a report in October 2016 that global wildlife populations decreased by 58 percent between 1970 and 2012. If this trend continues, we could lose "more than two-thirds of wildlife by 2020. . . . The rapid rate of decline is attributed to rising human populations, habitat loss and degradation, hunting, and climate change."[10]

But that is not all. Research conducted by Oregon State University found that humans posed the greatest threat to animals on the threatened species list. Hunting and trapping—whether for meat, pet trade, medicine, or ornaments—has put over three hundred species at risk of extinction. Large species and small are being impacted because the balance of prey animals is upset (and increases) as larger animals decrease. Furthermore, loss of seed-spreading animals, animals that keep insect populations down, and pollinators all impact human food supply.[11] In the study, conservation scientist John Fa commented that commercial hunters "with high-powered rifles and motorized vehicles" are having an enormous impact on this extinction to profit from the international bush meat trade. The study discussed hunting both on protected and unprotected areas, affecting "126 primates, 26 bats, and 65 ungulates such as deer and wild pigs." When these mammals disappear due to human exploitation, ecosystems will collapse.[12] It is clear that wildlife need rescue from humans—for both animals and humans to survive.

Trophy Hunting and Trapping

The cruel and illegal killing of Cecil the lion in Zimbabwe caused an international uproar. It wasn't that people had never heard of trophy hunting before; it was that people are reaching their saturation point of senseless deaths. The American, Walter Palmer, paid $50,000 to hunt and kill a lion, and he claims everything he did was legal, with permits. However, luring Cecil out of the national park where he was protected was not legal.

Cecil was a well-known and loved distinctive-looking lion, fitted with a GPS collar for research by Oxford University's Wildlife Conservation Research Unit since 2008. While Palmer was not charged with any crime, the Zimbabwean professional hunter he hired was. People around the world felt Palmer knew full well that what he was doing was illegal. In fact, he had previously pled guilty for illegal acts when he killed a black bear in 2006. In that case, he also killed the bear outside an approved area, moved the bear back in, and lied to U.S. wildlife agents.[13]

Trophy hunting has been decimating wildlife populations. Most trophy hunting—usually canned hunts, where wild animals are raised on game ranches, usually have no fear of humans, and cannot escape—happens in South Africa. Six hundred of the seven hundred lion trophies imported into the United States annually are from South Africa. As of October 2016, the U.S. Fish and Wildlife Service will no longer allow these imports into the country, since the African lion is listed as threatened and endangered.[14]

There are only 20,000 lions living in the wild. Much of the trophy hunting is done through canned lion hunts, which are repulsive. Lions are cornered, or led by the "guides," for the hunters' guaranteed kills.

In 2014, trophy hunters killed 999 captive lions in South Africa, 664 of them killed by Americans. Countries may argue that hunting fees are part of their national income, but both Kenya and Botswana have prohibited trophy hunting and they have growing tourism industries.[15]

But, trophy hunters don't need to travel overseas to kill an exotic animal to mount on their walls. Texas and Florida have dozens of ranches where wildlife, including endangered animals, are bred for canned hunting. Some of these animals are so tame, they will walk right up to the hunters. Animals such as giraffes, zebras, lions, African antelope, blackbuck, and others can be shot with high-powered rifles or a bow and arrow. The U.S. Fish and Wildlife Service regulates endangered species, and it has given permission for many of these animals to be hunted legally. These include "dama gazelles, scimitar-horned oryxes, Arabian oryxes, red lechwes, barasinghas and addax antelopes," animals born on the ranches or bred from animals from zoos.[16]

Another famous wildlife killing was of Pedals, a disabled bear who was killed in October 2016 in New Jersey. In 2016, New Jersey permitted the killing of almost one third of the state bear population, including mother bears and their cubs. People around the world followed Pedals on the Internet and were shocked that someone would slaughter him for a trophy. New Jersey allows baiting, which lures bears to garbage piles where they can be killed while eating. Only thirteen states allow this practice, which creates a situation where bears move closer to human residential areas to find easy food. Many states have outlawed this practice, and new legislation has been introduced in New Jersey to stop the bear hunts and remove black bears from the list of game species. Furthermore, the bill calls for measures to reduce human–bear conflicts.[17]

Millions of animals also die from trapping every year, which is a more brutal hunting method than shooting or bow hunting due to severe injury, trauma, and slow, agonizing deaths. According to an undercover investigation by Born Free USA in 2016, hunters in New York and Iowa were documented trapping in areas where it was not permitted; setting traps too close to roads, people, or residential areas; damaging beaver dams where not permitted by law; using illegal trap types; leaving bait uncovered; and other illegal measures. Wildlife was trapped for skins, and coyotes were trapped to be used in dogfighting.[18]

There are many organizations and individuals working to end the barbaric practices of hunting. Members of Wolf Patrol, for example, are committed to exposing trophy hunting of wolves, bears, and other wildlife by following hunters and making sure they aren't breaking any state or federal regulations. They only operate within the law and do not interfere with any hunts, including if animals are caught in traps. When they find poachers or hunters operating outside the hunting season, they report them to authorities. They hope to change public policy and encourage people to think more about the cruelty of hunting.[19]

Organizations such as The Humane Society of the United States (HSUS), Humane Society International, Born Free USA, International Fund for Animal Welfare, and others are all working to change federal and state laws, government regulations, and public opinions about wildlife and our need to coexist.

Private Ownership of Wildlife

People have a fascination with wildlife, and want to be close to it. However, they don't think it through—that wildlife requires certain diets, enough space to live species-appropriate lives, and that wildlife can be dangerous—even deadly—to humans. Millions of people in the United States keep wild animals as pets in their homes, yards, or caged outside their businesses. In 2011, the scene in Zanesville, Ohio, was devastating, as a man released his private collection of fifty lions, tigers, cougars, bears, and primates. Authorities were forced to hunt down the animals and kill them as they roamed the community. In 2012, Ohio legislators passed the Dangerous Wild Animal Act, which restricts ownership of wild animals, as most states do. Alabama, Nevada, North Carolina, South Carolina, and Wisconsin still do not have any restrictions on owning wildlife as pets.

We have endless documentation of maulings, attacks, and human deaths caused by wild animals such as tigers, reptiles, and monkeys in these forced interactions.[20] According to the Born Free USA Exotic Animal Incidents Database, "since 1990, more than 344 people have been injured by exotic pets in the [United States]."[21] It makes no sense whatsoever—for the humans or for the animals—to force wild animals into human spaces (homes, yards, entertainment pits, or cages). The animals will never be able to live as they do in the wild, and even in the best of circumstances, they will never live a "normal" wild life, with the appropriate environment and species behaviors. What benefit could this possibly be for humans?

Sadly, there is a thriving trade in wild animals as pets, estimated as a multibillion-dollar global industry. The trade is in animal products such as tusks, horns, skins, and fur, as well as for pets. Nadia, who is now in dog rescue, has seen this: "I began animal rescue work with captive big cats and wolves kept in apartments or private homes or sold through newspaper ads."

In 2016, Born Free USA issued its investigation into online sales of exotic (not domesticated) pets, an unfortunately growing, *legal*, and easy way to buy thousands of primates, exotic cats, canids, snakes, and others. They found baby animals under one year of age were the most popular, and that little to no information on animal care or well-being was offered. Though these animals posed safety risks to potential buyers, sellers rarely mentioned any possible risks. Born Free USA reports, "In fact, an estimated 15,000 primates, 10,000–20,000 big cats, 13.3 million small mammals, and 9.3 million reptiles are owned in homes across the nation as 'pets.'" Numbering in the millions, we can see this is big business for disreputable animal dealers.[22] An estimated 210 million animals were imported to the United States for "zoos, exhibitions, food, research, game ranches, and pets in 2005 alone," representing a doubling of animals in the past fifteen years, according to the U.S. Fish and Wildlife Service.[23]

One area where the exotic pet trade flourishes is online. Online sales are easy, fast, and show animals to prospective buyers that are not available in pet stores from breeders and dealers. Social media sites and online classified ads are largely unregulated, which means both the animals and the buyers are unprotected.

Sadly, wild animals as pets will suffer from isolation, confinement, and inappropriate diets. Breeders will take babies from their mothers, and apart from their own species, animals often develop mental and emotional illnesses. Add to this the handling and transportation they endure, these animals become highly stressed. They may be in tiny cages, tethered, or restrained, and many will have teeth, claws, fingernails, scent glands, or venom cruelly removed to control them. This is a horrific life for a wild animal.[24]

Sadly, our present legal response has been a hodgepodge of laws, some restricting wild animal ownership, some restricting only particular animals, some requiring pet licensing, and others with no regulation at all. This is clearly no way to protect these animals from suffering or, for that matter, to protect humans from harm.

Zoos and Captivity of Marine Life

When we see wild animals in homes as pets, or in entertaining acts such as circuses, zoos, or marine parks, we forget they are *wild*, and that they are in an unnatural environment. We forget they have their own needs and behaviors, because someone has shaped them into some caricature of our own projection—the monkey in a suit on a tricycle or the dolphin jumping through a hoop on fire. We don't see the constantly rocking elephant or the pacing lion in its cage. These animals are going crazy and living in fear. Captive animals often develop "zoochosis," forms of psychological disturbances seen in repetitive movements, body rocking, and outbursts of aggression. Animals in captivity, including captive orcas, are often given Prozac.[25]

Captive animals face different kinds of health problems than in the wild, but it is hard to argue that they are healthier. Elephants, for example, no longer traveling thirty miles a day over logs and streams, develop terrible arthritis and foot infections. They live shorter lives and have lower fertility. Often animals bred in captivity have genetic defects. Captive orcas develop bacterial infections and viruses they do not have in the oceans, and dorsal fin collapse—which never occurs in the wild—is common in male orcas. Orcas in captivity may attack each other, and boredom in their small tanks is a constant problem.[26]

It is hard to argue that captive animals teach children much about these animals. Their behavior is not the same as in the wild, and being in captivity is more likely to convey the message that animals are *for* our entertainment and use. Nature films give a much more accurate idea of what these animals are like in their nature habitats, with others of their species around them. Studies have shown that zoos do not create more compassion in children. In one study of 2,400 children visiting the London Zoo, 62 percent said they did not learn new facts about animals or feel they could engage in conservation efforts.[27]

Many zoos will argue that they contribute to conservation or breeding, but these outcomes are often quite weak. Captive wild animals do not necessarily breed, and wild animals raised in captivity do not behave the same as those in the wild. Those programs that are truly for rehabilitation and release rarely breed animals, and the animals are not on display to the public.

An interesting fact is that it is far less expensive to protect natural habitat for wild animals than it is to keep animals in captivity.[28] Removing big animals, such as elephants, from their native lands rarely benefits the people who live with these animals, and their consent is rarely obtained. One study found that money spent on conservation efforts or local investments was less than 5 percent of the total income of U.S. zoos.[29]

Breeding programs are going poorly in terms of genetic diversity for large mammals, and the survivability of the tens of thousands of species that are threatened with extinction is impossible to guarantee. What zoos do provide is money. The trade in zoo animals is profitable, much like other commodities that are traded—people, guns, drugs. Both legal and illegal trading in wild animals is big business.

Since the documentary *The Cove* was released in 2009, the world has learned of the extreme exploitation of dolphins hunted from September to March in Taiji, a coastal town in Japan. These sensitive, intelligent, and self-aware animals are driven into a small cove, where some are separated to be sold to marine parks and aquariums all around the world, while the others are killed for their meat. *The Cove* recorded one of these heartbreaking slaughters.

Dolphins captured in Taiji are separated from their families and trained through starvation and punishment to perform "tricks" for audiences who marvel at their beauty. But this is surface only. Dolphins become depressed in captivity, swim in endless circles, or lie motionless in their tanks. Before delivery to their performance destination, dolphins might have tubes placed down their throats to hydrate them and keep them healthy, since they are now on the feeding schedules of their trainers.[30]

Under public pressure, and with declining profits (partially fueled by the outrage from the documentary *Blackfish*), SeaWorld announced in March 2016 that it would end its orca breeding program, and phase out orca theatrical shows by 2019. Other marine parks are shifting from an emphasis on displaying captive dolphins and whales, as well. The National Aquarium in Baltimore, for instance, has plans to move eight bottlenose dolphins to a sea sanctuary they plan to build by the end of 2020.

Orcas, in particular, have a very rough time in captivity. Ordinarily they can swim one hundred miles a day in the ocean. In captivity in tanks, they will be lucky to swim one hundred laps. Sometimes they are not shielded by hot sun in shallow tanks; other times they are put in tanks with other orcas that attack and wound them. In captivity, orcas need antibiotics, fungal treatments, and antidepressants; not so in the wild. Boredom, depression, and illness (along with shorter life spans) are common among captive sea life, as we find with wildlife in zoos.

Orcas live in families, so family separations are emotionally brutal. Releasing them back to the wild is no easy matter. They need family members to live with and hunt with. Orcas do not live well as solitary creatures. According to David Kirby, a writer for *TakePart*, "Of the fifty-six orcas in captivity [around the world], only a small number were taken from the ocean; the rest were bred in captivity."[31] Even guaranteeing the family members of these few orcas could be found is a gamble.

Advocates are working on plans to build seaside sanctuaries to retire orcas to, but this is both a risky proposition and expensive. The idea is the orcas would learn to fish on their own, and live in a bay or cove with anchored netting where they could do deep dives and swim around a group of small islands. However, they would not have families to reunite with. On the positive, they wouldn't be in barren tanks, and there would be no roaring crowds. Not surprisingly, SeaWorld is opposed to these ideas, and the various locations for sanctuaries. They claim the risks of human pollution, disease exposure, and breaking of established human relationships would be irresponsible, and could cause stress or death.[32]

Wildlife Sanctuaries

There are all kinds of rescues, not just for cats and dogs, as I discussed earlier in this chapter, or the ocean sanctuaries mentioned above. There are also wildlife sanctuaries for birds, small animals, wolves, elephants, and so forth. Alexis, a study participant, volunteered with wildlife:

At eighteen, I applied to be a volunteer at Wildlife Haven [Rehabilitation Centre] in Manitoba, after dropping off a bird with a broken wing at the facility. I don't volunteer as often as I wish I could, between work and university, but when I can, it is always a fulfilling experience. There, I prep food for various animals: squirrels, turtles, rabbits, the barn cats, and mostly songbirds and corvids. As a vegan, I have a hard time prepping some plates—for example, feeding crows—because I have to cut up frozen baby rats and smelt. I wonder if I'm being "too vegan," as my sister jokes, but I do it, aware that it is nature and the crows must be fed somehow.

Finding the way to restore—to the extent possible—a balance caused by the disruption between humans and wildlife due to habitat loss, injury, hunting, and captivity is a goal of sanctuaries. There are many wildlife sanctuaries in the United States, though not all of them function in the best interests of the animals. A true sanctuary will not breed them, sell them, or buy them. If there are public tours, the fee goes into the care of the animals, not to make a profit off them.

One example of true wildlife rescues is The Elephant Sanctuary in Tennessee, which is the largest African and Asian elephant sanctuary in the United States. Elephants are only managed with positive reinforcement, and the sanctuary is closed to the public. Another, Performing Animal Welfare Society (PAWS), was founded in 1984, as three sanctuaries in Northern California. These elephants, tigers, bears, primates, African lions, and mountain lions are formerly abused, and retired wild animals.

Big cats and bears can be found at the International Exotic Animal Sanctuary in Texas. In Alpine, California, Lions, Tigers & Bears is a sanctuary for surrendered and abused big cats and bears. Both sanctuaries give scheduled tours for public education and awareness.

Born Free USA Primate Sanctuary in Texas opened in 1972. Macaques, baboons, and vervets are among the six hundred abused, displaced, and exploited primates provided for, rehabilitating and enriching their lives. The Center for Great Apes in Florida operates for chimpanzees and orangutans. Other sanctuaries provide for wildcats (Wildcat Haven Sanctuary in Oregon, Big Cat Rescue in Florida, and the Wildcat Sanctuary in Minnesota). All provide natural environments for the animals, enrichment, and education that reinforces that these animals should not be in captivity or used for entertainment.

The work in rescue and adoption that countless volunteers are doing is remarkable. The commitment to the well-being of the animals is enormous, though what the volunteers receive back in love, devotion, and satisfaction *from* these animals is also huge. The range of activities is impressive. Marge takes rescue dogs to a nursing home for pet therapy, "which is therapy for everyone involved, especially for mill dogs." Jocelyn fosters for one rescue, and also for a TNR group where she heads up a project that builds shelters for free-roaming cats. Liz B. gets the word out that the Humane Society of Southern Arizona has a program where the pets of survivors of domestic violence can be fostered while the women go to shelters (which rarely take pets).

Celeste, manager of Kitty City, the cat program at Wildhorse Ranch Rescue, monitors food, litter, bedding, critters on or around cats (such as fleas, ear mites, cockroaches, and scorpions), health, heating and cooling, and "anything a cat would need." Her view is these cats should be treated "like you would in your own environment, your own kitties." This is a sentiment widely shared by these volunteers.

Many care about wildlife, but have fewer opportunities to directly interact. Sea Shepherd volunteers do often work directly with ocean animals. Otherwise, their advocacy is mostly through raising awareness, petition signing, boycotts, social media networking, and financial donations, all crucial activities for rescuing animals.

As we move to chapter 5, we'll be examining how volunteers and staff view animal work as connected to other social justice issues, both philosophically and thematically. Our in-depth discussion will focus on a wide range of animal cruelty issues. We'll look at Justice for Tiger, documenting cruelty cases, domestic violence and animal abuse, the USDA Wildlife Services' killing program, wild horse roundups, and instances of other animal cruelty in everyday life. These impact not only the individual animals, but businesses, law, the environment, and people.

5

SOCIAL JUSTICE CONNECTIONS

*At one time, they were just blacks, just Jews, just women. The time of
'just animals' has passed.* —Nicole

[F]or animals, it is a daily holocaust. —Sybil

*I see connection between the way humans elevate themselves above
the natural world and its members—other species—[to] the way humans came to see each other the way this culture does, racism, sexism, ableism, ageism, and our destruction of this planet.* —Scout

I was curious if people who volunteered time, money, resources, and
energy to end animal suffering saw animal well-being, broadly defined,
as a social justice issue. Did they view this as complex, involving political, economic, and social institutions? Was this about power and power-
lessness? Were animals being dominated by humans? Are some people
problems very similar to animal problems? Were some of the solutions
to societal inequalities also solutions for animals? Did these individuals
also work on people issues, and if so, which ones?

I asked three related questions on the survey: "What other issues/
causes besides animal work are you involved with?"; "Do you connect
animal work with other social justice issues?"; and, "Do you feel the
oppression or abuse of animals is similar to other inequality issues, such
as sexism or racism, or to other issues of violence such as war or domestic violence? Why or why not?"

SOCIAL JUSTICE INTERESTS

Eighty-two individuals, or 40 percent of those surveyed, focused exclusively on animals. But 60 percent are giving time and resources to other societal issues besides animals. Sixty-three different issues were listed. The most popular issues that study participants were also working on included: environment, deforestation, water conservation (thirty-three); women's rights and issues, breast-feeding, reproductive rights (twenty-five); homelessness, hunger, and poverty (seventeen); lesbian, gay, bisexual, and transgender rights (sixteen); human and civil rights (eight); domestic violence and rape (seven); and politics (six). Most of the other issues were mentioned just once, but a few had two or three people involved. These topics ranged from children's health to sports coaching, from dignity in death to Team Plant Built (athletes who train, compete, and educate to show compassionate veganism), and from immigrant rights to literacy. Animal advocates are involved in a wide range of issues including health, peace, labor, poverty, elder rights, mental illness, religion, organ donation, museums, and libraries—spanning an array of social justice issues.

Let's examine what people had to say about the connection between working for animal well-being and other social justice issues. Most study respondents saw a connection in terms of "how you treat one is how you treat all." Kathleen K., a vegetarian/vegan meet-up organizer, said what many others echoed: "The worth (positive or negative) we place on animals directly correlates to how we treat one another." Thinking more specifically, Julie, a volunteer with Farm Sanctuary and a vegan nutrition counselor, stated, "The same principles of individual liberty apply to any group, be it a [group focused on a] certain kind of animal, all animals, or a subset such as humans, women, whomever. Each individual should be free from confinement and harm."

Rosanne, a cat and dog rescue volunteer, and Christi, volunteering with cat rescues, both saw similarities in populations with little power. Rosanne commented: "I think animal work is very connected to other social justice issues. If we can find compassion in caring for animals, we can channel that compassion into care for people, particularly those who have little or no voice." Christi saw vulnerability as key: "I do think there is a correlation between the abuse of animals and people, in that the weakest and most dependent are the most vulnerable to abuse."

Lilia, outreach manager with Sea Shepherd, takes a systems approach:

> *I subscribe to the motto "Until all are free, none are free." I believe*
> *the liberation of all animals (human and nonhuman) and landscapes*
> *are tied together. There are so many connections, you can't look at*
> *any of these issues—social justice, ecosystem collapse, animal exploi-*
> *tation—in isolation. You will always find connections.*

Eric, from Homeless Animal Rescue Team (HART), also views the connection on a broad scale. "We see a direct correlation of animal work within the community, as it is linked to law enforcement and social work. As we rescue animals and do TNR, we connect with the public on many other social issues, from hoarding, to poverty, to animal cruelty."

Izabela, animal rights activist and engaged in vegan outreach, expressed a common sentiment: "I believe there is no difference between human rights and animal rights." This is because, as Alicia, Latino outreach manager with PETA, said, "Arbitrary discrimination is wrong, whether it's against a human or an animal."

I saw this sentiment expressed in the comments people made about specific social problems. For example, Miranda, Humane Society of Southern Arizona volunteer, mentioned, "I believe feminism is linked to the way cows are treated on dairy farms." Looking at worker rights, Jeffrey, executive director of Jewish Veg, points to the "labor conditions on factory farms and in slaughterhouses." Diana, PETA's senior youth marketing coordinator, expands on this idea: "One of the factors that really affected me was reading how factory farms and slaughterhouses exploit illegal workers who have no voice. If they object or try to stand up for themselves, they are fired or deported, [and] this in one of the most dangerous jobs in the country!" Steve, on staff with Vegan Outreach, emphasized the inhumane treatment of workers in animal food production, where "workers in the industry are largely treated as replaceable cogs in a machine." Even worse, Susie C. refers to factory farming and slaughterhouse work as not only "desensitizing," but as "psychologically traumatizing." Susie C. oversees Farm Sanctuary's three sanctuaries in California and New York.

This is what Amber, who volunteers with several dog rescues, had to say about the connections between animals and homelessness:

I believe you can define a society and its people by how well they treat animals. I also find that issues like homelessness, underemployment, poverty, etc., lead people to be unable to care properly for animals—leading to lack of spaying, proper nutrition, and proper medical care. I find chronic homelessness connected to being an animal owner, since too few shelters or transitional housing programs allow animals. People chose to be on the streets with their dogs rather than accept housing.

Nancy, cofounder of Furever Friends Rescue, looks at another angle of the connection between low social class status and pets: "People on fixed incomes benefit from pet ownership, but are often unable to afford the care associated with having an animal. Age and financial status should not preclude an individual from having an animal to enrich their life."

Steve feels there is a strong social justice connection between basic health and the animal food industry. He writes: "The animal exploitation industries have diminished millions of peoples' quality of life in the most basic way: by taking away their health." Margaretta, humane society volunteer and foster, is also concerned with the social justice connection between health and animal agriculture. She says, "[A]n example would be the unhealthy food offered in schools, prisons, etc., that is tied with the meat and dairy industry, as opposed to clean produce and organic food, etc."

Concerns with animal agriculture and the environment were often referred to. Isabella, taking photos of animals for Berkeley, California, area shelters, and a member of Direct Action Everywhere, sums this up: "[T]he enslavement and slaughter of animals is a leading cause, if not the leading cause, of greenhouse gases, deforestation, ocean destruction, and mass species extinction."

The most frequent social justice connection made, however, concerns animal abuse and violence against people, specifically domestic violence. Carla, who started The Foundation for Homeless Cats, spoke for many when she wrote: "Certainly, as we know animal cruelty is linked to domestic violence, elder abuse, child abuse, and violent crime." Elizabeth Buff, in an article for One Green Planet, writes, "One study found that animal abuse occurred in 88 percent of homes where child abuse had been discovered. Another study found that up to 83 percent of women entering domestic violence shelters report that their abusers also abuse the family pet. In fact, animal abusers are five times more likely to abuse people."[1]

Betty, volunteering with cat rescues, like most of us, has heard of the cases where "many criminals or children crying out for emotional help start by harming animals." She continues, "[W]e need to keep reinforcing the concept that animals feel pain, and that we need to treat all animals better." While not all people who harm animals go on to kill people, we know of cases where murderers did start out by harming animals.

Kathy S., cofounder of Save the Cats Arizona, reminds us, "There is a connection between learning compassion for animals and showing compassion to fellow humans." Robin, an animal rights activist, writes, "[S]uffering and injustice are connected between animals and people, but the animals have the severe disadvantage of needing us to be their voice."

Similarities

I asked a question about similarities between animal issues and other social justice issues. The responses fell into five groups: abuse of animals as similar to abuse of people; all justice issues having a similar root cause; power or privilege rankings; animals seen as property or commodities; and a small group who did not feel there were similarities.

While many respondents specifically stated they did not see similarities between animal abuses and sexism or racism, others did. But, overwhelmingly, respondents did see a similarity between cruelty to animals and cruelty to humans. For example, Celeste, manager of Kitty City at Wildhorse Ranch Rescue, states, "People who do not respect animals, or abuse them, may also have no regard for their fellow human beings and their welfare." LeAnn, a volunteer with Furever Friends Rescue, echoes, "Those that are cruel and bigoted toward animals are usually cruel and bigoted toward people who are disenfranchised as well."

I received many comments on the similarity of root causes of inequalities, some referring to speciesism, which Shannon, who volunteers with dogs at two rescues, defines as "the assignment of different values, rights, or special consideration to individuals solely on the basis of their species membership." She continues:

Replace species with any one of those words (race, gender, home country, sexuality, etc.) and it is the same. I believe the majority of humans need to express their dominance through violence, whether that is war, domestic violence, rape, or factory farming. Eating animals is the socially acceptable violation of another being. We show our "superiority" through using animals for our enjoyment. For some, that means the zoo, and for others that means killing animals for the pleasure of consuming them.

Many others have a similar view, such as Izabela: "Animal suffering and slavery is not much different than what human slavery used to be. Sexism, racism, and *speciesism* are based on the same lack of understanding that equality was meant for all, no matter what gender, sexual orientation, or species." Kathleen K. says, "Because when we value one animal over another, saying this chicken is worth $2 a pound, and that dog can be bought for $350, it's an easy leap to say this homeless human is worth less than that celebrity." Ginny, a vegan dietitian who volunteers with animal shelters and several other animal organizations, also feels that this boils down to the idea that "certain lives matter less."

Robert, director of Free from Harm, brings up a most basic similarity:

The victims are different. The methods of oppression and the justifications that defend them are the same. The exploitation of animals was the precursor for the exploitation of certain human groups. There is no "us" and "them." We are part of a continuum of animal species that all share a common ancestry, a fact we have known since the time of Darwin. To deny this connection is to deny the basis for any scientific understanding of biology, evolution, etc.

Betty sees this exploitation and violence as similar, "whether that violence is domestic, animal fighting, or even puppy mills for profit." Janine, doing independent animal rescue and volunteering with a local shelter, further states: "The selfish, egocentric attitude that says our human wants, desires, and needs are more important than the well-being of other sentient beings is what allows us to accept institutionalized cruelty on factory farms and laboratories."

The idea that animals are property or commodities, rather than sentient beings with their own desires, relationships, and families, also figures prominently in the notion of similarities between social justice issues. Heather, working with PETA's Community Animal Project, states, "Yes, animals are considered property, which means they are often ignored and abused. This is the same fight children, women, and many races fight." Alka, PETA's senior laboratory oversight specialist, tells me, "Our mistreatment of animals is rooted in the (incorrect) perception that animals exist for humans—just as sexism is rooted in the notion that women exist for men, and [in racism] that people of color exist for white people."

Gwen, a volunteer with Mercy for Animals, believes we must "suppress and deny our natural compassion for other beings" in order to eat and use animals. She acknowledges an extension of this dynamic to other justice issues: "This suppression and denial also enables us to perpetrate the same kind of abuse on each other in the form of sexism, racism, war, domestic violence, and human trafficking."

The idea of a hierarchy of the strong (humans) over the weak (nonhuman animals) was discussed numerous times—more than any other social justice similarity between issues. Hierarchies involve a sense of "entitlement by a dominant group" (says Amber), where "[o]ppression and abuse, inequality, and injustice is meted out on the most vulnerable or suppressed of society" (says Elaine, who monitors a pig plant). According to Rosanne:

> We always seem to find ways to justify our treatment of animals as long as it suits our purposes and our comfort. They are "the other," in the same way that people from other cultures, genders, races, etc. are "the other." We can convince ourselves that "the other" is something inferior, and unworthy of our care and concern.

Diana easily associates animal rights and other social justice issues:

> Anyone who cares about human rights should care about animal rights. Anyone who has been treated as lesser, been taunted, called a faggot, a slut, a wetback, or any other slur that derides them as a lesser being based on their inherent traits, should feel compassion for the animals in slaughterhouses, laboratories, circuses, and any other animal whose lives are used and disregarded in an attempt to profit.

Lindsay, managing undercover investigations at Mercy for Animals, simply states: "[A]nimals are the epitome of oppression." Julie agrees:

"A stronger sect applies brute force to a minority or weaker sect, and subjects them to terrible treatment so the powerful sect can gain some fleeting incentive, [for example], food, pleasure, entertainment, etc."

Lack of Similarities

Not all the study participants saw these connections and similarities, however. A big difference for several people was that animals "do not have a voice to speak up with and defend themselves," as Lynne, a Sea Shepherd volunteer, says; that animals are more defenseless. Mike C., expressing animal rights through music, mentioned that "animals can't be heard, and they can't express themselves more than raw emotion, which, unfortunately, humans can't really read fluidly."

Alessa, a volunteer with the Humane Society of Southern Arizona, sees the treatment of animals by humans as a trust violation, not a type of inequality.

> We are their 100-percent, absolute stewards. Humans have violated this trust. There was, and always has been, an unspoken sacred contract for human beings to protect their lesser kin, and we have unconscionably violated that trust in many ways. . . . Since we continue to kill and abuse animals without regard for their sacred lives, we continue to operate at a much less evolved stage of consciousness than we could be at. . . . For example, this is manifest in an acceptance of the naturalness of meat eating, and the widespread forms of animal abuse.

Others saw animal issues as just different. To Darril, rescue and fostering volunteer, it's a "moral issue, or a cultural issue." He continues, "[S]ome people are raised to not care for animals, just raise them as livestock; some have never had pets and just don't understand what it is to have someone love you unconditionally."

Kathy W., a volunteer with Furever Friends Rescue, doesn't see it as an inequality issue. "Either you love animals or you don't," she said. Denise, with Friends for Seals in Washington state, felt it was different because, for example, "People who choose to hate a specific race, etc., do so for various reasons, while people who abuse animals typically don't do it because they hate individual animals or animals in general." To Yossi, staff with Let the Animals Live, "[E]ach issue is unique. There is complex system of differences and commonalities in power relations, oppression structures and methods, ethical issues, etc."

ISSUE FOCUS: ANIMAL CRUELTY

One of the reasons animal cruelty exists is because most people do not see nonhuman animals as equal to humans in terms of rights, sentience, or reasoning/thinking. If that is the way you think, you can use animals for entertainment, food, or experimentation, and treat them any way you want—as treasured companions, as backyard guards without adequate food and shelter, as objects or commodities to be used regardless of the result to the animal.

Justice for Tiger

A case that really took the spotlight is Justice for Tiger. I don't know if you could be on the Internet, and interested in animals, and not know this case. In April 2015, Texas veterinarian Kristen Lindsey shot and killed Tiger by shooting an arrow through his head. Tiger was an orange tabby who had the misfortune of being spotted by Lindsey. She posted a photo of herself on Facebook holding the arrow with Tiger's limp body dangling, along with the comment, "My first bow kill LOL. The only good feral tomcat is one with an arrow through its head! Vet of the year award . . . gladly accepted." This repulsive attitude was only compounded by the fact that Tiger was a family member, and his family lost their kitty in such a needless, gruesome way. And it goes without saying that no feral cat would deserve such a cruel death.

The Justice for Tiger Facebook campaign, along with Alley Cat Allies and the Animal Legal Defense Fund, were active in pushing for Dr. Lindsey to lose her veterinarian license to practice. Her action is certainly outside the scope of her oath to prevent and relieve animal suffering. After her Facebook posting, Lindsey was fired from her job, a practice that focused on equine medicine. Alley Cat Allies was clear that this act of cruelty is so unacceptable that few animal owners would ever trust her. The organization filed an amicus brief, pushed for license revocation, and kept the case alive on social media.

On August 20, 2016, two Texas administrative law judges recommended a five-year suspension of Lindsey's license, plus completion of continuing education on veterinary jurisprudence and animal welfare, as well as one hundred hours of community service at a cat rescue, free spay/neuter clinic, or other animal service. In this recommendation, Lindsey can practice as a vet under supervision after one year. The full Texas Board of Veterinary Medical Examiners met on October 18, 2016, and ruled to temporarily suspend Dr. Lindsey's veterinary license, a decision that is an insult to Tiger's family, and is inadequate to punish such severe animal cruelty. The ruling was a major disappointment to the thousands of people following the case, who were hoping that a strong response to animal cruelty would be taken.

The Justice for Tiger case is an example of what most people think of with animal cruelty or abuse—the mistreatment, often deliberate and outrageous, of individual animals, usually by individual humans. I read daily of these cases—dogs with acid poured on them, cats with their eyes glued shut, animals shot with weapons, dogs tied up with the chains or ropes digging deep into their necks, causing festering wounds. Farm animals may be starved, wounds and infections of animals go untreated, or animals may be beaten or even raped. Dogs are sometimes left in closed cars during the summer where they die of the heat; in the winter they may lack shelter in freezing weather.

I broaden the range of cruelty consideration to include animal suffering that results from deliberate policies, businesses, and practices. This includes the Bureau of Land Management's (BLM) wild horse roundups and U.S. Department of Agriculture (USDA) Wildlife Service hunts; commercial enterprises of animal fighting; circuses, puppy mills, horse soring, and horse-drawn carriages; and large-scale animal hoarding and widespread cat declawing. All of these create outcomes of suffering that are either accepted practice or, if illegal, still widespread in the culture.

I start with a discussion of new Federal Bureau of Investigations (FBI) data that tracks animal cruelty cases as a demonstration of how public attitudes are changing in regard to human treatment of animals. Study participants frequently mentioned animal abuse and the penalties associated with it; it taps into their compassion for animals, and how no sentient being should ever experience such suffering. They want a soci-

ety that clearly communicates that this abusive behavior is not acceptable.

FBI Animal Cruelty Documentation

A step in the right direction was taken in the fall of 2014, when the FBI
announced it would start classifying animal cruelty as a Class A felony,
joining arson, assault, and homicide. Starting in January 2016, the FBI
tracks four categories of crimes against animals: simple or gross neglect,
intentional abuse and torture, organized abuse (such as dogfighting),
and animal sexual abuse. The FBI defines cruelty to animals as
"[i]ntentionally, knowingly, or recklessly taking an action that mistreats
or kills any animal without just cause, such as torturing, tormenting,
mutilation, maiming, poisoning, or abandonment." Previously, animal
abuse cases were counted in the "other" crimes category, and not considered serious by the FBI.[2]

Another significant positive of FBI data collection is that animal
cruelty has been affirmed as a major vice, similar to other serious
crimes. Law enforcement training is in progress on how to investigate
these crimes, and how to better allocate resources on these cases, to
track cases, and to follow trends. As well, in the public mind, we see
animal victims treated more similarly to human victims. Legislators may
have a new understanding of the seriousness of these crimes and the
need for tougher penalties, one of the frequent comments I heard in
my study.

While local law enforcement reporting to the Uniform Crime Report is voluntary, the FBI, national and local animal welfare groups, and
the National Sheriffs Association (NSA) all consider this a major step in
understanding and responding to major crime. No national statistics
have been kept related to torture, abuse, or neglect of animals. It is well
documented that many serial murderers and people who commit violence against other people have abuse, torture, and murder of animals
in their backgrounds. This new data collection can help us document
and understand these patterns.

As a caution, however, Cat, cofounder of Children and Animals Together Assessment and Intervention Program at Arizona State University, reminded me in an interview that we need to be careful about
assuming there is a progression from animals to people. It isn't enough

to only ask, "Did they ever abuse animals?" These children may have been abusing people before animals, or engaging in property destruction, or involved in other acting-out behaviors. They are angry kids "striking out at whatever gets in their way." So, yes, absolutely look for this abusive behavior, but don't always assume there is a 100-percent predictive value based on animal abuse.

Legislative Responses

Domestic violence is a particularly sensitive area for victims and their pets, because often threats of violence, or actual acts of violence, are perpetrated against the pets, thus making it near impossible for victims to leave their abusers for fear of what will happen next. As many as 25 percent of victims return to abusers because they are worried about their pets. As a control mechanism, harm (or threats of harm) to pets is very effective.

In the meantime, a felony is also being committed against the animals. In March 2015, the Pets and Women Safety (PAWS) Act was introduced into Congress. This bill, H.R. 1258, expands federal coverage of protections to pets of victims of domestic violence, and establishes a federal grant program to help shelter these pets. Currently only 3 percent of domestic violence shelters take pets. This bill was sent to committee in June 2015.[3]

In May 2015, a new bill was introduced into Congress, the Prevent Animal Cruelty and Torture Act (the PACT Act; H.R. 2293). In December 2016, the Senate version (S. 1831) passed, and that bill has gone back to the House. This act would give the FBI and U.S. attorneys the ability to prosecute animal abuse cases that cross state lines.

Presently there is no federal anticruelty statute, and the PACT Act will hopefully be the first of many such federal bills. For example, this act would allow for criminal prosecution of those who run puppy mills, as well as people "who intentionally drown, suffocate, or otherwise heinously abuse their animals." Every state has felony-level malicious animal cruelty laws, but the federal government has the resources to deal with multistate cases.[4]

These federal laws are much-needed steps in ending animal suffering and holding perpetrators accountable. They will help animals and people. But their focus is primarily on cats and dogs; thus, many daily animal abuses will continue to be ignored. One reason they are ignored is that many people in society condone these practices—the public, food industries, and researchers. As Evelyn Nieves, writing for Alter-Net, discusses with regard to the new FBI tracking reform, there are still a number of widespread practices derided by animal welfare and protection groups. They include allowing animal torture and prolonged suffering in research labs; the widespread killing of wildlife by feds on public lands so that private ranchers can graze livestock; a lack of in-spectors for and monitoring of puppy mills; extreme confinement of animals in factory farms; and horrific conditions in animal slaughter-houses, to name some obvious examples of extreme conditions animals endure on a daily basis.[5]

This reality certainly demonstrates that while we may abhor the suffering of dogs and cats, we accept (or view as less horrific) the suffer-ing of farmed animals and laboratory animals, because we have justified their service to us. In other words, this behavior is integrated into our lives. Many animal advocates are speaking up for these animals, and working to end their suffering as well.

U.S. Department of Agriculture Wildlife Services

I believe most people would be shocked to learn that between 2004 and 2011, the USDA's Wildlife Services program killed over twenty-six mil-lion wild animals to protect agribusiness (primarily cattle grazing) and bolster hunting opportunities. Every year, $100 million of our tax dol-lars are spent on this killing. These animals are snared, trapped, poi-soned, denned (killing pups in their dens), or shot (usually from heli-copters and planes) by Wildlife Services. We are talking about coyotes, bobcats, river otters, foxes, prairie dogs, raccoons, rabbits, vultures, red-tailed hawks, black bears, wolves (including endangered Mexican grey wolves), a few bald and golden eagles, and millions of other birds. Some of these animals are "targeted," and others are "accidently" killed. In 2013 alone, over four million animals were killed.[6]

The supposed purpose of Wildlife Services is to eliminate invasive species, but the killing is largely indiscriminate. Each method of killing also creates enormous suffering for the animals. Habitats have been put out of balance by the practice, such as the killing of wolves and bears, which allows deer populations to increase, which then leads to more tree destruction from the deer, which then harms other animals.[7]

The Humane Society of the United States (HSUS) is opposed to the lethal methods of Wildlife Services. For example, coyotes are often baited with a lethal poison, compound 1080; HSUS notes that "[d]eath lasts five to fourteen hours. Victims suffer convulsions and ultimately die from cardiac failure or respiratory arrest."[8] The HSUS claims that while the program is funded primarily with our tax dollars, it benefits a small number of special interests—those who graze animals on public lands, factory farmers, industrial timber operations, and commercial fish farmers.

In an op-ed piece in the *New York Times* on August 11, 2016, Dan Flores wrote that coyotes stand alone (with wolves a close second) in their persecution as a species for eradication, with a half a million killed yearly. Coyotes have adjusted to this relentless kill campaign by spreading out in territories, by having large litters, and by beta females breeding after alphas are killed. They are not endangered. But, as Flores points out, coyotes are murdered for one main reason—for the sheep industry.[9] Does this coyote suffering make sense?

In October 2016, a federal court approved a settlement agreement in favor of WildEarth Guardians in its case against the activities of Wildlife Services in Nevada. This agreement was the outcome of a U.S. Ninth Circuit Court of Appeals ruling the year before that WildEarth Guardians had interests that were injured by Wildlife Services, and had standing to bring the program to court. WildEarth Guardians claimed the reliance on twenty-year-old data analysis for Wildlife Services decisions about native wildlife was outdated and disproven science. According to WildEarth's press release,

> The settlement requires the program to no longer rely on the outdated twenty-two-year-old Programmatic Environmental Impact Statement (PEIS). The program will conduct a new environmental analysis of its activities in Nevada, and will update all analyses nationwide that rely on the 1994 PEIS. The program will also cease all killing activities in designated Wilderness and Wilderness Study Areas in Nevada—over six million acres of public lands—at least until the new analysis is complete.[10]

Other pending cases that challenge this program's killings seem promising given this victory for wildlife in Nevada.

Wild Horse Roundups

Another government program that is shocking relates to wild horse and burro roundups, as well as cruel horse slaughter. According to the American Wild Horse Preservation Campaign, these animals are found on government-designated "Herd Management Areas" in ten states. There are fewer than thirty-three thousand wild horses left—from a population of over two million in 1900.[11] One of the common reasons given for roundup and removal is that wild horses degrade public lands. However, a study by the National Academy of Sciences found that livestock consumed 70 percent of public land grazing resources, while wild horses and burros consumed less than 5 percent.[12] Catering to ranchers' grazing interests, thousands of wild horses are harassed by helicopter to force them into government holding pens. In the process many horses are injured and even die. Families are separated, the horses are branded, and then they are held until they are sold in auction, or they just continue to live out their lives in these holding pens. Burros face a worse fate—burros found in Herd Management Areas are routinely shot in an eradication program, according to the Wild Horse Preservation Campaign.

Kim Meagher, founder of Wildhorse Ranch Rescue, spoke passionately to me about the politics involved in wild horse roundups. Bureau of Land Management (BLM) representatives are "mostly ranchers," and it is in the ranchers' interest to remove the horses. "They're making millions of dollars every year, rounding up our horses, and we pay for that. . . . The cattlemen's association is a huge lobbying group." While ranchers argue there are too many horses on the land, Kim argues that "we have twice as many horses in long-term holding pens" than running free.

Another consideration is the genetic viability of the herds. "If you've got under 1,500 head . . . that's not enough to genetically sustain them. They start inbreeding. Those horses are going to end up extinct," Kim said.

The cost of this wild horse management program is "expected to reach $80 million in taxpayer money" in 2016.[13] Horse auctions are held regularly, and some buyers are individuals looking for inexpensive riding horses. But most buyers represent horse slaughterhouses. They purchase horses cheap, and ship them without food or water to slaughterhouses in Canada or Mexico, where the food is then sent to European markets.

Horses sold for slaughter come from these BLM auctions, or are former racing horses, work horses, and companion horses that people no longer want or can afford. These horses are otherwise perfectly healthy. Horses endure long and cruel trips to slaughterhouses. The horse slaughter lobby in the United States tried unsuccessfully for years to receive the federal funding for inspections at slaughterhouses, but President Obama blocked them. This is why horses are shipped to Mexico and Canada. Eighty-seven percent of the horses slaughtered in Mexico come from the United States. No huge surprise: in 2015 the European Union suspended horse meat imports from Mexico, citing food safety concerns including the conditions of the horses during transport and the unregulated use of drugs in horses not raised for human consumption.[14]

Because horses are very skittish animals, with a flight response to fear, injuries at slaughterhouses are rampant. HSUS reports: "As a result, horses often endure repeated blows and sometimes remain conscious during dismemberment—this is rarely a quick, painless death." Broken bones, gaping wounds; it is horrendously cruel.[15]

According to a national public opinion poll, 71 percent of respondents were aware of wild horses and burros. Seventy-two percent supported protecting them, and 62 percent opposed the sale and slaughter of wild horses. In addition, 66 percent believed the BLM wild horse management approach was a waste of taxpayer funds.[16] Clearly, government policy and public opinion are at odds once again on an animal-related issue.

Soring

There is widespread use of animals for human financial gain, whether profit is made by charging admission, through betting, in competitions, or through sales. Soring is a cruel practice inflicted on show walking horses to produce the "big lick," chest-high step. Caustic chemicals (kerosene, diesel fuel, and mustard oil, for example) are applied to a horse's limbs, then the limbs are wrapped with plastic so the chemicals burn into the skin. One form of soring, pressure shoeing, involves cutting into the hoof and shoeing the horse so that any pressure put on the hoof causes terrible pain. Hence, the horse will step high to avoid this pain momentarily. Soring does cause burns, so to avoid detection, trainers will often burn off that evidence, causing more pain. Other methods of avoiding detection include numbing the horse so it doesn't react to being touched on the leg, training the horse to stand still by beating it, or using electric prods so it will stand still at inspection to avoid further trauma, causing pain in another area of the body to detract from the pain on its legs—or even switching horses so the inspected horse isn't the one in the competition.[17]

Soring was outlawed when Congress passed the Horse Protection Act of 1970, with punishments of fines and even imprisonment. However, while horses are sometimes pulled from competition, the practice continues to be widespread due to use of industry insiders as inspectors, and the fraudulent methods mentioned above to avoid detection. Ironically, competition winners earn about $300 at most, which is a small sum for so much pain inflicted, causing horses to moan in pain and to clearly fear humans. Successful trainers and owners may earn future fees for breeding and training.[18]

Due to the ineffectiveness of the Horse Protection Act, new regulatory action has been introduced, S. 1121, the Prevent All Soring Tactics (PAST) Act. This bill has been pending for over six years. In April 2015, it was referred to the Senate Committee on Commerce, Science, and Transportation. In July 2016, the USDA, responsible for enforcing the Horse Protection Act in the first place, announced a proposed rule to end walking horse industry self-regulation and ban the use of the painful devices used in the soring process. These are key components of the widely supported PAST Act. This bill was introduced largely because the USDA hadn't acted to fix these problems.[19]

Animal Fighting

The most common animal fighting operations are dogfighting, cockfighting, and hog-dog fighting. These tend to be highly secretive activities, and difficult for law enforcement to infiltrate. While it is believed that thousands of dogfighting operations exist in the United States, with tens of thousands of trainers, breeders, property owners, spectators, and gamblers involved, and often drugs, weapons, and money-laundering activities involved as well, there has been no data gathering, nor is there the ability to connect criminal activities together in any coherent way. The new FBI tracking, discussed above, will help with this. Tens of thousands of dollars can exchange hands in a single dogfight; this is very big business going on every day.

Fighting dogs are raised in isolation, usually outdoors, wearing heavy chains, forced to run treadmills, fed steroids to increase muscle mass, and often starved or given drugs to make them more vicious. They usually undergo ear cropping and tail docking to give an opponent less to grab onto, as well as eliminating body language cues of intentions. Females are subjected to rape boxes. Losing dogs are usually killed, or left without treatment for their injuries. As we saw with the Michael Vick case, killing can be through hanging, shooting, beating, electrocution, or drowning. Training involves using bait animals, which are procured from shelters, ads offering puppies or kittens for free, stolen dogs and cats, or by setting up a phony rescue organization.[20]

Dogfighting is a felony in all fifty states and in the District of Columbia, Guam, Puerto Rico, and the U.S. Virgin Islands. In most states, even possessing dogs for this purpose is a felony, and being a spectator at a dogfight is illegal. The penalties vary by state. There are also federal laws, including the Animal Welfare Act (AWA) of 1966, which criminalizes animal fighting activities that are interstate or use mail service. Congress passed the Animal Fighting Prohibition Enforcement Act in 2007, which amended the AWA and added felony penalties for aspects of dogfighting and cockfighting, and penalties of up to three years in jail and a fine of $250,000. Part of the 2014 Farm Bill (Agricultural Act) addressed animal fighting with the inclusion of the Animal Fighting Spectator Prohibition Act. In addition to making attendance at any animal fight a felony offense, it includes penalties for bringing a minor under age sixteen to an animal fight.[21]

The federal-level Michael Vick case brought the horrors of dogfighting to national prominence in 2007. Vick started his Virginia fight operation, called Bad Newz Kennels, when he was twenty-one and in his rookie year in professional football. He became a registered dog breeder. He had over fifty pit bulls in the kennels, and once search warrants exposed the full extent of the operation, all the familiar trappings of

SOCIAL JUSTICE CONNECTIONS

dogfighting were evident—chains, car axles, skeletal remains of murdered dogs, syringes for drug injections, the rape stand, a blood-stained fighting area, treadmills, parting sticks to pry open dogs' mouths during fights, and other signs of the organization, including paperwork. Vick (who originally denied any knowledge or involvement in the operation, including that he personally had killed dogs) and three associates went back and forth with evidence and testimony, on state and federal charges. Ultimately, the judge said Vick "played a major role by promoting, funding, and facilitating this cruel and inhumane sporting activity." The judge sentenced Vick to twenty-three months in prison. Vick also received three years' supervised probation during which he could not buy, sell, or own dogs. He was fined $5,000. Vick was also ordered to pay $928,073 as restitution for the fifty-three dogs seized from his property. He was required to enter a drug/alcohol treatment program and pay for the cost of treatment.[22]

The coconspirators received eighteen months in prison, twenty-one months, and two months (this last to Tony Taylor, who had cooperated and given evidence). Vick was released from Leavenworth after eighteen months, and served two more months in his home. His electronic monitoring ended in July 2009. As part of his release, he was required to do public speaking in an anti-dogfighting campaign with the HSUS. He was reinstated to the National Football League and resumed his multimillion-dollar career. In 2010 he became quarterback for the Philadelphia Eagles, with a salary of $5.25 million.[23]

Forty-nine of the dogs, meanwhile, had been evaluated by the American Society for the Prevention of Cruelty to Animals (ASPCA). It is usual for dogs seized in these fighting operations to be euthanized due to aggression. However, forty-seven of these dogs were able to go to sanctuaries or to foster homes to be socialized for adoptions. Twenty-two of these Vicktory Dogs went to Best Friends Sanctuary in Utah. A documentary was made and several books have been written about these remarkable dogs.[24]

In cockfighting, specially bred roosters, called gamecocks, are placed in a pit where they fight to the death. They are often trained on obstacle courses, on treadmills, have practice fights, and before a fight have their feathers plucked and their wattles (combs below the beak) cut off. Gamecocks have gaffs—three-inch-long curved daggers—attached to their legs. These are sharp enough to puncture a lung, poke out an eye, or break bones. Cockfights are held anywhere and everywhere, and not surprisingly, weapons, drugs, gambling, and other crimes are often associated with them. Hundreds to thousands of dollars can be won through the illegal betting.

Cockfighting is illegal in every state, and is a felony in forty states and Washington, DC. The possession of birds alone is illegal in thirty-eight states and the District of Columbia. Being a spectator is illegal in forty-three states and in Washington, DC. The Animal Welfare Act also criminalizes interstate transport of animals to be used in animal fighting, including cockfighting.[25]

It is impossible to understand why these cruel events are seen as family fun. However, this is big business: one cockfighting operation busted in Alabama in August 2016, drew over 400 people a week, with the potential to bring in more than $1 million through the fight season, not counting betting on the side.[26]

Last, in hog-dog fighting, feral hogs are put in a pen for dogs to attack. In hog catching, the dogs are timed at how long it takes to pin the hog down. Many attacks are fatal to the hog, who has had its tusks removed. In hog baying, how long it takes the dog to corner the hog is timed. As to why these animal fighting activities persist even when illegal, the Animal Legal Defense Fund writes, "Attendees consider the events to be family entertainment."[27]

Circus Animals and Roadside Zoos

Animals in the circus—whether elephants, tigers, lions, monkeys, bears, or horses—do not do "natural" tricks or acts. They are forced to perform in ways they never do in the wild. Recently, I saw a video of baby bears chained to a wall by collars around their necks that force them to walk upright. If they try to go on all fours, they are choked. It is heartbreaking to watch this "training." And for what?

All circus animals are trained through fear and punishment. Whether a bullhook or a whip, the animals are beaten or threatened with beating. Animals are also starved to give them an incentive to perform. When they aren't performing, these wild animals are kept in small, barren cages, and are never allowed anything close to a natural life with others of their species, or healthy environments and activities. Elephants, for example, suffer widespread foot infections because they are forced to live on concrete rather than foraging for miles on grasses and over logs and rivers. Depression, anger, and loneliness are common problems with contained animals.

Public pressure to retire elephants from circus acts did result in Ringling Bros. and Barnum & Bailey Circus "retiring" their elephants. In fact, Ringling Bros. is closing down in May 2017, in part due to the decline in ticket sales after retiring its elephants. But most people do not know that these elephants aren't going to an elephant sanctuary. Instead, they are going to a Ringling facility where they will be chained most of the day and used for breeding and cancer research. Bullhooks will still be used to keep them obeying trainers. While many sing the praises of the circus's Center for Elephant Conservation, where elephants get better food, for example, others say the center has little outdoor stimulation for the animals, and that they will still be chained up at night. [28]

The circus is not the only arena where animals are trained using food deprivation, punishment with whips or prods, and fear of trainers if they don't perform. Animals used in Hollywood movies, advertisements, and television also face fear and stress, loneliness, cramped cages, and difficult transport from location to location. Animals are separated from their mothers, and from others of their species. PETA is one organization exposing training cruelties, and urging a shift to computer-generated imagery (CGI) or sophisticated animatronics. *Rise of Planet of the Apes*, *Noah*, and *The Jungle Book* all used CGI after urging from PETA to avoid animal cruelty. [29]

Roadside zoos are particularly cruel venues for their animal captives. They include unaccredited menageries; petting zoos; pony, elephant, llama, and camel rides; and photo-ops with baby tigers. These animals might be a solitary attraction behind a store or at a truck stop, or they might be a larger collection of animals where people pay a fee to pet, take pictures with, take rides on, or just view the animals. The USDA does have oversight of these venues to try to ensure minimal standards of care; however, the USDA has about 136 inspectors for over fifteen thousand facilities. Under the federal Animal Welfare Act, wild animals such as bears, big cats, and primates can be kept if an "exhibitor license" is obtained from the USDA. [30]

These roadside zoos generally provide substandard housing for their animals. The lack of appropriate diets, veterinary care, and species-appropriate activities, and the trauma of isolation and forced interaction with the public, make the lives of these animals unbearable. Tiger cubs bred onsite are taken from their moms, starved, dragged, beaten, and drugged to ensure compliance with photo opportunities. These babies have a young life of misery, and when they get too old, these cubs are sold in the exotic animal trade.[31]

Puppy Mills

Most people know (on some level) that most stores selling dogs get those dogs from puppy mill operations. As discussed in chapter 3, many breeders with "certifications" actually are puppy mills. These mills keep females continuously pregnant; dogs and puppies live in crates or cages with wire floors for excrement to fall through; they have minimal health care resulting in ear and eye infections, dental infections, skin infections, and extreme hair matting; and there are other untreated medical complications. This is a life of misery for the dogs. It is a common story for new owners to face immediate vet bills.

Media exposure of puppy mill rescues has raised awareness of the dire situation of these puppies. According to the HSUS, sixteen states have no state regulations for puppy mills "such as a requirement to provide basic care." Another aspect of missing legal regulations is that no owners are charged with the rescue costs when the HSUS, or other entity, raids a puppy mill operation, and the costs then fall to the taxpayers and animal rescue groups.[32] Because many owners of puppy mills run Facebook pages for their businesses, they sell direct to the uninformed buyer.

Horse-Drawn Carriages

Since use of animals is thoroughly integrated into our lives, we usually are simply unaware of its impact on animals. Many of us have been brought up to see rides in horse-drawn carriages as a fun, vacation-related activity. Maybe we've seen these horses while we were on a visit to relatives, or at certain historical monuments. Perhaps it was a romantic moment shared.

Horse-drawn carriages are anything but romantic for the horses that have to work in all kinds of weather, and on hard pavement in traffic.

This can be very stressful and unhealthy. They can develop respiratory problems and leg problems. Not only are horses injured through this work, but sometimes there are accidents that harm people. Horses can also be hit in car accidents. When they become too old or sick to work, these horses are usually slaughtered for dog food or sent overseas as food for humans. Horses aren't protected by the Animal Welfare Act, which means local animal control is the only check for their welfare.[33]

Animal Hoarding

Some cruel animal-related activity is individual and private, but is extensive because it's found throughout the country. Many of us who volunteer or work with animal rescue have experience with hoarders. In a previous chapter, Kathy S., with Save the Cats Arizona, described sixty cats living in one woman's trailer. These cats were in remarkable shape given the overcrowding and lack of medical care. Others are not so lucky.

In most hoarding situations, animals are abused by neglect, and by lack of food, sanitation, and medical care for infections, skin lacerations, or other complications. Sometimes animals are so emaciated and sick they must be euthanized. One of the worst issues with hoarding is the waste matter—urine and feces may cover every surface. This creates serious health problems in terms of respiratory and skin infections, as well as contaminated food.

Hoarders often start out with sincere intentions to help animals. The situation gets out of control due to natural breeding, illness, and lack of resources to care for the animals' needs. According to the Animal Legal Defense Fund (ALDF), probably 250,000 animals are victims of hoarders annually. While farm animals can be hoarded, mostly it is cats and dogs. ALDF sees hoarding as "the number one animal cruelty crisis facing companion animals in communities across the country."[34]

The ALDF speaks to the difficulty of stopping hoarding. Many states have no legal definition of hoarding (only Illinois and Hawaii have laws that specifically address animal hoarding), and there are no laws forcing a hoarder to cover the costs of rescues. Therefore, costs are born by the rescuer or rescue group. Also, there is near 100 percent recidivism with animal hoarding, and it is viewed as connected to mental illness, much like other addictions. According to the ASPCA, there are nine hundred to two thousand new cases of animal hoarding discovered every year.[35]

Cat Declawing

Declawing is one example where a totally preventable mutilation occurs to suit human laziness. Individuals who declaw their cats usually do so to keep the cats from scratching at furniture or curtains; they may also believe it will reduce fighting between their pets. Usually these people truly believe it is a harmless surgery that does not impact the cat at all. However, this is no simple procedure. Bone, tendon, and nerves are cut through to amputate the first segment of the cat's toes. To a human, the equivalent would be cutting off your fingers at the first knuckle. Cats use their claws to stretch their shoulder and leg muscles, to shed old nail layers, to mark territory, to reduce stress, and when necessary, to fight.

Declawed cats are at a distinct health disadvantage. They may become more aggressive, walk differently as they are balancing without their toes, and they may have difficulty using a litter box (or ignore it altogether).

Instead of declawing, cats can be provided with a range of scratching posts made of sisal twine or carpeting, or with scratching cardboard boxes. Their nails can be trimmed regularly, or they can be trained to stay away from furniture, such as with water in a spray bottle.

This cruelty impacts an astounding 19 to 46 percent of cats. Declawing is illegal is Australia, several European countries, and at least seven cities in California. Currently, New York and New Jersey have pending legislation to make declawing illegal.[36]

To a certain extent, there are differing opinions on what animal abuse is. Some treatments might be unanimously agreed upon as deplorable and cruel, but others might be seen more as a context issue, or as acceptable given what humans want. For most people involved in animal work, animals do deserve justice, and their suffering does deserve consideration. As I have already mentioned, how we are socialized within the context of our culture holds particular weight in how we view animal use. I think there can be no doubt that every case I have described causes animal suffering. What remains is for us to decide whether we stand with the animals and step in to reject these human choices, or whether we continue to allow these uses regardless.

In the next chapter, we will look at the personal impacts on individuals who volunteer or work with animals due to their experiences. How has their thinking changed? Have their lifestyle decisions been impacted? What have they gained as a result of their experiences? We will see a range of impacts. The issue focus will be on vegetarianism and veganism as activism—in some cases this *is* the animal work people are engaged in. For others, their diet may or may not be impacted by volunteering to help animals out.

6

PERSONAL IMPACTS

Since I have worked with animal rescue and investigations, I have seen some terrible cases of human-caused suffering. I am haunted by some of the things I've experienced, and I have struggled with not losing my faith in humanity and being overwhelmed with depression and sadness. Knowing the reality of life on earth for billions of animals makes it hard for me to really be happy. No matter what joyful thing I may be experiencing, the pain of their suffering is always throbbing away, like cosmic background radiation. —Janine

I no longer care about material things. I do not care about furniture or nice clothes. Every spare dime I have goes to food or medical care for cats. I know that sounds insane, and people like me are made fun of and looked down on, but I do not care. I no longer want approval from people, because I see their ambition to acquire money, cars, and status symbols pointless when there is so much need in the world, human and animal. —Rachel

I am my work. —Gay

LIFE HAS MORE MEANING

A common response to the question, "How has this work impacted you?" is that life has more meaning. Some short examples are: "Seeing a saved animal living a happy life makes me feel like I've done something worthwhile" (Rebekah, volunteer with Furbaby Rescue); "It's rewarding to place animals with people who fall in love with them" (Tom, independent rescue); "I feel I am making a difference one animal at a time" (Katherine D., volunteer with Cozy Cat Cottage Adoption Center); "Animal advocacy has added a lot of meaning and joy into my life" (Jon C., Vegan Outreach staff); and "Spending time with the cats at the adoption center has given me purpose and a sense of doing good for the right reason" (Christi, doing cat adoptions and care).

For many individuals, this satisfaction is based on being part of the solution. Elizabeth K., of Animal Rights Hawai'i, states, "It has made me feel like I am truly contributing to something bigger than myself, and speaking up for those who can't." Dan B., active with the San Francisco Vegetarian Society, shares, "I like being part of the solution, doing what I can in my own little ways." Andrea, active in a variety of animal issues, echoes Dan B., "I feel like I'm contributing to the solution, and that makes me feel less guilty because I'm not just sitting feeling sorry for these animals, I'm helping improve their situation, even if it's something as simple as giving them some love and affection at the shelter." Jasmin, who cofounded Our Hen House, tells me the work "[g]ave me a purpose much greater than myself."

For others, it is helping individual animals. Mary S., cofounder of Ironwood Pig Sanctuary, wrote:

> I get a great deal of satisfaction being able to say "yes" when someone calls or e-mails with a pig that needs a home, and I am able to provide that home. I love seeing these rescued pigs enter their new lives and become comfortable with where they are living, and their new friends. . . . [They] no longer live in the horrible conditions that we find them in. . . . [T]hey now have the freedom to be pigs!

Liz B., a Humane Society of Southern Arizona (HSSA) volunteer, commented on helping dogs: "I love working with animals, as I frequently get frustrated with people. It gives me satisfaction to get the dogs out for a walk, when they spend twenty-three-plus hours a day in a small kennel. Not only does it help the dog get exercise and time outdoors, but it makes him or her calmer and more easily adoptable."

VALUES CLARIFICATION AND PURPOSE

In some cases, work with animals helps clarify values. For example, Alessa, active with HSSA, stated, "My volunteering and animal advocacy activities have helped strengthen and clarify my beliefs and feelings about my own values and life purposes. I continue to evolve and raise my own awareness in this regard."

Kim Meagher, founder of Wildhorse Ranch Rescue, has found that her work running the rescue "has allowed me to be my authentic self. I was ridiculed as a kid for my views on animals and vegetarianism. To this day, I've lost friends over my compassionate and passionate views on animals."

Nanci's life was changed by volunteering with animals: "I started putting them ahead of myself, and found that sacrifice was really rewarding and helping was so wonderful." Nanci volunteers with Save the Cats Arizona.

Sheila, who volunteered with Cat Haven and Save Our Strays, learned the meaning of "unconditional love. I've learned to accept myself as who I am, and rest in the knowledge that, even if only in a small way, I have made a difference."

Richard H., The Pig Preserve founder, is "a better man and a better human being for having spent twenty-five years working with the pigs. The more I deal with humans . . . the more I appreciate the pigs (and the dogs and cats we also rescue). These marvelous creatures teach me something new about life each and every day."

Ryan, associate director of International Youth Outreach with People for the Ethical Treatment of Animals (PETA), feels a sense of purpose because of his work. "Watching someone read an animal rights leaflet for the first time, and observing their eyes opening widely as their mind is opened, is a transformative experience."

Mike W., who has spent years in undercover investigations and works for Compassion Over Killing, echoes the idea that the work can be a unique experience. "This work most definitely changes you. You can't un-see the things that you have seen, or undo what you have had to do. It takes a large emotional and mental toll, but the feeling of self-satisfaction from being able to complete it is unparalleled."

Sandra Higgins, founder of Eden Farmed Animal Sanctuary, has turned the knowledge of animal suffering into an absolute commitment:

Regardless of how difficult it is to bear witness to some of the most horrible suffering on the planet in the residents who live at Eden, I look forward to getting out of bed each morning to be with them and care for them. I might set out with the idea of rescuing an animal from a torturous situation, but within a short time of that animal arriving at Eden, there is so much more pleasure, joy and love in my world because of that being.

I am more motivated to continue this work than I have ever been in my life. I can't rest knowing the suffering that other animals endure at human hands, and I am not content unless I am doing something to help relieve that suffering.

I believe LeAnn, volunteering with Furever Friends Rescue, sums up this purpose and satisfaction very well when she says, "There is nothing better in the world than feeling that you brought comfort to a creature that is suffering and scared."

LIFE'S WORK

LeAnn says that helping animals has "become a way of life for me." For so many, alleviating animal suffering is a way of life or a calling. Susie C. of Farm Sanctuary, feels similarly: "My work is my life. I cannot imagine doing anything else."

This sentiment is also expressed by Dolores, with Stray Cats About Town in British Columbia: "My whole life has been dedicated to veganism and the rights of animals." Jamie, a Help A Dog Smile volunteer, said: "Animal rescue is my world. It's not just a hobby, it's a calling. If I see an animal that needs help, I will find a way to help."

Nancy, cofounder of Furever Friends Rescue, doesn't consider herself "particularly religious or spiritual, but this is a calling for me, in every sense of the word." Batya, independent animal activist, has also devoted her life to animal liberation. "I spend most of my days at my computer doing advocacy work."

Young and old feel these commitments. Joyce M. started volunteering at Arizona Chihuahua Rescue at sixty-five, "and soon all of my free time was taken by dogs. When I retired at seventy, the rescue became my life's work."

Animal rights "greatly changed" the life of Richard S. "Now that I am eighty-one years old and retired, it is the thing I spend the most time on." Richard S. is affiliated with Jewish Veg.

Jon C. has been working in animal advocacy for the past ten years. He says, "I agree with Alice Walker's quote, 'Activism is my rent for living on the planet.'" Jon C. is sure his time is well-spent and "we really are making a difference."

The sense of how important this work will be for their entire lives is quite strong. Hope, on staff with United Poultry Concerns and a volunteer with Compassionate Living, expresses it this way: "It's not a part of me, it *is* me." Izabela, doing independent vegan activism, claims, "I see working for animals as my main life passion. I don't think I will ever stop."

Diana, senior youth marketing coordinator at peta2, supports this view: "I know even if I were to stop working at an animal rights organization, I would never stop being an animal rights activist."

Becky, working at the PETA Foundation and volunteering with San Francisco's Animal Care & Control, helps us understand this passion. She told me, "It's my whole life. . . . I do know, to me, it's the most important social movement of our time. It's human rights, it's human health, it's the environment and, of course, it's animals—the beings with whom we share this planet. And there is nothing bigger."

Mike W. told me the following:

> I love what I'm doing; I feel very lucky to be in this position. If I'm doing the same thing for the same place for the next however many years until I die, I'll be very happy. I love [the animals]. Honestly, I took a little break from my time in the field before coming back into it, and I was just doing normal nine-to-five stuff, and I felt like I was dead inside. There's no comparison. Once you're doing something that you have so much compassion for, there's no comparison. It doesn't feel like a job.

SENSE OF COMMUNITY

Another commitment factor people mentioned, beside satisfaction, is feeling a sense of community and being around like-minded people. For Maria, volunteering with both Save the Cats Arizona and Lost Our

Home Pet Rescue, the like-minded people became "great friends." Lori W. of Animal Place found the like-minded people "helped me focus." For Amber, meeting like-minded people while volunteering at the HSSA increased her "sense of belonging and community." About her time working for PETA, Robin said, "It was wonderful having such a motivated and committed group of outstanding people to work with and learn from."

Sandy B., volunteering with Save the Cats Arizona and Desert Paws, found that expanding her network of animal-loving friends brought her to meet "a broad array of friends from a vast array of backgrounds. That in itself has been mind-expanding and fun."

For Charlee, on staff with Compassion Over Killing and a volunteer with Poplar Spring Animal Sanctuary, meeting like-minded people meant meeting people she "can talk to about how I am feeling and [who] will easily understand."

Miranda, a Humane Society of the United States (HSUS) volunteer, stated that "being around other people who like animals has helped me see that not everyone has a disinterest in their well-being." Helen K., from Vegan Haven, also feels more positive:

> I also think I have gained a sense of hope and community through my involvement. Before starting to volunteer I felt very alone, and like no one in my life understood my views. By working with like-minded people on a regular basis, I feel much more hopeful for the future.

CAREERS AND SKILLS

For many people, exposure to animals led to particular career choices, or the building of specific skills. Jeanette, volunteering with Viva! and Animal Justice Project, found a new direction: "The more I got involved with animal issues, the less devoted I felt to my previous job, which is why I finally quit, and am now retraining as an animal campaigner to do this work full-time."

Alicia also changed direction:

> Growing up, I always thought I would be a teacher, and was in a PhD program thinking I was going to be a history professor. When I got involved in working for animals, I realized that the problem was

so urgent that I needed to dedicate my life to working for animals,
and I left school to work at PETA.

Sarah H. returned to school for a degree in Nonprofit Studies "so that I could continue to help and learn how a good organization was run." Maggie, a Save Our Strays volunteer, took an online course in grant writing to be more effective in her organization. Tracyene decided to return to school to become a vet tech: "I want to be part of a team that enables low income families to afford vet care." Mikayla's love for animals influenced her college major: "I am a Vet Science major, with a minor in Wildlife Conservation. My hope is to make a career for myself where I can be involved in an organization that helps and rehabilitates animals that have been abused."

Ginny knows that her devotion to animals has influenced her career:

I've been a dietitian for thirty years and, were it not for my commit-
ment to veganism and animal rights, I would most likely have
changed careers at some point in my life. I've remained in this field
primarily because I feel that, with the nutrition knowledge I've
gained over the years, it's where I can do the most good.

Commitment to animals also influenced Denise's business decisions: "It's led to opening my business five years ago, of bath and body products with no animal ingredients, approved vegan, and no animal testing."

Josie, who started out as a dog walker ten years ago, has never really left the animal field. "After ten years, I was finally able to mesh my corporate career skills with an organization that advocates for farm animals, and now I'm living my dream working for HSUS helping animals every day."

Sandra Higgins, founder of Eden Farmed Animal Sanctuary, has also blended professional work with animal rights: "Most of my clinical work is now devoted to compassionate mind training that includes living a vegan lifestyle."

For others, animal concerns have been integrated into the arts. Mike C., for example, has this to say: "The way I'm trying to make animal abuse and world issues known is through music I play in my band, and I try to educate people whenever the opportunity arises. I try and protect and preserve the earth as well as I can."

Isabella has chosen a deliberate focus in her photography. "My work has become more focused on animal liberation, and has expanded to accommodate all relevant strategies." Gwen, also an artist, has "begun to make visual art pieces that call attention to the plight of animals used for food."

In terms of concrete skills, numerous people mentioned improvement in their speaking and writing skills, and in their fund-raising abilities, as an impact of this work. Kitty, of Tailless Cat Rescue, learned "to build websites for a local shelter," which later helped her in her job. Francis learned "basic fundraising skills" as a volunteer with Full Circle Farm Sanctuary.

Ginny improved her "skills as both a writer and a speaker as a result of my work." Author and vegan activist Will Tuttle feels the work "has opened my heart and helped develop speaking, writing, and musical abilities." So many others—Lia (a Humane League volunteer), Libbi (a foster and involved in independent rescue work), and Amanda (a teen volunteer with HSSA), among them—feel more confident and effective when speaking with others about animal issues.

On another note, Brooke, who started volunteering as a teenager at Wildhorse Ranch Rescue, says: "Volunteering at such a young age has forced me to mature and learn concepts that most children my age don't acquire till later in life. It has turned me in to a responsible, dependable person, only further advancing me in life."

HELP WITH DEPRESSION, HOPELESSNESS, AND SHYNESS

Many study participants talked about how volunteering or working for, and with, animals helped them with depression or hopelessness. Kathy S., for example, had this to say about volunteers in a rescue she co-founded, Save the Cats Arizona:

> While I knew I'd love rescuing cats, I've come to realize how much this work rescues people as well as cats—many of our volunteers have expressed to me personally how much working with the cats has meant in their lives, giving their life more meaning or helping them overcome depression.

Diane P., at HSSA, "suffered from depression. I feel volunteering has helped me a lot with that. It gives me self-worth." Similarly, Jasmine M., with Blackhat Humane Society, feels having dogs in her life has made an enormous difference: "I have had chronic depression all my life, and often my dog is the only reason I have to get me out of my bed in the mornings. Having several fosters keeps me focused on them, and active, which improves my quality of life immensely." Jessica B., independent activist, states this even more strongly:

> Becoming an activist literally saved my life. I've been dealing with depression all my life. I was very shy and quiet; I often felt like if it weren't for my companion animal, Matilda, that I'd have nothing to live for. As soon as I became an activist, I felt like dealing with my depression became easier. When I do things like tabling or protests, I feel happier with myself and it makes other things easier to deal with.

For others, working with animals helped address feelings of hopelessness. Francis shared: "During times of frustration, it's been important to keep the individual animals in my mind's eye, in order to not get caught up in the small stuff. The sanctuary has served as a way to alleviate the hopelessness I feel when looking at my Facebook feed, and working in such an anti-animal culture."

Gwen found hope in her vegan activism: "In a world where it is easy to feel hopeless about one's ability to make positive change, I am happy to be practicing and promoting veganism, which is a way to make a difference every day, many times a day."

According to Cindy, who volunteers with local rescues, animal advocacy "has made me a better person. Although it's a long way off, for every animal I save or help save, or for anyone I can help get behind bars—or more—for abusing an animal, a star shines a little brighter and gives me hope."

Numerous people mentioned the personal impact of gaining interpersonal skills and abilities. Michelle L., a rescue kittens foster and volunteer with HSUS, feels the work "has definitely increased my ability to interact with all types of people, and be more accepting of our differences. I have gained self-confidence and pride." Shelley, who volunteers with Kiss for Kittens and Kitsnkats Rescue, also feels she has "learned how to work with groups of people from many different backgrounds."

Eric, who, along with his wife, cofounded Homeless Animal Rescue Team (HART) in Arizona, says:

> *We have found that we have become more patient with people, as we have worked with the worst . . . from people who discard their animals, to those who have disdain for cats, and even abuse animals. We have realized that not everyone is on the same wavelength, and that education and exposure can help bring about change.*

For others, overcoming shyness was a major result of their work. Jon C. found his work with Vegan Outreach helped in this way: "Around the time I got involved in animal advocacy, I was going through a shy spell in my life. Getting out and leafleting, giving talks, etc., forced me to interact with a lot more people, to work on my social skills, etc. This was a big positive for me."

Sandra Higgins considers herself "a shy person by nature." But she has "gained courage from this work, knowing that the animals need us to speak out on their behalf."

Similarly, Steve, with Vegan Outreach, found "[b]eing an activist has drawn me out of my shell. My discomfort at approaching people and asking them to make a change is nothing compared to what the animals are going through."

Organizing and advocating for animals has been transformative for some people. Kathleen K., Fargo/Moorhead Vegs organizer, shares: "I used to have social anxiety, so much so that sometimes I would be unable to talk with people, and I would have to excuse myself in the middle of conversations. No more! I can even talk some to crowds now!"

Lilia, who works for Sea Shepherd Conservation Society, says her activism has helped her "develop from a very shy introverted person to someone who is much more capable of dealing with confrontation and engaging in public outreach, and taking a stand in my own personal affairs also. Standing up for other creatures has definitely taught me how to stand up for myself."

EMOTIONAL KNOWLEDGE

It comes as no surprise that study participants state that they learned more about animal suffering and animal welfare issues because of their involvements. For example, Leah, an independent rabbit advocate, says, "I have learned a lot about the horrific way animals are treated." Laura J., vegan advocate, echoed, "I've learned more about the hidden animal abuse than I could have ever imagined."

Often this new knowledge leads to increased commitment, as with Mikayla: "Knowing what I know about the industries that abuse animals makes me just want to fight harder for their rights."

Some knowledge truly expanded people's scope. Amy says, "I knew next to nothing about bunnies when I started working with Leaps and Bounds [Rabbit Rescue] five years ago. Now I can educate people and be knowledgeable about it." Andrea has learned "about the legal processes associated with getting policies and laws put into place to protect animal rights." Jeanette tells me, "I'm aware of more pressing issues that people tend to conveniently ignore, [for example], the effect animal agriculture is having on climate change."

But along with knowledge and experience also can come heartbreak, despair, and anger. Dove, an independent advocate, feels "heartbreak on a daily basis." Molly F., experienced in international animal rescue, feels "a great deal of pride in what I do, even though it's an extremely emotionally draining way to live." John, the Baltimore/Washington, DC, Sea Shepherd volunteer coordinator and founder of Peaceful Fields Sanctuary, agrees that "[c]ombatting burn-out and staying positive can be a challenge, but it is highly rewarding to be part of a calling to make a difference for better."

Elizabeth S., concentrating on animal rights law, shares a common story:

> When I became more heavily involved in animal activism, I went through the usual first stage of being so overwhelmed by the terrible cruelty that exists, and my inability to change the entire world, that it was hard to function sometimes. But that has gradually been replaced by a determination to do something useful, whatever it may be.

The emotion of anger is common and needs to be acknowledged, but also must be contained for advocates to stay effective. Jackie, engaged in dog rescue, had "to take small breaks from time to time, because you get frustrated and angry." Isabella said: "I feel a lot of anger, and that I've been betrayed by my own species; that all those years I thought humans were basically good, and I don't know where I stand on that anymore. But I'm very angry about this continuing atrocity that we are carrying out on every other species on this earth."

Others also are angry with humans. Nina, involved in rescue work, claims, "It has also made me more cynical and less hopeful about humanity, because we really see the worst of what people do." Novette, working on all things cat (rescue, transport, fostering, and TNR) adds, "The human race is completely irresponsible." Izabela feels this anger as well. But she tries not to put all the blame on people. Instead, "[i]t's the industries [that] profit from animal suffering."

Mike W. has an emotional reaction to animal cruelty, such as "kids burning kittens. . . . If they're abusing cats, they're clearly not going to care about farm animals." He sees crush videos as "a huge signifier of how terrible our society is. . . . When I see that kind of stuff, it makes me despair."

But these negative emotions are balanced by the powerful good these volunteers and staff are doing. Tracyene keeps on: "The more I learn about the worldwide situation of animals, the more depressed and hopeless I get. I try to focus on my community and the changes I can make personally, or the larger changes I can help facilitate." For Lisa L., doing independent rescue, when she is saddened by animal cruelty stories, this "compelled me to try to help the best I can." Mary S. reflects on the challenges:

> The work is very hard and emotionally trying. Pigs die and are sick, the hours are long, I have little balance in my life, and hiring and keeping good employees who care about the animals is difficult. But still, when I see these animals come to the sanctuary, and roll around in their mud wallow, and run free in a large field, there are rewards indeed.

For some study participants, stress and hard physical demands resulted in negative impacts from their work. Not many people mentioned this, but it is real. As Alison, focusing on dog rescue, says, "Animal rescue takes a toll," but at the same time it is incredibly rewarding. Faith (from Wee Paws Animal Sanctuary), Carol (volunteering at a local shelter), and Nadia (founder of Golden Bone Rescue & Rehab) all mentioned health-related issues stemming from their work. Elaine, a pig plant monitor, mentioned, "I am fifty-one years old and I am tired." Judy McG's husband thought she might need a counselor because she was so worried about a feral cat colony being moved due to mall construction: "It was making me physically ill because I was always concerned about their well-being."

But for virtually everyone, the feeling about making a difference, "no matter how small," as Judy McG said, allowed them to continue on.

LIFESTYLE IMPACTS

In describing the personal impact working on animal issues, or with animals directly, had on study participants, there were two major categories: (1) I became vegan or vegetarian; and (2), my new knowledge affected my consumer choices.

The primary reason for these changes had to do with reducing animal suffering. For example, Margaretta, who works with Farm Sanctuary and her local humane society, says: "Being vegan has affected all of my life choices for the better. I can live everyday knowing that I am trying to do my best to live as clean as possible for all animals, and the earth as well. Having little impact on the earth's resources, living as one with animals, brings me self-confidence and happiness."

Susan S., who volunteers at many rescues and her local shelter, tries "to avoid products made by companies that test on animals." She also tries to avoid products with palm oil which negatively impacts orangutans.

People also wanted to be ethically consistent in their lifestyles, in accordance with their new knowledge. They did not want to be a part of animal abuse. Daya claims her independent animal rescue work "changed how I live, what I consume, what my values are, and even how I think of and act toward human animals."

For Dana, knowledge of pet overpopulation and where these animals come from, as well as shelter issues was important: "My volunteering has impacted my diet choices significantly—and also the number of animals I have adopted. I would never purchase a pet again—only adopt them from a shelter."

Overwhelmingly, this group of animal advocates and activists are checking to see if products they buy have been tested on animals. Eighty-nine percent are checking personal care products, makeup, or cleaning products. There are many aspects to the testing on animals—some of it is medical testing (of highly dubious value, even according to the National Institutes of Health), some is product testing, and some is psychological or scientific testing of various types. The Animal Welfare Act (AWA), passed in 1966, was supposed to protect and regulate the welfare of *all* warm-blooded animals used in experiments. However, in 1972, birds, rats, and mice were specifically excluded: that is their status to this day, and 90 percent of all animals in U.S. labs *are* birds, rats, and mice. Other animals experimented on include primates, cats, dogs, sheep, pigs, rabbits, gerbils, guinea pigs, goats, and more. What is the point of this "welfare" act if the majority of these sentient creatures have no protection in terms of their care and treatment?

The AWA also legislated that alternative procedures to the stress and pain caused animals must be considered. This does not apply to the excluded birds, rats, and mice, however. There are pending lawsuits against the U.S. Department of Agriculture (USDA) to include these animals based on the original intent of the act.[1] In the meantime, millions of animals suffer.

In June 2016, the Frank R. Lautenberg Chemical Safety for the 21st Century Act was signed into law by President Obama. This bill aims to modernize testing of chemicals for safety, and to promote alternatives to the use of animals. Hopefully both these goals will be reached.

Amy Clippinger, associate director of the PETA International Science Consortium, is optimistic about the shift to nonanimal cell-based and computational testing approaches. Animal-based tests, she says, "are time-consuming, very expensive, and not especially human relevant," along with having ethical considerations. These changes will be cost- and time-effective for the tens of thousands of chemicals in products now on the market that have never been tested.[2]

When asked if they wear products such as leather, fur, or feathers in shoes, jackets, clothing, or accessory trims, 70 percent of study participants said they did not. Some who qualified their "yes" answer said, for example, that they had trouble with their feet and wore leather shoes.

The move away from products that use animals is most likely based on more information circulating about dogs being skinned alive for their fur; alligators and crocodiles raised in filth, stabbed, and cut to try to destroy their spinal columns, and often skinned while alive to make shoes, handbags, and wristbands; mink overcrowded in wire cages and gassed with carbon monoxide, electrocuted, or crushed between boards to kill them for their skins and "faux fur" which, according to a recent HSUS exposé, was actually real animal fur on clothing and accessories.[3]

Fifty-nine percent of study participants are vegan (45 percent) or vegetarian (14 percent); 41 percent eat meat. In replying to this open-ended question, some of the meat-eaters stated they eat meat, or told me they are working toward being vegetarian, that they like meat, that they eat chicken and fish but no red meat, that they eat the "regular diet," the "normal diet," or that they eat very little meat. A few people commented that they buy humane meat, cruelty-free meat, eggs from cage-free chickens, or that they responsibly source their food.

For some people being vegan *is* their activism. Their job or volunteer activity relates to vegan education, promoting veganism, or it is how they view their daily activism—saving animals and reducing cruelty through not eating or using animals. Some individuals are working on securing commitments from animal advocacy organizations to stop serving meat at fund-raising events. Others are organizing VegFests in their hometowns.

More vegans are found in the paid jobs in animal advocacy organizations, and in volunteering for relieving animal suffering in animals other than cats and dogs (for example, with farm animals or wildlife). Most of the individuals who eat meat are involved in cat and dog rescues: When I closely examined the data, I found that a full 90 percent of the people in this study who eat meat work with cats and/or dogs. Of the remaining eight meat-eating people, five did not engage in hands-on work with any animals. This finding supports the research and anecdotal evidence related to veganism and who is most likely to become vegan (in particular, not connecting animals we are close to, such as pets, with animals we don't know much about, as well as denial, social isolation, and lack of information), which are discussed below.

ISSUE FOCUS: VEGANISM

Jeff B., on staff with Vegan Outreach, recounts a fairly common experience in becoming vegan. He heard about animal suffering from friends while at college, and saw some posters on campus. He realized he was a product of his culture, and then started to do his own research. "At the time I believed the protein myth, and you kind of believe all the stories that you're told . . . to change your road, you have to research everything about nutrition. . . ." He became a vegetarian first and a vegan a year later, now sixteen years ago.

The vast majority of people who are vegans *were* meat-eaters; learning about animal suffering is usually what compelled them to change their eating habits. Occasionally, as for Amy, a volunteer with Leaps and Bounds Rabbit Rescue, that wasn't the case: "I wasn't informed enough. It wasn't because of factory farms, the environment, or anything. I thought eating dead animals was gross." Becky, now with her local animal care and control, was an aquatics director, and was challenged by a woman at the swim club. The woman was surprised that, as an athlete, Becky still ate meat, and she suggested Becky check out peta.org:

> I went back to my desk, and went to peta.org, and I was stunned by what I learned. I just never thought, like so many people—which is why I try not to judge people, unless the information is given to them and they don't act on it, or aren't curious. But, I changed. It was a light switch for me, an absolute light switch. So, I went from eating meat to vegetarian, almost vegan. . . . I switched; it was very easy; I felt great. As I said I'm an athlete: My body felt stronger, my recovery was better, all that. I felt much better about my life.

Some vegans prioritize environmental reasons for eating less (or no) meat. Helen K. wonders, "Does the planet have enough time? Eating meat isn't sustainable. Maybe it will be too little, too late. The earth will survive, but maybe not humans."

Jessika A., involved in international animal nongovernmental organization (NGO) consultant work, also challenges animal agriculture as sustainable. While a vegan world may not happen in her lifetime, she feels "[w]e don't have a choice on this": go vegan or face extinction. "We may not be 100 percent vegan, but I don't think there is any other option for the survival of the species."

The appeals to veganism (discussed at length below) are many, but most vegans feel moral or ethical motivations. Laura, a vegan activist, writes, "For me, it's ethical, and needs to be that way for anyone to remain vegan for the long term. Health benefits are obvious, but that's not enough for people to not eat animal products the rest of their lives."

Nina became a vegan in 1995:

> I had tried before, when I was a freshman in college, but I ended up on a very limited diet and didn't do it the right way, and developed anemia. When I decided to do it again, I tried to make sure I was getting a very balanced diet. I did it for the animals. I came to realize that just being vegetarian didn't mean my diet was harmless, and there was immense suffering in dairy and eggs as well.

Knowledge about animal agriculture is crucial, yet we live in a culture that hides that information. It is a common refrain that vegans "didn't know" the extent of the suffering, or even the most basic ways we "get" food. I personally was a vegetarian for seven years before going vegan, and I had no knowledge that the dairy industry actually causes more suffering for longer periods of time to cows than cows headed to slaughter for meat. I didn't know they were forcibly impregnated, and then had their babies taken from them right after birth—so that you and I could have the milk intended for their own offspring. Male calves became veal, and female calves became dairy cows. It never occurred to me that dairy cows were treated as commodities, and not as living creatures with their own families.

Molly F., working in the international wildlife rescue field, confirms this:

> I became vegetarian for ethical reasons, but I never really knew about factory farming 'cause I didn't pay attention to it. I wasn't eating meat and I thought that was enough, I was taking a stand. And the veganism thing: I had a bit of misinformation on that. When I was in college I had some friends who had been vegan and spoke horribly about it, and I thought, "That's too extreme, I can't do that." I knew nothing, and as you said, I think [for] cultural reasons. I had it in my head that certain products or animal things were OK, or you needed them, and I wish I had known or seen the light earlier, but I

didn't. And that's just how it is. Once I became aware of it, there was
no turning back.

Vegans as "Extreme"

Occasionally, meat-eaters will say that vegans are snobs, or think we are superior because of our ethical position. Esther, a writer, artist, and therapist, sees it this way:

> *When people learn we are vegan, they know we are acting more*
> *morally. That brings a defensive reaction. They know we are more*
> *moral and they aren't willing to do it. Cognitive dissonance results.*
> *Somewhere deep down they know they should not eat meat, and they*
> *feel bad, so they have to react by saying "You're too extreme," or*
> *"You think you're better than me."*

Mike W. wonders about the "extremist" label as well. He told me:

> *It's ludicrous that we're the ones who embrace compassion and try to*
> *reduce suffering, yet we're the ones labeled as extremists. And the*
> *norm [are] the ones who are slitting throats, causing the torture and*
> *suffering, out hunting. That's normal? Hunting an animal, shooting a*
> *bow through them and letting them suffer, is normal? Meanwhile,*
> *just eating vegetables is extremist?*

Alka, senior laboratory oversight specialist with PETA, turns this labeling on its head: "[I]t seems like the decision to eat meat, or the choice to eat meat, is saying my palate preference is so important that I would kill another animal for that. That is a superiority complex at its most extreme. *That's* snobbery, like 'I'm so important.'" Of course, this may not be a conscious attitude. Alka continues, "Sometimes, when people know they are contributing to something horrific, they can't see the ethics of it. Their vision is clouded because they have a palate preference for animal foods. and so their ethics become clouded and they can't see it."

Alexis reminds us that, "We need to present ourselves as compassionate people to all beings, including the people who speak disrespectfully toward us. We need to be empathetic, just as we are to animals, onto people, and remember what it was like to not be vegan and why."

This is a point I try to remember, since I myself grew up eating meat. And again, it serves us to be reminded that culture "normalizes" our practices, even if they are not actually normal behaviors.

Julie, a nutrition counselor, puts it this way:

> *Yes, extreme! Killing a perfectly healthy young animal, charring its flesh until it becomes carcinogenic, and eating that instead of something nutritious is what seems odd to me. . . . Have you seen a documentary called* Forks over Knives? *It is about diet. A cardiologist [Caldwell B. Esselstyn] who left his surgical practice to treat his CVD [cardiovascular disease] patients with nutritional therapy, said something in that [documentary] that I love (paraphrased here): Some people think the plant-based whole foods diet is extreme. Half a million people this year will have their chests carved open and a vein cut out of their leg and sewn into their coronary artery. Some people would call that extreme.*

Meat Consumption Levels

How much meat is our culture eating? How many vegetarians and vegans are there in America? According to *MarketWatch*, "The average American now eats roughly 193 pounds of beef, pork, and/or chicken a year (or more than 3.7 pounds a week), up from roughly 184 pounds in 2012."[4] This increase can be attributed to cheaper prices, the popularity of diets such as the paleo diet, the millions more farmed animals and, to some extent, government sanctions through farm subsidies and recommendations. For example, the latest USDA guidelines critiqued sugar intake, but when it came to meat, only suggested eating leaner meats. The agency didn't discuss consuming less meat.

As meat consumption increases in the United States, other countries are cutting back. According to a *Mother Jones* article, the Netherlands Nutrition Centre issued new guidelines calling for cutbacks of red meat and fish for health reasons and sustainability. Sweden, Brazil, and the United Kingdom have all called for less red meat-eating in their populations. This is having an impact.[5] More than 1 percent of the population of Britain (around 542,000 people) are vegan, according to a poll commissioned for the Vegan Society and *Vegan Life* magazine—an increase of 360 percent in ten years.[6] The Chinese government wants its population to reduce meat consumption by 50 percent by 2030. This is in response to an enormous rise in rates of diabetes, cancer, and heart disease.

The benefits to world health costs, to saving lives shortened due to disease, to reducing greenhouse gas emissions, would be staggering in the positive direction. According to a Food Revolution Network blog post, "Currently, the average Chinese person eats 63 kg of meat per year. The new guidelines call for reducing this to 14 kg to 27 kg per year—which would be the most rapid drop in meat consumption by a population even remotely near this large in world history."[7]

Numbers of Vegetarians and Vegans

A 2008 survey by *Vegetarian Times* (using Harris Interactive) found "3.2 percent of U.S. adults, or 7.3 million people, follow a vegetarian-based diet. Approximately 0.5 percent, or one million, of those are vegans, who consume no animal products at all. In addition, 10 percent of U.S. adults, or 22.8 million people, say they largely follow a vegetarian-inclined diet."[8] When asked why they limited animal product intake,

> over half (53 percent) of current vegetarians eat a vegetarian diet to improve their overall health. Environmental concerns were cited by 47 percent; 39 percent cited 'natural approaches to wellness'; 31 percent cited food-safety concerns; 54 percent cited animal welfare; 25 percent cited weight loss; and 24 percent weight maintenance.[9]

According to a Gallup poll in 2012, 5 percent of American adults considered themselves vegetarians. There was similarity in the different population segments, with slightly more vegetarian women than men, and older, as opposed to younger, adults being vegetarian. The main difference was that unmarried adults were more than twice as likely as married adults to be vegetarian.[10] A 2011 Harris Interactive phone survey commissioned by the Vegetarian Resource Group found "approximately 5 [percent] of the country say that they never eat meat, fish, seafood, or poultry. About half of these vegetarians are also vegan."[11]

A slightly different slant on asking about vegan or vegetarian eating was taken in this 2015 Harris poll. The Vegetarian Resource Group asked about eating behavior, not labels for that behavior. Over a third of respondents (36 percent) eat at least one vegetarian meal per week; 3.4

percent said they always ate vegetarian meals; and 15 percent of those were vegans (no eggs or dairy). [12]

Different responses were found in the "2015 Special Diets Report" released by the *Nutrition Business Journal*. Eric Pierce, director of Strategy and Insights for NEXT Trend, feels there has been a significant shift in the perception of vegan eating and living. He said in an interview with Hannah Sentenac of *Latest Vegan News*:

> If you ask consumers to self-define their dietary preferences, I've actually found among the general population of U.S. consumers, about 6 percent will say they're vegan and about 7 percent will say they're vegetarian. . . . What's really exciting is that there's this bucket of flexitarians, or lessitarians, or pescetarians, or just consumers who wouldn't identify with any of those terms, who would say "I'm choosing to eat less meat," and what I've found in, again, a brief survey, is that about 26 percent of the U.S. population has said they've consciously chosen to eat less meat in the last twelve months. [13]

Denial

The numbers of vegetarians and vegans in our society is small, but it really depends on how strictly you are defining vegan and vegetarian. Perhaps the most significant measure is how many people are reducing meat consumption and adding more vegetables and fruits to their diets. These shifts are closer to one third of Americans.

But, at the same time, we know meat consumption—by those who are meat-eaters in the standard American diet—is increasing. Since we know for a fact that meat-eating is related to the major illnesses of heart disease, diabetes, high blood pressure, and premature death—and therefore preventable through diet changes—why is the vast majority of our culture consuming meat at increasing rates? Even putting aside the issues of animal suffering, why is the compelling health information not enough to turn animal agriculture around?

Vegans see and hear denial frequently. For example, Mikayla shares, "One of my friends—I was following her on Twitter—she was all about the Chinese dog festival, and all these zoos and animal testing. And she said I'm definitely an animal rights enthusiast. And I said, 'You eat meat; how?' And she said, 'That's different.'"

Even people working to end animal suffering share this contradiction and often eat meat, as mentioned earlier. Sandy W., Furever Friends Rescue staff and volunteer, tells me, "I say, 'I'm against animal cruelty,' and they say, 'Do you eat meat?' I'm like, 'Yeah.' But I don't know . . . in my mind, there's something between killing a deer, and killing a cow that was raised for beef. I don't know, it's screwy, I guess."

Will, a vegan, devotes his life to planting seeds and helping people realize that:

> [W]e're all forced to eat meat from our upbringing. If you want to be free and be healthy, then we need to be free to question the official stories of society. . . . [Let] people, on their own, decide what they want to do. That way they have ownership of it; I'm not trying to influence them. I'm just basically saying what I discovered for myself. I was just eating meat and dairy because I was forced into it, and I realized it's definitely not a good idea.

But challenging the cultural messaging and practices is no easy task; resistance is strong. Rosanne, volunteering with HSSA, No Kill Pima County, and other shelters, uses social media to spread information. She shares:

> I know a lot of people react very negatively to posts on social media about the awfulness in the animal agriculture industry. And people have said, "Don't post those things." I've seen this: "Please don't talk about this, please don't post those images, those videos, I can't take it." So I respect that. At the same time, I want to tell them there's a reason they should be seen, because you need to know what your role is, what your responsibility is in that cycle. And if you're avoiding that, then you're staying on a course that's very destructive, not just for the animals but for the planet.

Jessica B. is a harsher critic. "People don't want to educate themselves," she says, adding:

> Nobody wants to watch a video about monkeys having all these ridiculous experiments done on them. People don't want to see dogs hooked up to hoses of these smoking experiments. People don't want to see it. I don't want to see it. I've already seen it, which is why I don't support the things I don't support. Other people don't want to

see it; it's hard to get them to know enough to want to do something about it.

This may be true—it *is* difficult to watch footage of suffering animals with injuries, or the horror of slaughter, and so forth. Most people would rather not know. Lindsay has encountered this repeatedly:

> *Like with the videos, so many people say, "I don't want to watch, I don't want to hear, I don't want to see it. I'm just going to go to the store and buy all these products." That's what frustrates me the most, the people who want to be oblivious, and want to live in that world and be fine with it. That's so frustrating. How can they be OK with that?*

Another factor, touched on by Jessika A. and Becky, is that when we are socialized into our culture, there are many "givens." One of these "givens" is that it is OK to eat meat, which is thoroughly integrated into our daily lives. If people are challenged with the idea that "meat-eating is wrong," then, as Jessika A. says, they are confronted with "everything [they've] ever known is wrong."

Becky, who volunteers at an animal care and control facility with small animals—rats, mice, chickens, rabbits—shares this story. Advocates often brought chickens from Chinatown who escaped slaughter into the facility. There was one volunteer playing with a chicken, eating a chicken sandwich.

> *He was great, he loved the chickens, nice young fellow. But I had to say something. That's kind of amazing, what I'm seeing here. He was embarrassed, but I said it nicely. "You realize you're eating Jake's, like, brethren." He said, "Oh my goodness, I never thought about it." People don't. . . . They're just not ready to look.*

Social Isolation

For many who do look, there are still many blocks to examining our daily use of animals and changing eating habits. Often this is related to social isolation, if our families, coworkers, and friends are eating meat. Even if, as a vegan (or vegetarian), you are ethically "right" for not contributing to animal suffering due to your food choices, most people "don't want to be different," according to Molly F. She continues: "I think it just comes down to the fact that the farther outside [of the norm] you get, the more extreme [you're seen]. Veganism is like that. People see it as such an extreme lifestyle."

Nina, describing having dinner with vegan friends, concurs:

> *We started talking about the success of the local "vegan pledge" program. One reason it's successful is that it provides social support. We realized that many people out there would prefer to be wrong if it meant fitting into the crowd, and [they] find it very hard to take an unpopular or misunderstood action. So providing social support is vital to getting people to that point where they can be as kind to animals as they want to be in their hearts.*

Yossi, on staff of Israel's Let the Animals Live, also cited concerns of social isolation as a "common obstruction" to people reducing their animal consumption. In addition, he saw fears "of changing habits, of admitting guilt, of having nothing to eat, of giving up food [that] is tasty or emotionally significant." Giving support to new vegans was an important step, in his opinion.

The staying power of individuals who start a vegetarian or vegan diet is not high; in fact, it is embarrassingly low. According to Faunalytics (formerly the Humane Research Council), 84 percent of vegetarians and vegans add meat back into their diets. This study of over eleven thousand adults found that 86 percent of vegetarians return to meat-eating, and 70 percent of vegans do. Half claim they are interested in trying vegetarian or vegan eating at some point in the future.[14]

In examining the dynamics that contribute to these lapses, Ginny Messina wrote on her blog, The Vegan r.d., that veganism is not yet "normal." She cites findings from a Cornell study that meat-eaters do not want to be seen as "extreme," and that this has implications for vegan outreach. As new products enter the market, people reducing their meat intake, as well as those with the goal of completely eliminating it, may find comfort in using the mock meats and veggie cheeses that look and taste much like the animal products. The more these products are readily available in restaurants and grocery stores, the more "normal" veganism will be, and the less uncomfortable new vegans will feel.[15]

"Humane Meat" Myth

"Humane meat" is a myth that soothes many individuals who continue to consume meat because they believe the animals were raised and/or slaughtered "humanely." If there was no serious suffering, then why not continue the familiar and comfortable personal and cultural practices?

However, undercover investigations have shown there is no such thing as "humane" when it comes to animal agriculture.[16] Animals in "humane-certified" operations still are overcrowded, live in ammonia-soaked environments, are subject to physical procedures such as de-beaking and detoeing without anesthesia, are bred to gain too much weight too quickly, and so forth.

If you examine the main "humane" certification labels, such as the American Humane Association's Humane Heartland, you see that, by and large, they support the industry standards. Undercover investigations continue to find problems such as overcrowding, windowless sheds, no access to sunlight, and so on. Nathan Runkle, founder of Mercy for Animals, calls Humane Heartland "little more than a scam."[17]

Lately there has been media coverage of major poultry corporations, such as Sodexo and Perdue, announcing they would be transitioning to cage-free egg-laying chicken operations. While taking ten or more years to reach this goal, the idea is to get chickens out of overcrowded wire cages and allow them to stretch their wings, dust bathe, and sit on perches. While this sounds like a much better alternative to the cages, it is not the same as free roaming outside, does not end debeaking, and certainly does not end cruel worker treatment, such as when they load chickens for transport to slaughterhouses, or during the slaughter process. Are these really "humane" eggs that are being produced?

Furthermore, there is the question as to whether *any* slaughter of an animal can be stress-free even under the best of circumstances. Gay Bradshaw, founder of The Kerulos Center, in an interview with *The MOON Magazine*, says, "'Humane' is not congruent with any kind of practice whose ultimate aim is to kill."[18]

The fact that humans do not need to eat animals at all to be healthy is another challenge to why animals need to be raised and killed for us. Could it be humane to sacrifice animals in this way? Jamie C., volunteering with Poplar Spring Animal Sanctuary, considers "humane":

I think one big problem that is hindering the movement today was the industry's creation of the supposed "humane meat" phenomenon back in the '90s, to combat the attitude that people were upset for how the animals were treated. The big problem here is that many animal groups have decided to work with the industry to promote the supposed "humane" treatment of animals, which is so unfortunate. They have helped the industry change the focus from "Is it right to eat animals?" to "What is the right way to raise animals for food?" This has helped these groups widen their donor pool at the expense of the core issue. People who might have given up eating meat, dairy, and eggs don't have to do so to feel moral if they buy into this myth. They can buy these supposed humane products and think they are helping animals.

You cannot help animals by eating certain animals. And no matter what anyone says, there is no humane way to raise animals for food. It is impossible. All end up being killed and scared to death. Most of the animals at Poplar Spring [where I volunteer] are from these small—supposedly kinder—farms, and there is horrendous abuse there. People are buying the myth that smaller, organic, supposed cage-free operations are humane, and they are not.

Molly F. agrees with Jamie C. and feels "it just reduces some of the conflict in their heads and it justifies their continued consumption." She continues, "I have multiple friends on Facebook that are always posting things [like] 'Well, this was a happy chicken, so it is OK I'm eating it.'"

Lia also sees this rationale:

I think [there is] a huge disconnect [in] "humane" meat. While I am a champion for welfare issues, I do believe a lot of people see positive examples of welfare (that so-and-so has gone cage-free or whatever), and then the consumer feels it is enough. I get hit over the head with "I get my meat locally," and people think they are immune and that their animal didn't feel pain or have a horrific life.

Lia, Molly F., and Jamie C. share a common view among vegans, but it is also important to know that many, many vegans and vegetarians support improved welfare for all factory-farmed animals while supporting the eventual vegan goal for society, because for each individual animal, whether in a larger cage for months or experiencing an improved procedure (perhaps ensuring stunning at slaughter, or reducing antibiotics in feed), that step *does* improve the life for that animal, and that is a positive step. But the question remains: If I were raised in a cage, would I prefer a larger cage? Maybe yes, maybe no.

Vegan Food Options Moving into the Mainstream

Alternative vegan options on the market, whether in supermarkets or at restaurants, have been exploding. Eric Pierce, in the *Nutrition Business Journal*, reported how the public views the vegan diet, as stated in an article by Hannah Sentenac:

> When Pierce and team asked general U.S. market consumers what they associate with a vegan diet, 35 percent said healthy/health food. Following that, 23 percent said animal welfare, 13 percent said cleaner ingredients, 12 percent said weight loss, 11 percent said environmental responsibility, and 8 percent said social responsibility. [19]

This suggests veganism is not only viewed as an "extreme" diet or associated with activist extremists, but is increasingly seen as positive for health and animal well-being.

In fact, now, the market is flooded with plant-based choices. For example, Gardein, a company that offers meat-free chicken, meatballs, fish fillets, breakfast scrambles, pizza pockets, and so on, is now sold in "over 23,000 stores, 5,000 food service establishments, and 150 colleges and universities in North America alone."[20] This same article in *Latest Vegan News* reports that 36 percent of people are open to a plant-based diet, and that vegetarian menus have grown 66 percent in the past three years.

Vegan eating is in the mainstream. Mintel, a leader in market intelligence, reports that meat alternatives sales "are expected to reach $5 billion by 2020."[21] This is not surprising given that, according to Mintel, 30 percent of millennials consume some meat alternative product every day. According to the Specialty Food Association, currently "[o]nly 7 percent of U.S. consumers say they are vegetarian, but the vegetarian market is a $2.8 billion-a-year industry and about 22.3 million people say they are inclined to follow a vegetarian diet."[22] Marketwired reported, in 2015, that plant-based proteins will probably take one third of the protein market by 2054.[23] Burger King, Panera Bread, Subway, Superiority Burger, 7-Eleven, White Castle, Wendy's, and Taco Bell are among the many establishments offering vegan ingredients and vegan options. On Taco Bell's website, the company reports, "Taco Bell sells 350 million vegetarian items a year and about 7 percent of all items ordered at Taco Bell are either vegetarian-friendly or made vegetarian-friendly by substitution or removal."[24]

Serving Meat at Animal Organization Fundraisers

With this kind of mainstream reach, it is no surprise that many vegans are shocked when an animal organization, such as dog and cat rescues and county shelters, hold fund-raisers that serve meat. To them, it is a contradiction at best and speciesist at worst—caring for one kind of animal while participating in the exploitation of another. Janine, doing independent rescue and fostering, writes in her survey:

> I actually quit volunteering with the local humane society after they started selling hamburgers and hot dogs for fundraising at the local shelter. Talk about mental disconnect!! How is it ethical to help one animal while harming another? I tried to discuss this with the members but was shouted down by the group.

Lindsay found something similar at a bird rescue: "in shelters and different rescues, they serve meat at many different functions, and it's always confusing to me how they don't make this connection. This bird rescue, an exotic bird rescue, served chicken at one of these fundraisers, and it's exactly the same thing." Dana attended a shelter fundraiser and wondered, "We were raising money to stop dog-eating in other countries, but we'll eat cows here. How can they care about these dogs but not about the cows?"

Isabella has been active in her city animal shelter in Berkeley, California. Here is what she reports on her very public efforts to end the serving of meat to raise money for an animal shelter:

> Over two years ago, when the Berkeley city animal shelter (Berkeley Animal Care Services), where I volunteer, announced a fundraiser where they would be serving hot dogs and hamburgers, I was chagrined—it seemed hypocritical for an organization whose mission is to save the lives of animals to contribute to the slaughter of animals.

Since then I have lobbied, cajoled, and begged for the shelter to adopt an animal-friendly menu at events. This has involved numerous communications with the shelter director and the organization that raises money for the shelter (Friends of Berkeley Animal Care Services), to no avail. I have created a petition and collected 500 signatures, over 150 in the San Francisco Bay Area, and twenty-eight from shelter volunteers, citing animal welfare, environmental concerns, and human health. The item went before the Berkeley City Council, where it came close to passing but was then referred to the Berkeley Animal Care Commission.

I was then appointed to the animal care commission, and the item was discussed at four meetings. The majority of the commissioners were vehemently against it despite the fact that dozens of members of the public have spoken eloquently in favor of the motion, while only less than a handful have spoken against. At the last meeting, the president of the commission substituted a motion to "provide vegetarian options at events." I tried to amend the motion but was told that I was not allowed to speak or make any further motions, clearly a breach of Robert's Rules of Order by which the commission is meant to abide.

Since that meeting, two of the three vacancies on the animal care commission have been filled by animal liberationists. At the next meeting I will make a motion for the shelter to provide animal-friendly menus at events. If the third new commissioner votes in favor, the motion will pass. If not, it will fail. However, it is only a matter of time until we succeed.

Animal Place runs a campaign called Food for Thought that helps shelters, rescues, and animal-focused organizations adopt vegan or vegetarian menu policies at their organization events. They provide support, sample menus, sample policy language, and even a one-time grant to get started. Their number one reason why animal organizations should make this move:

To act in accordance with your mission: Animal rescue and adoption agencies are driven by their mission to help animals. Rabbits, chickens, pigs, and other species suffer immensely on farms—far worse and in greater numbers than dogs and cats. They deserve our consideration, too. A veg-friendly menu policy is a chance to align your actions and values with your mission.[25]

Marketing Appeals

Good intentions, ethics, health, the environment, love for animals—
there are many reasons why people become vegans and work toward
ending animal suffering. But a reality is that there are powerful political
and corporate interests that use money and influence to stop reforms in
animal agriculture, and to stop the loss of market share in animal food
products. Julie, a nutrition counselor, observed one aspect of this influence in her field of work:

> *A few weeks ago I attended the Arizona AND (Academy of Nutrition
> and Dietetics) conference, [as] required to maintain professional cre-
> dentials in nutrition, and again most of the speakers and the events
> were sponsored (paid for) by the Arizona Dairy Council, the Nation-
> al Pork Producers Association . . . and on and on with the meat
> producers. The most respected academic journal in nutrition, the
> American Journal of Clinical Nutrition, is funded by the same food
> producers. The USDA, along with every single producer of meat and
> dairy, contribute hundreds of millions of dollars per year in lobbying
> and funding to create and distribute industry-friendly marketing,
> promotion, and research to encourage the consumption of animals as
> food, and perpetuate the myth that doing so is healthy and necessary.
> Food companies spend billions of dollars every year on "education"
> promoting eating meat and dairy, and this greatly overshadows all
> vegan films/books/marketing spending. When one adds in the unseen
> political exchanges and intense lobbying, any vegan education pales
> in comparison.*

Between the industry lobbying to keep and increase animal agriculture
and animal by-product use, and the cultural pressures to fit in and be
like others, it's important to understand what appeals are more likely to
work to interest people in changing their lifestyle. There is growing
interest in veganism, as shown by a 32 percent increase in Google
searches for the term "vegan" from 2014 to 2015.[26]

   To the animals, it does not matter which rationale leads a person to
become vegan, or reduce animal intake, or in other ways help animals.
But it does matter to us—what appeal should we be using? Jeffrey,
executive director of Jewish Veg, mentioned this to me in our interview:

One thing that's so powerful about the vegan movement is that there are different doors into the movement. There's the health door, such as the raw food cooking classes . . . which is a big one; there's the animal door, which is probably what you came through; there's the environment door; and for us, the religion door. It's not necessarily analogous to the other three doors, but it makes those doors wider. We can tell people authentically that all these other reasons are supported by the Torah. In fact, the Torah is explicit we should be eating plants and not meat.

Jasmin, executive director of Our Hen House, has a focus on media outreach. There is no question that more information is needed about our culture's use of animals and the impact on the animals and the environment. She says:

[W]hat's needed is a multipronged approach, involving undercover investigations; media covering those undercover investigations; grassroots activism; media covering grassroots activism; legal and policy reform; media covering that legal and policy reform; more vegan food businesses; media covering those vegan food businesses; and independent media (like Our Hen House) shedding light and providing commentary on issues that the mainstream media largely ignores.

When Elizabeth K. thinks about a vegan world, she believes it will take many aspects coming together:

[L]egal advances (a la Nonhuman Rights Project-type lawsuits), legislative changes (tougher penalties for animal abuse, getting rid of common farming exemptions, etc.), and changes of the heart (consumers have to stop turning a blind eye to what they know to be true: that their dinner suffered terribly). I think changes of heart will come about by grassroots activism (bringing vegan cookies to work, having vegan dinner parties, having serious but not heated conversations about why we are vegan with family/friends/coworkers, etc.).

Ginny Messina, interviewed for this book, but responding to an interview found on the Vegan Street blog, echoes the importance of sharing vegan food. "I think it's much easier to get someone to hear a vegan message once they know that vegan food is good. . . . I'm a very big fan of food activism."[27]

Learning about appeals that will reduce animal exploitation is very important to the advocates, activists, and organizations that promote less or no animal food consumption. But this turns out to be complicated by cultural habits, traditions, socialization into what is considered normal practice, and psychological issues of fitting in, cognitive dissonance, and what researchers in this next study call "willful ignorance."

Jared Piazza, of Lancaster University, and Steve Loughnan, of the University of Edinburgh, were interested in the impact of animal intelligence on whether study participants thought it was okay to eat animals. They compared knowledge of the intelligence of three animals—dogs (which Americans do not eat), a fictional animal that some fictional people ate elsewhere, and pigs (which many Americans do eat). We know that pigs are as intelligent as dogs, or even more so. Basically, knowledge of the intelligence of the dogs reinforced that participants should not eat dogs, knowledge of intelligence of the fictional animal led participants to feel they should not be eaten, but knowledge of pigs' intelligence, which they were already eating, did not impact their eating choices. Researchers concluded that it was in the interest of the meat-eaters (eating pigs) to continue with their behavior, and so they discounted the intelligence information (which the researchers referred to as "willful ignorance").[28]

In 2015, Piazza et al. published research looking at the "meat paradox"—that so many meat-eaters have pets, love animals, and say they oppose animal suffering. To handle this paradox, these researchers studied the psychological mechanisms people employ to rationalize their inconsistencies. The most common rationalizations were what they termed the 4Ns, that meat eating is natural (humans are supposed to eat meat), normal (everyone does it), necessary (we need that protein), and nice (it is enjoyable to eat meat). Here they built upon the work by Melanie Joy, who wrote about the 3Ns (natural, normal, necessary) in her 2010 book *Why We Love Dogs, Eat Pigs, and Wear Cows*. They added "nice" to account for the fact that so many people claim "meat tastes so good."[29]

This research (six different studies reported on in the article) indicates that meat-eaters adhere to these psychological rationalizations more strongly than vegetarians or vegans. They were less likely to be moved by ethical arguments, did not see cows as intelligent, were more tolerant of social inequality, held more speciesist views, ate animal products more frequently, and so on. The mechanisms of the 4Ns were quite effective, and only show how important vegan messaging is in trying to break through our meat-centered culture.[30]

In terms of what the actual research tells us about messaging, we can look at three reports by Humane League Labs. First, when we look at what farm animal photos work best at interesting people in vegan eating, researchers found the most effective type of photo was of sick or injured animals. The second most influential photo was of animals who were dead or being killed, and the third most effective was of animals in tight confinement. Photos of pigs were the most compelling, with chickens and turkeys next. Photos of individual animals were more effective than photos of groups of animals, and photos of baby animals more compelling than adult animals. This has relevance for the many brochures and leaflets that are distributed to interest people to consider vegetarian or vegan meals.[31]

Another Humane League Labs report was titled, "Is Animal Cruelty or Purity ('Abolitionist') Messaging More Effective?" This research was interested in the debate as to whether outreach should focus on animal suffering on factory farms, or focus on the rights of animals and the ethical considerations of how to treat animals. Study participants were shown different flyers that focused on either cruelty to animals, animal rights, or the environmental impact of meat consumption. Participants were asked, after viewing the flyers, if they might change their diets. Animal cruelty messaging and environmental messaging were both more effective than the animal rights/ethical flyer. This is an especially interesting finding because most vegans will say the ethical issue is most important in staying with the vegan diet, and many of my study participants spoke passionately about the moral reasons they themselves were vegan. However, according to the study results, "[T]he flyer with cruelty messaging led twice as many people to want to change their diet as the flyer with purity ('abolitionist') messaging (51% percent versus 27 percent)."[32]

Susie C. of Farm Sanctuary spoke to me about her parents, and trying many strategies over the years to move them toward a vegan diet. Her experience reflects what many have gone through:

My parents are not vegan, but they have reduced their meat by well over 50 percent—not because I work with animals, not because

they've been to the farm, but because they saw Forks over Knives.
And I got my dad The China Study *first, because of his interest in
history. We've been to China multiple times, we've been to Japan
multiple times . . . if I had bombarded them with video of bad images,
they physically could not watch that. They won't. So me being, "You
have to see this," won't do it. Some people—they cannot do it, and it's
not going to change who they are, it's just going to upset them more.
We assume because it changed us it will change them, but it doesn't
work that way. I think you have to meet people where they're at. My
parents are professors, they're older, they're worried about their
health. So, give them something about their health, that's proven, and
shows that their health issues are being caused by, or are linked to,
the meat in their diet. And it actually worked. I tried everything,
including the force thing, and I saw this was never going to work,
they're never going to be vegan, but they did reduce. And reducing is
a lot better than not reducing.*

On the other hand, Alka spoke to me about a different view of the
health-based approach reflected in the film *PlantPure Nation*:

*All these people have heart disease, and diabetes, and cholesterol,
and it is inspiring to see people get a handle on their health. But I
bristle a little at that. I sort of feel like we have not done our jobs if all
we're doing is getting people to be more self-interested. You know,
people clapping because some guy has dropped in his cholesterol
level. It's not that I'm not sympathetic to what it means to a family if
a member of that family is not well, and is on all the statin, choleste-
rol-lowering drugs—it's not that I'm not sympathetic to that—but, I
sometimes do feel that we give too much credence to—and credence
might not be the right word. But there's so much value ascribed to
the human story and no value ascribed to the animal story.*

*And I think that we lose a lot. There's an opportunity here for
people to see that our interests are tied up in their interests, and their
interests are tied in ours, to see this oneness, this connection. And
that, to me, is the message. So if we're just saying eat a vegan diet,
there's no cholesterol in a vegan diet, blah, blah, blah, that's good,
and it's going to motivate a lot of people because people are selfish,
but that's not the endgame to me, that's not it, the prize.*

A third study by Humane League Labs examined the language of requests for diet change, comparing vegan, vegetarian, eat less meat, cut

out or cut back on animal products. I personally know countless individuals who believe in abolition (end of factory farms), but speak most often in terms of "cutting back on consumption" to reach people. In this study, 1,594 college students were given a short survey and different types of veg booklets reflecting the different appeals. Then there was a follow-up survey, which 601 of the initial participants completed. Researchers found that the "combination message of 'cut out or cut back on' meat and other products appeared to work best" in reducing animal product consumption. This worked better even than using the words vegetarian or vegan in reaching people, and in getting them to change their eating patterns.[33]

This finding does not sit well with Casey T. Taft, author of *Motivational Methods for Vegan Advocacy: A Clinical Psychology Perspective*. According to Taft, it is well known in clinical psychology that behavior change is best reached by having specific long-term goals. For example, goals that relate to ending violence would never be stated as "end some violence," or end one type of violence but not another (such as physical but not psychological). To Taft, it is a losing proposition for mainstream animal advocacy groups to not speak explicitly in terms of veganism as the goal (and ending all violence against animals). Because Taft feels science is on his side in terms of behavior change, we should not "compromise the vegan message by suggesting that anything less than veganism is acceptable or ethical as an end goal." Taking steps toward the goal is one thing (such as Meatless Mondays), but the goal should be clearly stated (to end meat-eating).[34]

Taft is an example of one kind of reasoning and approach to veganism. Others, however, stress that cutting down on meat-eating has a profound impact on the animals right now. For example, Andrea Gunn of the Humane League talks about how one vegetarian can save the lives of thirty-seven animals per year. Cutting meat out (while still eating dairy and eggs) does make a difference.

Regardless of whether one feels veganism should be based on ethics, or health, or environmental sustainability, and whether one should support gradual or partial meat reduction, or no animal products at all, what is clear is that appeals to reducing animal consumption to some degree (or completely) are part of everyday life.

I end this chapter with discussion of the Be Fair Be Vegan campaign, which started in New York City in mid-2016. With two hundred posters on the streets of Manhattan, plus two slideshows showing on high-profile billboards, the images and messages are geared to help viewers connect individual animals with personalities, lives, emotions, and relationships.

According to Lori Amos, Scout 22 marketing executive:

> Be Fair Be Vegan believes the overwhelming violence in the world is a sign that we need to examine the root causes of our problems, including the disturbing nature of our relationships with nonhuman animals. Many people are beginning to recognize that animals are no more meant to be our possessions than people with different colored skin, women, children, or any other living beings. [35]

One poster shows three young chicks under the heading, "Which chick should die for your omelet?" Each chick is labeled in one of these ways: "The spirited one?," "The quiet one?," or "The proud one?" The rest of the copy reads: "Male chicks are killed the day they hatch because they don't lay eggs." Another poster focuses on three sheep, "The daring one," "The loving one," and "The hopeful one." The question asked is: "Which sheep should die for your sweater?" The ending copy reads: "Sheep used for wool are killed at 3 or 4 when their fleece quality declines."

Campaigns such as Be Fair Be Vegan and Go Vegan World, mentioned in chapter 2, make appeals to consumers to consider animals as complex individuals, much like humans. Considering that plant-based foods are a top trend for 2016 (according to the global market intelligence group Mintel), this message seems to be making headway.

Our next chapter focuses on the study participants and their goals. What are they hoping to accomplish with their animal work? What is their vision? The Issue Focus is on animal use and the environment—climate change, soil, air, and water.

7

OUR GOALS

I'd like to live in a world where my sanctuary was forced out of business because there were no more pigs who needed sanctuary space. —Richard H.

I want animal liberation from all the exploitation and abuse we humans inflict on them. I want a total change in attitude, one that views animals as equals on this earth, with the right to live according to their own agenda, not ours. Meantime, until that is accomplished, I work for their protection. —Batya

Until animals are afforded some basic rights to be treated humanely, and until they are recognized as having emotions and feeling pain, we will constantly have to deal with thousands of individual atrocities (horse racing, horse slaughter, greyhound racing, farmed animals, domestic pet overpopulation, animals used in research, trapping, hunting, and on and on). Little by little this will happen, when the majority of the public agrees with the premise that animals can suffer and it is wrong to cause them to suffer. —Vernon

People volunteering or working for animal well-being may have short-term commitments or long-term dedication, may be focused on one specific issue or on many. But when they are involved with animals, they do so for a reason. I asked on the survey, "What are you hoping to accomplish by your volunteering/working with animal issues? What changes for animals would you most like to see?"

We start with the broadest change—the end to speciesism—and move to the more specific.

A NEW PARADIGM

Changing mind-sets is "about how we treat each other, animals, and the earth," as Charles, staff with Vegetarian Resource Group, said. In discussing an end to all animal suffering, Molly F., volunteer with international rescue groups, would "like to see more of a recognition from people that animals have value beyond what role they can play in providing for humans, and need to be respected because of that alone." Janine, doing independent rescue and fostering, also sees this as an issue of empathy, where humans would "care for animals as our family and fellow earthlings" and would "stop looking at animals as commodities or things." Volunteering at CJ Acres Animal Rescue Farm, Rebecca F.'s way of saying this is: "I want all animals to be considered equal, and be able to live the lives they deserve in natural habitats."

When speaking about speciesism, or human supremacy, Robert, director of Free from Harm, says:

> [T]here's no basis for it in rational thought. It's a prejudice, like judging someone on the color of their skin. So being of another species is just another thing that we can't control and isn't morally relevant to how we treat someone . . . to me it's very important to challenge that because it is so pervasive, and it comes up and manifests itself in so many different ways. . . . That's something that we have to challenge.

Shannon, volunteering with dog rescue organizations, shares how she is challenging this thinking:

> I feel very strongly that no law will suffice until our basic values change. Any argument cannot progress until all of us agree that animals are equal to us. After we can agree that they are not commodities, not for our consumption, then we can move forward with laws that support our values. I am often confused, frustrated, and overwhelmed by others' views on many issues. What I attempt is gently educating others, and setting an example. I try to promote brands or products or foods or experiences that do not exploit ani-

mals, in the hope that my example encourages others to change. I make it known that making that change in your life is not difficult, and is in fact very rewarding.

When I asked Unny, executive director of Compassionate Action for Animals, how he felt we could reach his goal of a transformation of society to one where fewer animals are raised and killed for food, he replied: "We need a broad cultural change involving ethics, culinary arts, food service, restaurants, religion, and other institutions that determine cultural norms and food policy. Activists can engage at many levels with different institutions to make change."

Speciesism isn't only between humans and nonhuman animals; a hierarchy is also applied when people consider different nonhuman animals—for example, comparing a rabbit to a cow or a cat. Leah wants to see an end to eating animals, but her main focus is as an advocate for rabbits. She shares:

Here's what goes on with rabbits. Many AR [animal rights] activists will not advocate for them because their meat is not as mainstream as cows, pigs, and chickens. And a lot of the AR activists will not advocate for an animal that is a pet. . . .[T]hen you have the pet community, cat/dog—hardly any of them advocate or help rabbits either, they only help cats and dogs. So then where does that leave rabbits, the most exploited animal on our Earth between their fur, meat, testing, after Easter dumps, dog bait, backyard breeding with the homesteaders, and the "farm-to-table" movement? Nowhere. Most of the rabbit advocates are rabbit rescuers that don't have time to advocate for them because they are too busy saving them from all sorts of horrid conditions.
Since rabbits are small, take up less space, and are more silent little animals, they are often bred in backyards. There are rabbit breeders everywhere. The animals are kept outside in wire-bottomed cages. Rabbits like to roam around freely, like all animals. Mine live free range in my home; they explore around just like any animal. Keeping rabbits in cages is like a jail cell for them. There is no way to get statistics on those rabbits that are eaten by people.

For Andrea, who volunteers on a range of animal issues, a paradigm shift in thought toward greater respect has to do with respecting animals' communication as equally in merit to human communication.

The point I'm trying to make is, there has to be an appreciation [for] different species having their own intellect, dialect, their own world of communication separate from humans. And just because we don't understand it doesn't give us the right to immediately dismiss it and claim superiority. . . . [We need] respect for other life-forms on this planet, and to end the belief that we (humans) can decide how those species get to live their lives, and what purpose their lives should serve [for] us.

Mary S. and Susie C., both managing sanctuaries (Ironwood Pig Sanctuary and Farm Sanctuary, respectively), feel the experience of actually being with animals advances this respect. Mary S. writes on her survey: "I hope that by supporting our pigs, and coming to visit the sanctuary, [people] will see that pigs, too, are wonderful animals that deserve respect and a life free of oppression."

To be practical, any major shift will require more than ideas. Also needed are viable options and alternatives. Josie, on staff with The Humane Society of the United States (HSUS), tells me,

The other part of the equation, too, is offering alternatives, even if we're talking about the circus. So, if people want to do something for entertainment, can we provide something that is equally entertaining but not cruel? And if people want to eat something that is exactly like mayonnaise but is not cruel, there need to be alternatives available.

Jamie L., volunteer extraordinaire with Help A Dog Smile, speaks about her friends who are moms, and who take their kids to the zoo on a summer pass. "[T]hey take their kids three times a week. They need other options and other things they can do with their kids, other than seeing animals taken out of their natural environments and put on display."

Ginny, vegan dietitian and writer, echoes, "On a more practical level, it will also take the development of alternatives—in vitro meat, alternatives to animal testing, widespread availability of vegan shoes, and the like—because people will be much more open to a message about ending animal use if they are familiar with the alternatives."

Amber, a Humane Society of Southern Arizona (HSSA) volunteer, is hoping that people can learn "to interact kindly and compassionately with animals." Charlee, Compassion Over Killing staff, also is looking for an outcome of compassion:

> I am hoping to shed a light on how we use animals every day in so many different industries. I want people to see the things I have seen, so they can understand the truth and feel compassion. I hope that, as a result, people will choose the cruelty-free options that organizations suggest. Options like going to an amusement park over SeaWorld, vegan cheese over dairy, cotton over fur, and so on.

We need these cultural and food alternatives to achieve these goals: "dignity and freedom" (Gay, author and founder of The Kerulos Center); compassion "regardless of the species" (Andrea); "no more death" (Susan L., executive director of St. Martin's Animal Rescue); to "stop their suffering" (Cat, Best Friends volunteer, founder of MildCats at Arizona State University, and director of Children and Animals Together Assessment and Intervention); to "end exploitation" (Farrah, attorney for an animal rights organization); for "better living conditions" (Emmy, vegetarian/vegan activist); and so that "animals will no longer be considered property" (Isabella, photographer of shelter animals and independent animal rights photography projects).

END SUFFERING

Volunteering with animals, especially at a dog and/or cat rescue, creates immediate hands-on satisfaction. For Dana, shelter dog walker and artist, "I would like to think that my volunteering helps these animals, who are already in a bad place, have better lives."

Brooke, teen volunteer at Wildhorse Ranch Rescue, feels that "[b]y volunteering I am able to provide the animals a sense of companionship and that someone cares for them." Christi, volunteering with rescue cats, "hope[s] to help cats be more adoptable through taking care of their daily needs, showing compassion and love, socialization, and grooming."

Volunteering with Animal Rescue Inc. in Maryland, and taking sick animals into her home, Rachel wants to "most of all, provide comfort for the sick, scared, hurting, and abused." Melissa R., volunteering with HSSA, concurs: "If they were abused or abandoned, and their world is upside down, I want to comfort them." This comforting and making a difference for each animal is a common desire, and as Fran, focusing on feral cats, writes, "I try to make my corner of the world a better place for all animals."

As we have seen throughout this book, animal suffering is found everywhere in our culture—on our dinner plates, in dogfighting, horse racing, roadside zoos, circuses, animal testing, horse-drawn carriage operations, wild horse roundups, trophy hunting, dog and cat abandonment, and more—and there are different positions as to how best to end this suffering. There is no one answer, no one magic wand or law or action.

I believe a good half of the study participants don't think much about the animal rights *movement*, and whether a strategy of "abolition" (campaigns to end all factory farming, animal captivity, animal entertainment or use by humans *now*), or a "welfare" approach (make incremental changes for the better for animal well-being, including efforts like Meatless Mondays, which reduces some suffering now and *eventually* might end all animal suffering) is better. But many individuals I spoke with did bring this up. Lori W., a volunteer with Animal Place, for example, told me:

> *I'm really for anyone who's helping animals in any way, or anyone who's getting the message out there about animals, anyone who's making the lives of individual animals better. So, I'm not someone who's going to go out and complain about how animal rights people are doing it because I don't, frankly, know the best way.*

Lori W. is a vegan, and one of her goals is to spread veganism. Still, like many others, she feels people should do what they want to do and can do for animals. Lindsay, on staff with Mercy for Animals, mentions in her goals' statement: "I want the world to no longer exploit/abuse animals in any way. Right now I support any change that benefits any animals."

Molly F. had a different experience. When I interviewed her, she was in a master's program in Applied Animal Behavior and Welfare.

> *I remember this moment of complete absurdity. It was the day we were doing all our presentations on what our dissertation projects were going to be, and someone was going over his project, which was*

to look at the effects of high fiber diets on broiler breeders. Do you know about broiler chickens? In order to reproduce, they have to starve the parents so that they don't get too big, because if they grow too big they can't walk and then they can't produce babies. So one of the projects was to give them high fiber diets so they can decrease abnormal behaviors, make them less hungry, blah, blah. And I was just sitting there thinking, I am in a room full of people who supposedly care about animals, and we are acknowledging the fact that we are withholding food from these chickens, so they are starving, so that we can use them to breed more chickens, so we can use them [for food], and no one has a problem with this. . . . That's animal welfare.

Molly F. saw value in an advanced degree as she pursues a career in wildlife rescue and rehabilitation, but was exposed to fellow students who would probably work for animal industries or in welfare-oriented organizations. She was one of only a few vegans, and does not believe in compromising or sacrificing some animals for the end goal of ending *all* animal suffering.

The "welfarist" approach is probably misnamed, and is often used in a negative, critical way by those who feel it dilutes advocacy for the true end of animal exploitation. These differences in approach exist, but the end goal is usually shared. Taking a step-by-step approach is seen as more realistic, culturally and legally, to welfarists, but not by abolitionists.

Most national organizations promote an eventual end to factory farms and veganism, for example, even if they are advocating for larger cages or better treatment. In addition, it is pretty difficult to scoff at the amazing changes for animals because of some organizations and their efforts to improve the lives of animals. The HSUS is probably the best known of the organizations that take a welfare approach. These would also include Mercy for Animals, Compassion Over Killing, People for the Ethical Treatment of Animals (PETA), Animal Legal Defense Fund, Farm Sanctuary, and others.

The HSUS, for example, in 2016 alone, helped lead initiatives for companies to commit to cage-free egg production, was involved in the end of elephant acts by Ringling Bros. and Barnum & Bailey Circus, helped Philadelphia ban the sale of puppy mill dogs, pressured Sea-World to end orca breeding, worked on Armani going fur-free, helped Nevada end its use of carbon monoxide gas chambers to euthanize shelter animals, and stopped bobcat hunting and trapping in New Hampshire.

The abolitionist perspective rests primarily on the premise that any *use* of animals is morally wrong, not whether *treatment* of animals is humane to various degrees. Gary Francione is a major proponent of this view, and wrote in *Turning Points in Compassion* that while we might personally take incremental steps toward a goal of, say, becoming vegan, "We should, however, never promote the idea that some forms of animal exploitation are morally acceptable or different from other forms of animal exploitation." Rather, it is a paradigm shift that is absolutely necessary to achieve the end of animal exploitation and suffering. To Francione, we should focus single-mindedly on "creative, nonviolent, vegan education." This focus will transform individual and cultural participation in animal exploitation, and no degree of animal suffering in any realm will be acceptable.[1]

A paradigm shift is more than an intellectual and value framework. The economy would require a huge transformation, for instance, as jobs in the food industries, fashion, hunting, animal testing, pet shops, and more would require new jobs created as alternatives. It would require changes in personal habits and behaviors, consumer choices, and traditions such as holiday foods or activities. This paradigm shift, therefore, is enormous, because animal use and abuse is thoroughly integrated into our lives. To get an idea of how mind-boggling and far-reaching these changes would be, consider that medical products, household products, and personal care items often have animal-derived ingredients.

I agree that the paradigm framing is key—there is a difference between accepting animal use while struggling to reduce the harm or suffering of animals, and taking the position that no use is acceptable. It is difficult to argue that no use is acceptable at the same time you are making agreements with corporations to slaughter in a less horrific manner (for example). For the time being, animal welfare is the dominant paradigm, and undeniably successes are reached that reduce suffering by degrees. However, as long as the challenge to human use of animals is seen as extreme and unrealistic, a genuine end to animal suffering will be elusive.

EDUCATION

Education was mentioned frequently in the survey's goals question, demonstrating the high importance advocates for animals place on it. Raising awareness about animal issues, and changing people's minds and behaviors based on what they learn, is part of most advocacy efforts.

Most study participants had specific issues in mind. For example, Kathy S., cofounder of Save the Cats Arizona, wants "to educate people on feline welfare, and change views on things such as declawing, letting family cats roam outside, cat abandonment, etc." Jocelyn is also focused on cats—ferals. "My community needs to be educated on free-roaming cats, and understand that TNR is the answer—not just gathering them up and euthanizing them. There will always be outdoor cats. We are trying to reduce the population by spaying and neutering."

Amanda, a teen volunteer with HSSA, mentions how important public awareness is to ending animal experimentation. "The public has the power to speak up against animal testing and experimentation, and make it a thing of the past."

Clare, who has interned with several national organizations, such as the Humane League and PETA, believes people "are just not aware" of the extent of rain forest depletion, including orangutan habitat. "I think people would be outraged," she said.

Education to raise awareness is "the number one priority" to Jocelyn: "Many people don't understand how poorly circus animals and puppy mill dogs are treated."

Ruth, on staff at Poplar Spring Animal Sanctuary, feels the culture is "definitely moving in the right direction." She became vegetarian back in the 1970s, and has seen amazing progress in the availability of vegan foods:

> [E]ducation, continued availability of vegan food, scientifically based health studies and publicity of them, advocates and activists working together to increase the public's awareness of [the] environmental impact and negative health consequences of non-vegan diets, and publicity of the cruelties inherent in animal agriculture, will move our society in the right direction.

A volunteer with Sea Shepherd Conservation Society, Lynne's goal is "[e]ducating people, and stopping overfishing and the slaughter of innocents." Margaretta's hope, while she works for Farm Sanctuary and volunteers with her local humane society, is for:

> [T]he end of animal cruelty all together by educating people on the problems with eating meat/dairy, breeding companion animals, and keeping animals in the pet trade who belong in the wild (i.e., all animals in pet stores and illegal, exotic pet trades). Also, educating [people] on the proper techniques with how to deal with wildlife and wildlife predators (i.e., shooting them is not a valid solution . . .).

Education figured hugely in influencing how people make choices. For example, Ryan, working for PETA's international youth outreach, writes:

> In my experience, the largest factor that determines whether someone makes a kind or cruel choice at the grocery store or the mall, is how much they know about the suffering that went into the product. When people are fully informed about the ways that cows on dairy farms are forcibly impregnated, and taught how their babies are taken away to keep the milk flowing, they are more likely to choose the almond or soy milk instead. Simply giving people information about what their choices mean can have a tremendous impact, because the vast majority of people consider themselves to be kind toward animals and want to put their money toward ethical companies when given the opportunity.

Elaine, who spent years exposing slaughterhouse practices in England, writes in response to the "hope to accomplish" survey question: "I have accomplished what I set out to do—film, photograph, and expose the reality for animals. My work is in the public domain; it is up to those who view it what they will do about it. Change can only happen with the free will of those who are no longer ignorant of the facts."

Sandra Higgins offers education that involves direct contact with rescued farmed animals at her Eden sanctuary:

> When doing vegan education, I introduce people to the intimate suffering that the residents at Eden are forced to endure when we are not vegan. I show the love, joy, [and] individual lives [animals] have at Eden, [which] are desecrated when we are not vegan. All of this is

in the hope of reaching someone somewhere, connecting with that
part of them that will care enough to become vegan.

Celeste, manager of the cats at Wildhorse Ranch Rescue, is "big on education." She hopes the next generation will "get it"—the "it" being the mistreatment of animals. She writes, "Our organization has open houses. We have an opportunity to show others what happens to animals who are not fed or cared for properly. We also make people aware of the animals who are not in our care, because they are now deceased because of human cruelty."

Many individuals spoke to me about the importance of education of young people in particular. Elizabeth S., specializing in animal law, wants to see "an educational system that teaches children compassion for all species." Laura J., an animal activist, laments, "No one tells kids the truth about where their food comes from. Like anything else, truth needs to be introduced at an early age."

Mary-Lynn, volunteer with the HSSA, believes we should "[c]reate an interest by taking kids to the shelters. . . . I'm sure people don't give kids enough credit—they love helping animals!" Kasey, teen volunteer with the HSSA, would like to see "the humane society and the shelters come to schools . . . and speak for the animals, and get people more aware of what is going on. I think that would be a great idea, especially if you start out young, because then you grow up with that awareness."

Dove, who has advocated for animals all her life, reinforces this idea:

> [W]e need to get people into schools with animals to visit—all differ-
> ent species of animals, with the young children, so we erase their
> fears; they form a connection. [We can] let them see, perhaps, movies
> of how animals act with their young, so that they see the connection
> between them living in families and animals living in families. [A]nd
> it starts in the early grades.

However, it isn't always so easy. Mary S. of Ironwood Pig Sanctuary tried to speak to a local 4-H program: "The nearby school has 4-H, and they raise pigs and then sell them at auction [for slaughter]. Some of us went to 4-H to buy the pigs. We got one for rescue. We asked if we could go in and talk about compassion. They said no. They let the humane society in, but not us. Why not? The meat industry is so powerful."

SPAY/NEUTER, BREEDERS, AND END PUPPY MILLS

Not surprisingly, many people mentioned mandatory spay/neuter in their goal statements. Jasmine M., of Blackhat Humane Society, wants to see "living standards improve for dogs on the reservation. . . . [Spay/neuter] clinics are very important, not only for sterilization but because they serve as an education and public outreach platform."

Sybil, a volunteer with Cochise Canine Rescue, is concerned about pet overpopulation. She has this to say about mandatory spay/neuter: "Until there is mandatory spay/neutering, with high fees for breeders, there will always be a severe overpopulation problem. But it has to be done in such a way—perhaps providing free spay/neuter to people as an alternative to turning in the animals—that the 'solution' does not create greater problems for the animals."

Eric, cofounder of Homeless Animal Rescue Team, wants to see "the overpopulation of pets dwindle significantly"; Joyce M., of Arizona Chihuahua Rescue, "would like to see an end to pet overpopulation and the resulting numbers of animals in shelters"; and Helen G., doing independent rescue with feral cats and kittens, wants people to "come together and offer protection from overpopulation by taking responsibility for a few cats, [to] get the overpopulation under control without killing them."

Breeders were mentioned by quite a few individuals. Amy, volunteering with Leaps and Bounds Rabbit Rescue, had this to say about bunnies:

> I don't agree with breeders, but a lot of people get their bunnies from breeders. While I don't agree with that, at the same time, [it would be better] if those people who sold bunnies to people also explained to people what you need to do to take care of your bunny, [that] you need to get [them] spayed or neutered when they get to a certain age, and what will happen if you don't.

Daya, doing independent rescue, "would like to see humans stop making animals suffer intentionally by breeding them into existence." Jodie, with the Feral Cat Coalition of Oregon, believes that in terms of meeting her goals of spay/neuter, "I think people should be required to spay/neuter their pets unless [they] have a license. Like being a licensed breeder. Work on changing laws to enforce mandatory spay/neuter.

[For example,] in my town, a local law was just passed that animals cannot be sold/given away for free on city/public property." Several people, such as Tracyene, in vet tech school, and Kim H., volunteer dog foster, mentioned the importance of free or low-cost spay/neuter, and vet care in general, to encourage responsible behavior.

Closing puppy mills is a big concern for many people. The cruelty and suffering for these puppies and their moms is horrific. The dogs are adopted by unsuspecting people, who then spend time and money trying to address the health needs of these animals bred for profit.

Jocelyn "would like to see an end to puppy mills. There are *so* many wonderful animals in shelters and with rescues. It disgusts me when someone buys a 'purebred' dog." Rita, doing TNR, echoes those concerns, "We need to stop this breeding at puppy mills."

HSSA volunteer Lisa McQ feels this is one issue she has hope of stopping:

> I think there is some momentum in "you should adopt rather than buy" nowadays, but three of my best friends bought their dogs from a breeder. And I was like, "What?" I thought my friends wouldn't do that. They wanted that type of dog. So I feel like getting the message out; those super sad commercials out. Maybe just more messages, more media, like, "You really don't need to go to a puppy mill, you can go to a shelter." And you [would] get so many animals turned over. I think it's beginning to work. And [shelters] get purebreds. That's something I did not know. The purebreds come into the shelter a lot. . . . [T]hat's what I mean by saying this one has momentum. People who aren't necessarily in the animal rights movement are starting to get it. So, I think we have a chance here. If people stop buying [purebreds], they'll stop making them.

SHELTER REFORM

Shelter reform is a common topic of discussion. JoAnn R., a volunteer with Animal Guardian Network, sums it up: "Killing healthy animals because there is no room is not acceptable."

Laurie (Pima Paws for Life and HSSA volunteer), Bryan (founder of Animal Life Rescue), Carla (founder of The Foundation for Homeless

Cats), Lynanne (volunteer with Little Rascals Rescue), and others all agree: "Never destroy an animal for space."

The volunteer work many are doing is toward the goal of no-kill shelters. Rosanne, for example, is part of a group in Tucson, Arizona, impacting change at the county shelter:

> *Well, it's going to take a little bit more effort in convincing manage-ment there're certain things to be put in place. They're still destroy-ing animals for behavioral issues that we think are manageable, or can be worked with. We think they can do more to network the animals that need to get out of there—the ones that are on an urgent list, that don't have much time. And I think they might still be de-stroying animals that have significant health issues, but again, these are things that we feel that can be managed and helped. And people who adopt them or foster them can be supported more in terms of taking care of those ill or injured animals. So, we're still working on it. They've come a long way and there's still some distance to go, and we're still letting our feelings be known.*

Maria, who works with two cat rescues, Save the Cats Arizona and Lost Our Homes Pet Rescue, talks about another dimension of pet surren-der—the fee. "As much as I despise killing innocent animals, there needs to be a place for people to surrender pets, for a minimal fee. I've been witness to people not having the money to surrender a pet, so the pet was left outside, to fend for himself," she stated.

Susan S., active with many rescues and a local shelter, lives in rural North Carolina. There, she says, even companion animals are seen as "disposable and replaceable." She continues,

> *State laws governing shelters reflect this attitude, and are cited by the county shelters to justify minimal standards of care. Shelter reform would include a state requirement that shelter animals be quaran-tined and receive basic vetting on intake; that shelter animals are assessed by someone qualified to make recommendations based on temperament (rather than automatically assume that a cat that hisses, swats, or cowers is feral, so kill it and sell its carcass); that shelter animals have access to veterinary care; that when euthanasia is required, it be carried out humanely, including anesthesia and an accurate determination of dosage by weight; that shelter animals be available to the public for longer than the current minimum of about*

twelve hours per week; and that the minimum hold time for a stray
animal be increased from seventy-two hours to at least one week,
among other things.

Carol's goal is to save lives through rescue and her local shelter. She
wishes "that there were funds for a bigger, better animal control facility,
to include an adoption center and clinic, and to be open on the weekends."

Novette, working with several cat organizations doing fostering,
transport, and TNR, sees shelter reform in a different way: "My first
step would be to have all government shelters and tax-money turned
over to rescues. . . . Rescues would better utilize and manage taxpayer
money as well as achieve an acceptable live release rate." While Novette's specific idea is unlikely, Alison, involved in rescue and some
fostering, has seen some real shelter change in her area:

To tell you the truth, social media in the past few years has had the
biggest impact on rescue efforts. It has enabled rescue groups to
mobilize faster, gain volunteers, find fosters, and raise funds faster
than any other means. Believe me when I say that when they kill
animals at the shelter now, the shelter staff and local commissioners
get a big *response from the community through e-mails, phone calls,*
and online comments. They are paying attention, too.

It is only with constant public pressure (sometimes gently, some-
times not) that [people] respond and implement changes for the shel-
ter animals. . . .[T]wo groups have had the biggest impact on changes
for animals in the past few years in Harnett County: Friends of the
Harnett County Animal Shelter and the Harnett Animal Welfare
Coalition. These groups are large and lobby locally for change. They
are very visible in the community and promote animal welfare here.
Several local rescues over the past few years have also stepped up,
and began rescuing all *of the animals at the shelter every week. Then*
out-of-state rescues became more involved, as well.

USE MEDIA FOR ANIMAL LIBERATION

Amanda "would love to see a day when tests on animals for cosmetics
are a thing of the past, and when animal experimentation has ended for
good." John, founder of Peaceful Fields Sanctuary and active with Sea

Shepherd Conservation Society, wants "to see the end of all killing, cruelty, and exploitation of animals, but especially start with testing and vivisection, since it is not only cruel but completely unnecessary, and a good step to start with for general public culture change."

Alka, whose job at PETA has the goal of ending animal testing and experimentation, talks about messaging:

> We recently had a meeting of my department, and we were looking at two questions: What is the most important message of our department, and what is the most effective method at our disposal? So, the most important message that we want to convey is that animals are not ours to experiment on. That is the most important message. But then the most effective method to get there is to point out that animals are not good models for human disease. So, it's this kind of crazy juxtaposition. What we know is the prize, and the prize is that animals matter. And what we know will be most effective [is] talking to people where they are, which is selfish, self-interested, not caring too much or seeing what the world is around them necessarily.

Jasmin, executive director of Our Hen House, talks about using podcasts, TV shows, online magazines, and more multimedia resources to get information out. She also recently wrote a memoir that "will use the power of personal narrative to open people's eyes to the plight of animals—and I hope that my book reaches far, far beyond the 'vegan choir.'"

Kim Meagher, founder of Wildhorse Ranch Rescue, also wants to see more mainstream media exposure for animal issues. "We need a TV show, we need billboards. . . . We need media, media, media. . . . To me it's marketing. We are not good at marketing this stuff. We have our tiny little groups but we all sing to the choir."

OVERALL COMPASSION

Many participants mentioned compassion, respect, or a kinder world as what they were working toward.

Kim Meagher says, "I'd like to see more people find compassion for the suffering of animals, and to make changes in their lives that will help animals in need." Shannon wants to see people viewing animals as "a brother or sister." She hopes to see changes in policy "so that animals may see a different, kinder world in the future." Nadia, founder of Golden Bone Rescue and Rehabilitation, claims: "For me, the core of all of this is creating a compassionate mindful population. We have to start with our children from the time they are six weeks old, and teach compassion."

More people specifically mentioned a vegan world as part of ending suffering than any other specific step or vision of what they were working toward. Keith, PETA's Assistant Action Team coordinator, wants to see people "shift their dietary and lifestyle proclivities toward making more compassionate choices."

Diana, PETA's senior youth marketing coordinator at peta2, feels that, with awareness, people can "choose cruelty-free products, adopt animals from shelters instead of buying them, and stop buying tickets to circuses that use animals." In addition, she is encouraged by the greater availability of vegan food in supermarkets, restaurants, and in fast-food drive-throughs, making it a "normal option." She writes, "America is based on profits, and I'd like to see popular opinion—and consumer spending habits—move in a more compassionate direction."

Kristin N., volunteering at shelters for the past several decades, sees a vegan world ending "the Hell on earth that animals suffer." To Jeannette, volunteering with Viva! and Animal Justice Project, this compassionate world is tied directly to veganism: "Veganism, to me, is the silver bullet to solving a lot of problems: climate change, world hunger, more empathy/less violence in general in the world, antibiotic resistance, zoonotic pandemics, cancer/diabetes/heart disease."

When Karyn, a committed vegan, reflects on her caring about animal well-being, she says: "Ideally, I would like all animals to be treated with compassion and respect. I would like to put a stop to the following: the killing of homeless animals, hunting, animal experimentation, and any abuse or killing of animals. I would like everyone to become vegan." Lia, Humane League volunteer, clearly states: "Helping people see a path to veganism is my main focus and what I would like to accomplish."

Jon C. (on staff with Vegan Outreach), Steve (also staff with Vegan Outreach), Robert, Will (author), Hope (on staff with United Poultry Concerns and a volunteer with Compassionate Living), and others agree with this comment from Jeffrey (executive director of Jewish

Veg): "Veganism as the dominant paradigm in society" is why they do the work they do. But, they also know we are far from that right now. As an example, Cindy, volunteering with local rescues, writes, "[T]here are so many kids involved with dogfights—fathers taking their little children—they grow up to think it's OK to mistreat them," and this presents a huge challenge to messages of treating animals as the sentient beings they are.

This is why education and role modeling figure so prominently in what these advocates and activists talk about. Working with the PETA Foundation, Becky's goal is "[c]hanging people's minds/educat[ing] others, as well as helping animals one by one, or by the thousands (being vegan, etc.)." Meghan, a volunteer with Farm Sanctuary and Mercy for Animals, writes, "I hope to set an example of someone who can live compassionately, and that this will cause others to do the same."

Helen K., a volunteer with Vegan Haven, similarly says,

> I hope that by being vegan, and participating in animal activism, I can be one of many making a positive change for animals in this world. I also hope to show people that each and every one of us can make a difference, and that the actions we take do matter. While I will never claim to be perfect, and there will always be ways I can have a better impact on the world, I hope to show people that it is possible for us to stand up for our beliefs, and represent our core values in our everyday behavior.

Rachel would like to achieve changing people's hearts and minds about the treatment of animals. I asked her, "How?" She replied (and I quote at length, because it touches on so many important ideas):

> This is the hardest question, because I do not think there is an answer. I think we can reach some people just by example, but many have cold, black hearts. I truly believe [that] "Times will not change until the hearts of men change" . . . We have laws on the books for animal abuse that are not being enforced. We, as a society, are materialistic and self-centered. We see anyone weaker than ourselves as an inconvenience and of lesser value.
>
> How do we change that in a consumer-driven society? I would say as a society we need to know Jesus, yet so many claim to be Christian but have never actually read the Bible, or taken the time to understand it. Ms. Lindsey [from chapter 5] herself claims to be

Christian, but doesn't see [that] the thrill she gets from killing is because she has a murderous heart, which is a sin in the Bible.

In the end, we cannot control others, we can only control ourselves. As advocates and rescuers we need to be loving and empathetic to everyone we come into contact with, even the terrible people, because no one responds to force. You cannot force people to be compassionate and just, even by laws. After all, it is illegal to abuse a child, but everyday children (like animals) are abused, neglected, and killed. I guess for me the "key" to change is: Be the change you want to see.

While many people spoke about being a role model and leading by example, Farrah reminds us of the structural levels of the animal industry. Ending the exploitation of animals is what she is working toward, and I asked her how she felt we could achieve that.

I think we have to fight it on three fronts. I think we're talking about corporations, governments, and culture. I think that corporations and government can be lumped together, because they facilitate each other. And, most people don't even have a basic understanding of what the system is, and it's meant very much to facilitate the exploitation of animals. In fact, it's meant to exclude from the process of change any stakeholder who does not agree with the industry. [By] the industry, I'm not just talking about factory farming, I'm talking about any big industry that's exploitative. That's a problem, and I think it requires people to think about why we have the government structure that we do. And on the legislative and litigation front, why do we have a history of legislation that has created complete opacity?

Also on the structural level, many individuals mentioned changing laws as part of their goals, and stated what they hoped to achieve by their work. Stacey, who volunteers with rescues and shelters, wants to "get better laws protecting animals, and harsher punishments for those that hurt them." Christi hopes for "stricter laws governing the humane treatment of animals and the laws being consistently enforced." She'd like "laws against keeping wild animals in captivity unless they are injured and would perish without intervention."

Rita had this to say:

Abusers now just seem to get a slap on the hand. No serious jail time, no matter how horrific the abuse. Individuals caught fighting animals should, mandatory, get at least ten years in prison, and possibly twenty-five-plus if they torture and kill the animals. Our society gives them a few months in jail, a fine, and community service. To them it is a joke. They get out and just begin all over.

We need serious laws in this country, with serious jail time. [Offenders] serve a short term, and then get out and are told they can't have any more pets, animals, etc., but they go right out and do it again. In Missouri, there was a young man who would take puppies and hang them on a clothesline, and bet his friends on a sports game. If his team lost, he shot and killed the puppies. No one did anything about it. I had one of my rescue dogs shot by a neighbor and nothing was done.

ISSUE FOCUS: ANIMALS AND ENVIRONMENTAL ISSUES

Animals relate to environmental concerns in major ways that impact the future of our planet and its inhabitants. Habitat destruction for the sake of growing corn or soy for animal feed in factory farming, or loss of tropical rain forests for grazing livestock for slaughter, impacts wildlife and extinction rates, as well as contributes to climate change. Factory farming itself is a major contributor to global warming. Pesticides, chemical fertilizers, and toxic manure all add to water and air pollution and contamination.

But most people are not thinking about environmental issues when they eat. It is a case of true lack of knowledge, as well as self-interest. A volunteer with Sea Shepherd, one of Melissa J.'s goals is to raise "[a]n awareness among humans that we are destroying the earth and all of its inhabitants, and that we can stop it." Rosanne "would very much like to see more people turning to veganism as a way to end animal agriculture, lessen global warming, save water, and feed the hungry."

The movie *Cowspiracy* led countless environmentalists to go vegan, and many vegans to consider environmental issues in addition to the ethical reasons for keeping animals off their plates. This movie looked specifically at the connection of animal agriculture to the environmental issues mentioned above, and exposed that most national environmental organizations focus on fossil fuels as a major cause of global warming rather than animal agriculture, which actually has a greater impact. It is, shall we say, more palatable to critique fossil fuels and continue to eat your steak, than to admit our cultural steak and chicken and pork habits have to go if we want to leave a habitable planet for our kids and grandkids.

The facts are astounding, and encompass many facets of life. According to Kate Good, writing for One Green Planet:

> [T]he global livestock system currently covers around 45 percent of land, uses 23 percent of available freshwater resources, and is responsible for more greenhouse gas emissions than the entire transportation sector. Not to mention this industry is also to blame for rampant deforestation, air pollution, water pollution—and, interestingly enough, despite all the resources being put into industrial animal agriculture, nearly one billion people still go to bed hungry every night.[2]

Journalist and environmentalist George Monbiot tells us more about the scope of the problem:

> One third of our cereal crops are used to feed [farmed animals]. This may rise to roughly half by 2050. More people will starve as a result, because the poor rely mainly on grain for their subsistence, and diverting it to livestock raises the price. . . . This might seem counter-intuitive, but were we to eat soya, rather than meat, the clearance of natural vegetation required to supply us with the same amount of protein would decline by 94 percent. Producing protein from chickens requires three times as much land as protein from soybeans. Pork needs nine times, beef thirty-two times.[3]

Monbiot continues, "A recent paper in the journal *Science of the Total Environment* suggests that our consumption of meat is likely to be 'the leading cause of modern species extinctions.'"[4]

I offer here a brief discussion of just a few facts of the pressing environmental issues as related to animals.

Water and Oceans

Concerns about water and oceans include the huge amount of freshwater resources used in agriculture to feed animals for slaughter; water pollution from the animal agriculture industry; ocean dead zones due to nitrate pollution, overfishing, and bycatch waste; mercury, heavy metals, and PCB contamination of fish; bottom trawling leading to depletion of marine diversity and the collapse of fish ecosystems; and the loss of sea beds necessary for feeding, spawning, and shelter. One fact that amazed me personally is that, of all fish caught globally, one-third is used as fishmeal to feed animals for slaughter.[5]

A single pound of beef requires between 1,850 and 2,500 gallons of water, whereas a pound of vegetables only needs 39 gallons.[6] Health and environmental advocate Richard Oppenlander uses even higher numbers of 5,000 gallons of water to produce one pound of beef, and between 20 and 60 gallons of water to produce one pound of vegetables, fruits, beans, and grains.[7]

Another water fact found on the *Cowspiracy* movie website, which speaks to the out-of-balance use of water resources for meat, is that agriculture (which goes mostly to *animal* agriculture) uses 80–90 percent of U.S. water consumption. Furthermore, 1,000 gallons of water are required to give us one gallon of milk, and 477 gallons of water are needed for one pound of eggs. Water usage alone is an astounding factor when examining animal agriculture and natural resources.[8]

The video *Planet Earth*, produced by Mercy for Animals, reports that animal agriculture is the number one cause of environmental destruction, including the creation of ocean "dead zones." This industry consumes one-third of all freshwater, and is the leading cause of the destruction of the Amazon.[9]

The Environmental Working Group issued a report in 2011 on meat-eating, and climate change and health. Concerning water the report states:

> Slaughterhouses dump millions of pounds of toxic pollutants—primarily nitrogen, phosphorus, and ammonia—into waterways. Eight slaughterhouses are consistently among the nation's top twenty industrial polluters of surface water, responsible for discharging 13.6 million kilos (thirty million pounds) of contaminants—primarily nitrates—in 2009 (EPA 2009). Nitrates are a significant source of drinking water contamination in agricultural communities nationwide. Excessive amounts of these pollutants lead to massive fish kills and oxygen-deprived "dead zones," where no marine life can survive.[10]

Concerns about overfishing, depleting fisheries, and bycatch killing, along with ocean pollution, toxic dumping, and plastics causing both ocean dead zones and death to fish whose stomachs get filled with plastic, are huge for environmentalists. While we refer to the over seventy billion animals raised and slaughtered for human consumption, there are trillions of animals every year taken from the oceans. The waste in fishing is astounding.

According to the United Nations Food and Agriculture Organization, "for every one pound of fish caught, up to five pounds of unintended marine species are caught and discarded as by-kill."[11] If you look specifically at shrimp, for every pound of shrimp eaten, more than twenty pounds of other sea creatures were caught and killed.[12]

Also found on the *Cowspiracy* fact page: "As many as 40 percent of fish caught globally every year are discarded," and "[s]cientists estimate as many as 650,000 whales, dolphins, and seals are killed every year by fishing vessels."[13] Another sobering United Nations statistic is that three-fourths of world fisheries are depleted or exhausted.[14]

Land/Rain Forests

The sheer amount of land used for animal agriculture is staggering. Half of the landmass of the United States is used for animal production—for grazing, living space, and growing crops to feed them. In the United States, that means 80 percent of all land for agriculture is dedicated to animals we eat.[15]

Animal agriculture has devastating impacts on the earth's land. According to the *Cowspiracy* fact page, "[L]ivestock covers 45 percent of the earth's total land."[16] To put this in perspective, we could grow twelve to twenty times the amount in pounds of vegetables, fruits, and grains for every pound of meat.[17] Is our land being used wisely, especially when adding in all the other negatives to the environment and human health when considering animal agriculture and meat-eating?

One-third of the topsoil in the United States has also been lost due to overgrazing.[18] One-third of the planet has experienced desertification, with animal agriculture as the leading cause. In terms of rain forest destruction, a World Bank study found "animal agriculture is responsible for up to 91 percent of Amazon destruction." This happens because one to two acres of rain forest is cleared for grazing animals, or for growing animal feed, every second.[19] Loss of rain forests also results in plant, animal, and insect species extinction.

According to Brazilian government figures, just in the past year (2016), deforestation in Brazil has gone up 29 percent, a 5 percent increase from 2015. While some of this is due to government abandonment of protected areas, and waiving of fines for illegal activity, the beef industry is mostly to blame. Trees are clear-cut so that beef cattle can graze. The livestock industry alone accounts for 30 percent of Brazil's greenhouse gas emissions. Another factor that Americans should be aware of is that Brazil exports much of the beef it produces. The United States imports about 200 million pounds of beef. Deforestation is related to Americans' food choices.[20]

In addition to cattle grazing, the demand for palm oil, found in over 50 percent of consumer products, has ravaged the rain forests of Indonesia. This has put orangutans, rhinos, tigers, elephants, and other animals at extreme risk of extinction due to loss of habitat, poaching, and trafficking. The loss of rain forests has not only created extreme risk for wildlife, but the slash-and-burn technique used for clearing those forests is responsible for 97 percent of Indonesia's greenhouse gas emissions (and daily average greenhouse emissions higher than those recorded in the United States).[21]

Greenhouse Gases and Climate Change

According to the United Nations Food and Agriculture Organization, animal agriculture produces more greenhouse gases than all the transportation sectors combined (based on fossil fuel use). The organization reports:

> All told, greenhouse gas (GHG) emissions associated with livestock supply chains add up to 7.1 gigatonnes (GT) of carbon dioxide equivalent (CO2-eq) per year—or 14.5 percent of all human-caused GHG releases. The main sources of emissions are: feed production and processing (45 percent of the total), outputs of GHG during digestion by cows (39 percent), and manure decomposition (10 percent). The remainder is attributable to the processing and transportation of animal products."[22]

In terms of feed production, the organization states:

[M]ost U.S. livestock are fattened on fishmeal, corn, soybean meal, and other grains. Grain production, in particular, requires significant quantities of fertilizer, fuel, pesticides, water, and land. It takes 149 million acres of cropland, 76 million kilos (167 million pounds) of pesticides and 7.7 billion kilos (17 billion pounds) of nitrogen fertilizer to grow this feed. Fertilizer applied to soil generates nitrous oxide (N_2O), which has 300 times the warming effect of carbon dioxide. Irrigation pumps, tractors, and other farm equipment also release carbon dioxide, but in relatively small amounts. Pesticides and fertilizers often end up in runoff that pollutes rivers, groundwater, and oceans. . . . The biggest impact [on global warming] is from the nitrous oxide emissions resulting from fertilizer application.[23]

Furthermore, the Environmental Working Group reports that "animal waste releases nitrous dioxide and methane, and pollutes our water and air, especially when it is concentrated." These concentrations are increasing, and in 2007, U.S. livestock produced "three times the amount of human waste produced by the entire U.S. population. . . . Manure is the fastest growing major source of methane."[24]

But climate change is also impacted by ocean ecosystems. Predator removal (sharks and most commercially caught fish) increases levels of carbon dioxide. According to researchers, widespread removal does not transfer carbon through the food chain. Carbon accumulates in small fish and zooplankton, and more carbon dioxide is produced. Marine biologist Rick Stafford writes,

> There are also studies that demonstrate the potential role of whales in climate change, by providing nutrients for phytoplankton—the "plants" of the sea—to grow, and therefore absorb, carbon dioxide. Whales achieve this by transporting essential sources of iron across layers of water that don't otherwise mix, by feeding at depth and defecating at the surface. This allows iron and other nutrients to come to the surface waters where phytoplankton live—and more phytoplankton means less carbon dioxide. And so by reducing whale populations, we risk increasing carbon dioxide levels, too.[25]

Thus, we see that global warming as related to ocean fish is more than about fish for human food, and like most wildlife issues, it relates to entire ecosystems.

Waste

Oppenlander tells us, "In the U.S. alone, chickens, turkeys, pigs, and cows in factory farms produce over five million pounds of excrement every minute."[26]

Monbiot also discusses waste (that then impacts global warming):

> Not only is livestock farming the major reason for habitat destruction and the killing of predators, but its waste products are overwhelming the world's capacity to absorb them. Factory farms in the U.S. generate thirteen times as much sewage as the human population. The dairy farms in Tulare County, California, produce five times as much as New York City.[27]

In the case of pigs, this waste is kept in lagoons that present huge pollution and human health challenges. When these lagoons are breached due to hurricanes, such as occurred in North Carolina, there is danger from contamination to groundwater, personal wells, tidal estuaries, bays, and the ocean. Hurricane Floyd, in 1999, for example, dumped tons of hog waste into the storm waters, resulting in "elevated nitrogen and phosphorous levels, algae blooms, and fish kills."[28]

With millions of poultry and pigs confined in concentrated animal feeding operations (CAFOs), and despite the hazardous waste they generate, the Environmental Protection Agency has been blocked by the livestock industry from effectively regulating discharge. Hurricane Matthew, which struck North Carolina in October 2016, killed millions of chickens and thousands of pigs, "sending potentially toxic animal waste coursing into waterways." All across the country, states do not even know where their CAFOs are located, and "[d]ecomposing manure releases toxic chemicals, mostly ammonia and hydrogen sulfide, into the air. Manure stored in lagoons releases methane and nitrous oxide, global warming gases more powerful than carbon dioxide."[29]

Livestock present other problems as well. Oppenlander reports that livestock production accounts for 37 percent of pesticide use, 55 percent of erosion, and 50 percent of antibiotic use, which all ultimately end up in our waterways as waste.[30] What ends up in our streams and rivers, eventually ends up in our oceans. This waste is then toxic to marine life.

Plastics are another source of waste products killing our oceans and marine life. Clare Groden of *Fortune* tells us, "There are 5.25 trillion pieces of plastic trash in the world's oceans, and each year, eight million tons of plastic are added to the count."[31] Plastics, found in every aspect of our lives, are included in many aspects of animal agriculture and packaging. In turn, plastics are impacting animals, especially marine life.

Food waste is another related animal waste. While not all food waste is of animal origin, an estimated 70 billion pounds of food waste is created in America each year, according to Feeding America. When we consider the issue of animals and the environment, it is staggering to realize that 25 to 40 percent of food grown, processed, and transported in the United States will never be consumed. Food, itself, is the largest waste product compared to any other single type of waste. Sadly, this waste becomes a significant source of methane, which is a much more serious greenhouse gas than carbon dioxide (that is, it has twenty-one times the impact compared to carbon dioxide).[32]

Environmentalists Need to Care about Animals (and Animal Advocates about the Environment)

It is clear that environmentalists need to know more about animal use, and animal advocates need more knowledge about animals' impact on the environment. These issues are impacting our lives and every aspect of the environment—water, land, oceans, air. Both policy decisions and individual choices need to be better informed. No longer can we pretend our personal choices make no difference to the state of the earth.

Journalist and activist Chris Hedges wrote an article about the environmental reasons that influenced him to go vegan. For him, the contrast between exploiting animals in our everyday lives and going vegan and living more sustainably was clear. He wrote, "A person who is vegan will save 1,100 gallons of water, twenty pounds CO2 equivalent, 30 square feet of forested land, forty-five pounds of grain, and one sentient animal's life *every day*" (emphasis added). Hedges feels we do not have any other option if we want to save the planet.[33]

I end this section with a quote from Lilia, outreach manager with Sea Shepherd and volunteer with Wolf Patrol. We can bemoan the resource destruction, but Lilia reminds us that this is tied to our framework, our assumptions, our desire for "more." She tells me,

> In my ideal world, I think most humans need to downsize their footprint massively. If we didn't have this constant demand for energy and new "things," then we wouldn't be losing so much habitat around the world. There are obviously humans around the world that do live with a very small footprint in their local environment, and for most of human history, most humans have been living this way. We have a lot to relearn by remembering how people used to live.
>
>   . . . I don't feel that we have to go "back in time" to a previous lifestyle, but we do have the intelligence to use the skills and tools that we have to live more simply. If we worked on building strong, healthy, and resilient communities in our local environments, I don't think we would feel the need to surround ourselves with so much "stuff," [which] our capitalist culture tells us we need (that really just results in us being separated from our communities, while fostering the illusion of making us feel more connected through social media, etc.). I think it's because of our social isolation and lack of community that we look to products and the media for company and satisfaction. And it's this culture that is driving demand for energy and all the things that demand massive scales of "resource" (animal, plant, and mineral) extraction around the world.

I couldn't agree more.

Next, I move to my concluding comments, thinking about all these ideas and challenges, goals and motivations. I want to us to work together to end animal suffering and help make the world more compassionate, livable, and sustainable.

CONCLUDING COMMENTS

People will say, "Can you believe that was what they were doing at the turn of the millennium with animals!?! Can you believe that!?!" Maybe it will be the way that people view cigarette smoking now, or maybe it will be actually not using animals as property, or some limited form of animal. I don't know exactly. But I do believe in my heart of hearts that I will see that time when people—when we [animal advocates]—will be in the majority. We will be seen as: Yes, that's the right thing for our world, our society, our culture. —Isabella

Everything about this planet is so amazing. There's nothing you can't look at and just feel awe. Everything is so wonderfully and beautifully made. And when you look at animals, I mean, how can you not feel awe when you look at a bird? And it amazes me when I look over and someone says, "Piece of shit pigeon . . ." —Scout

MY EARLY INFLUENCES

I became a vegetarian in 1975 at age twenty-two. I did this because I was a hippie, and many hippies heard about vegetarian diets. I thought it would be healthier than eating meat (health being an emphasis at the time for vegetarians). Though I was a politically aware person, I knew nothing about factory farms or, really, anything about animal rights.

In 1980, the person closest to me, a new boyfriend, was involved in animal rights groups in Boston (ARC—Animal Rights Coalition, and CEASE—Coalition to End Animal Suffering in Experiments). Because of him, I learned about factory farming, many animal issues such as fur and zoo captivity, and especially about vivisection.

The Boston-based New England Anti-Vivisection Society was quite active, and the demonstrations and rallies we held at the Boston Common commonly displayed posters of animals in labs involved in experiments. This was pivotal for me. CEASE invited Henry Spira to be a speaker at one of the rallies, and he stayed with us. I was so impressed with his efforts to end the Draize test on rabbits, with a focus on the testing by Revlon, I was inspired to become more involved.

I finally went fully vegan in 1982. I can say that animal rights has been a focus of my life since those days. My own path relied on exposure to the information about animal cruelty, role modeling of other activists, and to someone with national prominence, Henry Spira. This path is similar to many others' who are animal advocates.

WHAT IS "ANIMAL SUFFERING?"

The subtitle of this book uses the term "animal suffering." The book has been about people who address animal suffering and abuses, and shares acts of helping animals who are, in countless ways, at the mercy of humans. The book has covered a range of realities for animals that require intervention to end the practices, or to alleviate the suffering.

When I started out, I did not have an operational definition of "suffering." As I started to write, I realized the vast range of uses and abuses of animals all entail suffering. The main exception to this is pets—though some people do abuse their pets, the vast majority do not. In fact, they lavish their companion animals with food, treats, toys, medical care, enriched environments, and so forth. For so many, pets are family members. I know my six cats mean the world to me.

I have used this term—suffering—very broadly, and it encompasses most of the uses and abuses of animals throughout the culture. As I uncovered these uses and abuses in our everyday lives, I have realized that most people have not thought of these cultural practices as "abusive," as causing "suffering." But, I believe that they are. Whether it is the practices on factory farms for the meat we eat, declawing cats, killing animals for their fur, or caging wildlife in zoos, animals are suffering—and I, and countless others, believe we should help stop this suffering.

If we are against animal suffering, I feel it would be impossible to draw artificial lines as to which suffering is acceptable. None of it is. In fact, if we think about people, we clearly understand that suffering and pain is caused if we are stabbed, cut, beaten, or have pieces of our bodies gouged or burned out without anesthetic. When humans are placed in solitary confinement for more than a few days, that is considered a human rights violation.

Beth Levine, a psychotherapist, artist, animal activist, and anti-speciesist, sent a letter at the end of 2015 to twelve organizations that have missions to treat people with compassion and empathy. Her letter asks them to add nonhuman animals to their mission statements. These organizations include the Dalai Lama Center for Ethics and Transformative Values, Program on Empathy Awareness and Compassion in Education, and the Center for Compassion and Altruism Research and Education, to name a few. All these organizations focus on creating a just society for humans. Levine is asking them to include nonhuman animals in their visions of a peaceful world. In her letter she states the problem:

> Unfortunately, the reality is that many humans treat other animals as widgets; resources for our use, whether for food, clothing, entertainment, product testing, or vivisection, as opposed to treating other animals as individuals whose lives matter to them, just as our lives matter to us. Our cultural norms position nonhuman animals either as commodities to be exploited for our pleasure, or certainly as having interests "less than" those of humans.[1]

I agree with Levine that humans would benefit enormously by living in harmony with animals, and by acknowledging and honoring the emotional and physical well-being of animals as well as of humans. Her letter was signed by over thirty leading social scientists.

ANIMAL ADVOCATES: "BE THE CHANGE YOU WANT TO SEE"

Starting with the online surveys and then the follow-up interviews, this research has been humbling and inspiring for me. I am in awe at the range and depth of actions people are taking. Animal advocates show their compassion and love for nonhuman animals. They are role models and they are social change agents. Their efforts are to be celebrated.

There are many jokes about "crazy cat people." But, as we have seen in this book, these passionate individuals make a world of difference for cats. They are the ones educating others about spay/neuter, urging people to adopt pets from a rescue or shelter, engaging in trap-neuter-return (TNR), standing up for Justice for Tiger, volunteering at shelters and cleaning kennels at PetSmart, fostering kittens for rescues, and building shelters from the cold for ferals. As Lindsay Patton writes in her article, "Why We Need 'Crazy' Cat People": "It's the time and care these people give to cats that makes all the difference. Without their passion and love, there would be so many cats that would have much worse fates, that would not experience unconditional love, that would not get a second, third, or even fourth chance at life."[2]

You can call us "crazy," but we are saving cats' lives. I say, call us "compassionate," not crazy.

Animal advocates and activists are making a difference, but we also show strength in going against many cultural practices. The public opinion polls quoted in this book show that the majority of people favor animal protection and animal well-being. Yet, daily life, as discussed, demonstrates a disconnect—too many of the every day activities we engage in cause animal suffering. Yes, some of the animal advocates still engage in these actions themselves, but many do not. Vegans are often ridiculed, or someone may be pressured to buy tickets to the circus so her child can participate with other children in an outing. Advocates need to stand strong and keep animal well-being at the center of their decisions. Our actions for animals usually evolve over time, as we ourselves change our views as individuals and make new choices.

I think most of the people in the study would agree that it's empowering to help animals. On an individual level, we feel good about it. We might see the result immediately because we are working directly with animals. Or, the result might be more indirect, in terms of a law passed, funds raised, or leaflets distributed. It might show as a satisfying conversation with someone who decides to be vegan, or by attending a vegan thanksgiving for the first time. While the horror of animal cruelty shows up too often in the rescue of a starving horse, a wolf hunt, a pacing animal at the zoo, or an animal in a steel leghold trap, as individuals we are doing everything we can, within our means, to prevent more of these outcomes.

THE RELATIONSHIP BETWEEN HUMANS AND NONHUMAN ANIMALS

It seems useful to remember that humans are animals; animals are not only "the other." We have a bond with other creatures, partly biological (orangutans share 97 percent of human DNA), partly emotional (such as the feelings we all have related to our offspring; relationships among and between species; feelings about freedom and movement), and partly because we live in ecosystems that emphasize interdependence. Humans cannot survive without birds, insects, primates, large and small land mammals, and ocean life. Of course, none of us can survive without clean air, water, and land.

But there is a difference: Humans are directly responsible for the well-being of the planet, and we have entered a new age: the Anthropocene—the Human Age. Rob Nixon writes in a review of Diane Ackerman's book, *The Human Age*:

> For the first time in history, a sentient species, *Homo sapiens*, has become a force of such magnitude that our impacts are being written into the fossil record. We have decisively changed the carbon cycle, the nitrogen cycle, and the rate of extinction. We have created new atomic isotopes and plastiglomerates that may persist for millions of years. We have built megacities that will leave a durable footprint long after they have vanished. We have altered the pH of the oceans and have moved so many life-forms around the globe—inadvertently and intentionally—that we are creating novel ecosystems everywhere. Since the late eighteenth century, industrialization that marks the Anthropocene's beginnings, humans have shaken Earth's life systems with a profundity that the paleontologist Anthony Barnosky has likened to an asteroid strike.[3]

Humans control nonhuman animals in all ways, such as where and how they live—or if they will live at all. Hence, this immense influence should demand the utmost consideration. But, somehow, I don't believe that is what is happening, unless the consideration relates to profit. Humans should be asking: Do we get what we want at any cruelty cost?

Captive wildlife and lab animals are, to me, clear examples of absolute cruelty. With zoos, for example, we rob wildlife of their natural heritage. We steal babies from their mothers and families, slaughtering other animals in the process. We transport animals far from their native habitats. They are kept in confinement, often unable to move, in improperly ventilated, heated or cooled, environments, often with inappropriate diets. Confined animals often develop illnesses they rarely, or never, get in the wild. Often these animals have no, or few, of their own species around them, and they might live for decades in such loneliness and conditions; they develop zoochosis. Not only have we robbed their original habitat of their ecosystem contributions, but we have indelibly altered the well-being of the animals. I discussed zoos and their impact in chapter 4. Is it justified to cause this animal cruelty for the sake of creating venues for people to look at animals in unnatural environments?

It makes much more sense to save wildlife by stopping the destruction of habitat. If we want to stop the mental and physical deterioration of these animals, we can't keep kidnapping them for a life behind bars in a zoo. As Gene Baur says, "It is time for zoos to embrace the sanctuary model." If animals are unable to return to the wild, sanctuaries have a role in rehabilitating them, and giving them a home closer to their natural habitat, with others of their species. Sanctuaries rarely display their animals, and they do not exist for human self-interest. Baur echoes what Levine's letter evokes: "By respecting other animals, we also awaken human empathy. Kindness to animals is also good for people."[4]

DO ANIMALS HAVE RIGHTS?

When you work for animals you encounter a full range of attitudes toward them, whether cats, mice, pigeons, eagles, elephants, wolves, or others. For example, some people view feral cats as pests who mess in their yards, and yowl and fight in their neighborhoods. Others see them as having a right to live outdoors, free from harm and needing access to food, water, and shelter. In addition, it was humans who dumped them and/or didn't spay and neuter them in the first place.

Roof rats in your attic or mice in your pantry are problems to address. Will this be addressed compassionately, or with a call to an exterminator? Wolves, facing diminishing food sources, will find it quite appetizing to feed on an occasional penned sheep or chicken. Chimpanzees or bears in a zoo are there for our entertainment. Do these animals have rights to exist free from harm?

In 2013, the Nonhuman Rights Project (NhRP) filed lawsuits on behalf of four chimpanzees in captivity (Kiko, Tommie, Leo, and Hercules) to establish legal personhood. A legal person does not have to be a human being; legal personhood changes the status of "things"—which animals are now—to "persons," who can make claims of basic rights. For animals, these rights would include life; liberty; not being "owned" by private citizens, circuses, zoos, or marine parks; and not being tested on in labs. There is precedent for nonhuman "legal persons" that have interests to be protected. Maureen Mitra, writing in *Earth Island Journal*, cites these examples:

> Indian law recognizes the personhood of the Sikh holy book, the Guru Granth Sahib. In 2012 the Whanganui River in New Zealand was recognized as a legal person following years of advocacy by the Maoris. Here in the United States, corporations have been considered legal persons since the early 1800s, when the Supreme Court ruled that corporations have the same rights as natural persons.[5]

The arguments NhRP founder Steven Wise used are based on scientific research and societal changes. His lawsuits are "on behalf of animal species whose unusually high level of intelligence and self-awareness have been established by a growing body of scientific research. In addition to chimpanzees, the list includes gorillas, bonobos, orangutans, elephants, whales, and dolphins."[6] Wise realized that, without legal rights, nonhuman animals would be "essentially invisible to the law."[7] Wise had sanctuaries lined up to take in these four chimpanzees if their cases were won. The lawsuits have been winding through the appeals process in New York State.

It is fairly easy to deny animals any rights, or access to their own lives and relationships, if the law and the culture holds to beliefs that animals are not self-aware or self-interested. That has begun to change, with scientific research showing the high intelligence, communication methods, and self-awareness of many species. We know elephants mourn their dead, that dolphins attend to sick pod members, that baboons form lasting and deep friendships, mice laugh, cows solve problems and realize it. Cross-species empathy abounds with examples.[8]

Legal personhood would allow us to address widespread animal suffering based on recognition of animals' emotional and mental lives, which are actually so close to how humans relate to others, and feel and think about ourselves. The disconnect between our treatment of animals and their sentience is a huge chasm. It is time to change our thinking about animals in order to change our behavior toward them. As long as animals are viewed by us—and the law—as property or objects, we can do pretty much anything to them (and we do).

There is some precedent for legal personhood for nonhuman animals. Just a few of the examples include Switzerland, which in 1992 amended its constitution to categorize animals as "beings" and not "things." New Zealand granted basic rights to five great ape species in 1999, a change which ended their use in research. Germany guaranteed rights to animals in 2002.[9] This "legal life" that can be granted to animals allows us to view them as having an ability to live.

The original suits to grant the four chimpanzees a writ of habeas corpus were all denied. When the cases started in 2013, all four chimps lived in New York State. Tommy was owned by a man who rented and sold reindeer. He lived in a cage in the back of a used trailer lot. Kiko was also owned by a private family, and lived in a cage. Hercules and Leo were together at a research facility at Stony Brook University, but owned by the New Iberia Research Center.

Today, Tommy cannot be located. He had been given or sold by his owner to a Michigan roadside zoo (DeYoung Zoo) in 2015, but by late 2016 had not been seen. Litigation in his case is at a standstill. Kiko's appeals are moving forward, with another court date in the February 2017 term. In May 2016, the New Iberia Research Center released its decision that all 220 chimpanzees at its facility would be sent to the Project Chimps sanctuary in Georgia, which is currently being expanded. It will take years for this transfer to occur, and Hercules and Leo are still not in sanctuary, and they were never granted their legal personhood.[10]

WHY I BELIEVE ANIMAL SUFFERING CAN END AND CULTURAL CHANGE IS POSSIBLE

People overwhelmingly love animals. We love our pets as family members, and we are fascinated by wildlife. Most people do not want to cause harm and suffering. In fact, there is near-universal condemnation when abuse cases surface. The public opinion polls we've examined show that our society continues to increasingly move in the direction of animals having rights, showing compassion for the lives of animals, and wanting to help animals. Good Samaritans abound, who stop what they are doing to help an animal at the side of the road or in their neighborhoods.

People would care even more if they were better informed. We live in an information age, with incredible access to facts, documentation, and real-time video of animals and their treatment. Still, there is a bias in this information to only show partial reality for animals. The marketing campaigns of the meat, dairy, and egg industries dominate, and confirm our use of animals as food. If we don't move past "Milk does a body good," we will never understand that milk from a dairy cow only "does good" for her own calf. Not humans. If the suffering of dairy cows and the impacts of separation on their babies was as widely known as the marketing *idea* that cows' milk is good for humans, then I believe more people would be choosing the alternatives of almond milk, soy milk, rice milk, or other types. These milks are readily available and they cause no suffering.

One problem is that information about animal suffering, and alternatives to reduce or end it, competes with information "airspace." However, if we could match the reach of the "Milk. It Does a Body Good" campaign, for example, we might be more influential. I think that is where the campaigns like Be Fair Be Vegan and Go Vegan World have enormous potential.

I have also discussed that many of these ideas are met with cognitive dissonance, denial, and willful ignorance. People often don't *want* to know this information. These psychological responses are real, but I believe that, as other aspects of culture change, it will be easier for people to embrace these messages. I also believe the ethical considerations are very compelling, and I think people prefer to base their lifestyles and life choices on what is morally right. Ending animal suffering certainly resonates with this.

In addition to the pro-animal attitudes of individuals in the culture, the availability of vegan alternatives is exploding. People are changing their eating habits little by little. As we adopt these new eating habits and preferences, and as we buy more clothing and accessory alternatives that aren't literally off the backs of animals, and as we are exposed to more animal-friendly advertising, I believe there will be a cultural shift. That shift has already started. We haven't reached the turning point yet, but it seems possible for a whole culture to make deep changes in daily life. Slavery, once deeply embedded in daily life, ended in the United States. Same-sex marriage, once unthinkable as equal to heterosexual marriage, is now part of the institution of marriage, families, and legal rights. I agree with what Isabella says at the beginning of this chapter: We will reach a point of saying "Can you believe what we used to do to animals?!?"

There is data that supports broad culture change. Erica Chenoweth studied both nonviolent and violent social justice movements, and found that between 1900 and 2006, campaigns of nonviolent civil resistance were twice as successful as violent campaigns. She found that successful movements needed only 3.5 percent of the population to be successful in their pressure on government to change.[11] When I hear that, I think: Yes, this can happen. A small group can bring about astounding cultural change (and nonviolently).

CHANGE STRATEGIES

Earlier in this book, I discussed change that is taken in small, gradual steps, and change that is very broad, or macrolevel. Both of these approaches have the goal to end animal suffering, but have different levels of acceptance, of what can be tolerated, until that goal is reached.

For example, Wayne Pacelle of The Humane Society of the United States details in his book, *The Humane Economy*, cooperation with major food corporations to gradually improve the conditions for animals at factory farms. Animals are still suffering but less so.[12] On the other hand, other animal advocates and activists want to close down the factory farm. One way to achieve this is to make people so uncomfortable that factory farms cannot be tolerated another minute.

Alicia says, for example, that activists with Direct Action Everywhere would argue the only way to get people to change their minds is to make it uncomfortable—to make it that they cannot ignore you. That was part of the strategy with sit-ins in the 1960s, when you would have civil rights activists go into a restaurant and just sit there. They made people really, really uncomfortable, to the point of inflicting violence on the activists. But it got in the news—it got people talking—and just by getting people out of their comfort zones, really shaking them out of their comfort zones in a metaphorical sense, helps to push the moral conversation forward. I certainly think there's some value to these actions, and to this philosophy.

I personally don't think it's an either/or choice. Sometimes the most powerful influence is a simple conversation at the right time, when someone is ready to make a new decision for animals. People will support or engage in different approaches to bring about change. At the same time, many other elements of change are occurring, such as media campaigns and consumer choice changes. All of these push on the dominant paradigm to help us to get a new way of thinking. That is the key—a shift of assumptions about animals, which can lead us to an end to speciesism.

The Netherlands announced a major initiative to set the country on a path to be free of using laboratory animals by 2025, in order to completely halt the use of testing on animals (currently, six hundred thousand lab animals are used each year). According to the National Committee for the Protection of Animals (NCad), "in order to transition to research that no longer uses procedures that involve animals, it will be necessary to let go of existing attitudes and practices." NCad is developing transition strategies and suggestions for "a different approach to risk."[13] This is exactly the paradigm shift I have been describing in this book, and it opens us up to the realm of possibility.

Martha Rosenberg and Ronnie Cummins of the Organic Consumers Association wonder if it's time to end the system of factory farming, which they identify as the "malevolent profit-driver and lynchpin of industrial agriculture, GMOs, and fast food."[14] In their thinking, when people consider healthier, more humane, environmentally friendly food, this is the logical move. For all the reasons already discussed, boycotting the results of factory farming and buying alternative food will result in a massive change in society, not only in our eating habits but in the agriculture industry.

The interconnections Rosenberg and Cummins discuss—environment, humane treatment of animals, and health, in particular—are why I feel animal rights is a social justice movement. People and animals suffer from factory farming, and this is related to many broader issues of air and water quality, health care, and the like. The World Resources Institute (WRI), a group of consumer researchers, marketing experts, and behavioral economists, is researching how to make transitioning to a plant-based diet more appealing to people worldwide. The concerns are with the strain on natural resources, increasing greenhouse gas emissions, and feeding a growing global population, as countries are on a path to increasing meat consumption. For one example, the institute knows the word "superfood" increases food sales, while a word like "healthy" does not. This research is part of our paradigm shift.[15]

Andrea Gunn, managing director of the Humane League, spoke at the PlantPure Summit in 2016. In discussing social change, she cautioned against pushing people into your way of thinking, but instead showing them what is possible, being kind and respectful, and keeping communication open.[16]

Many of the study respondents said, "You must meet people where they are at." At this point, I think people are more ready to reduce meat and animal product intake, and even go vegan, than ever before. We are at an accelerating pace for ending animal suffering.

An example of positive change is the ending of greyhound racing. Once a very popular sport, greyhound racing is in decline. According to a report by GREY2K USA and the ASPCA, between 2008 and 2015 over eighty thousand young greyhounds were brought into the racing industry, and there were almost twelve thousand greyhound injuries, such as broken legs, crushed skulls, and broken backs. Over nine hundred dogs died. Cases of cruelty and neglect were found, involving dogs starved to death, kept in poor conditions, or denied veterinary care. Perhaps not legally negligent, the dogs are usually kept in crates stacked on top of each other, in poor ventilation, with little care and human contact. But change is coming.[17]

In the past ten years, gambling on dog races has declined 66 percent, and greyhound breeding has declined by 57 percent. Only six states

(Alabama, Arkansas, Florida, Iowa, Texas, and West Virginia) operate greyhound race tracks.[18] Arizona is the latest state to end this cruel practice. Public awareness of the cruelty of this form of entertainment, and advocates pushing to end racing in the state, led to legislation that went into effect the end of 2016, closing Tucson Greyhound Park. Three hundred to four hundred greyhounds are being moved to rescues and statewide organizations, looking for permanent homes.[19] No more cruel dog racing in Arizona because of the pressure of advocates and organizations.

WHAT YOU CAN DO

Hopefully, reading this book has given you the information you need to motivate you to action. There are probably numerous issues you feel passionately about right now. Hopefully, reading the stories and the words of animal advocates and activists has shown you what you can actually do, and the range of options to consider. These 204 people are role models for you.

If you aren't already, you can donate money to organizations in your community, or to national organizations, that do both direct animal rescue and care, and take actions such as work on legislation, raise awareness through producing educational materials, or engage in leafleting or other outreach. Appendix A has a listing of all the animal organizations, with website addresses, mentioned by the study participants. You can offer a skill such as carpentry, or make items like jewelry or artwork to sell at fund-raisers.

Many advocates keep up to date on issues by subscribing to updates that are delivered to their e-mail inboxes. This is an effortless way to learn about what is going on. There are links for online activism with petitions to sign. If you are particularly interested in taking a stand against animal cruelty, the site www.animalpetitions.org is one that you want to know about. Also, www.change.org has many animal-related petitions.

There are numerous ways to work online to help end animal suffering on a daily basis. You will also want to bookmark the Facebook pages of organizations you care about, to stay on top of their activities. You can share animal campaigns and information on your own Facebook page.

Volunteering at your county shelter or local rescue organizations is filled with opportunities, not to mention you will have an immediate impact on animals. Direct care can include dog walking, cleaning kennels, socializing with cats, playing with animals such as rabbits, helping injured birds, helping feed animals, comforting scared animals in new surroundings, doing administrative work, bottle-feeding foster kittens, fostering animals that need medicine or a break from the kennel regimen, helping with fund-raisers, being an adoption counselor, taking photographs to post new animals on adoption sites, keeping a website up to date, helping feed animals at a farm sanctuary, and so on. The opportunities are endless. Working together with other volunteers is a wonderful way to build community.

Some of you will want to volunteer or work in wildlife sanctuaries, be undercover investigators, or plan major media campaigns. Internships with a national organization or at a sanctuary might be a good way to go. Understanding your community resources and opportunities, as well as what possibilities exist outside your hometown, will help you make a good match.

If you want to be more independent, feeding feral colonies and doing TNR will keep you busy. I didn't know much about outdoor cats before I started the interviews for this book. But once I learned more and heard the experiences of individuals all across the country, I was hooked. It was easy to get connected with people active in my area, and today I am helping feed feral colonies, as well as trapping. The satisfaction of helping control cat overpopulation is enormous. I introduced this activism into my routine and have learned so much from it.

Most communities have meet-up groups that coordinate gatherings at restaurants that serve vegetarian and/or vegan food. That is a fun way to try new food, meet other people, and increase the meatless options on your plate. Other meet-up groups offer opportunities for volunteering at local shelters or rescue organizations. Check out www.meetup.org.

Another form of advocacy for animals is through your consumer choices. If you aren't already reading labels of your personal care products, you can start, to make sure you aren't buying products tested on animals or that have animal ingredients. There are plenty of alternatives to products that depend on animal suffering. You can find resources on the Internet, at any of the national organizations, about these options. A good place to start is www.ewg.org and www.peta.org.

Your consumer dollar also relates to food choices. If you don't want ducks to be immobilized and force-fed until their livers practically burst, don't buy foie gras. Learn about your food and make compassionate choices. If you want to go vegan, there are vegan (or vegetarian) starter kits at all the national organization websites. Maybe you want to leaflet for Vegan Outreach at a local college campus? Contact the group at www.veganoutreach.org/.

What's very important is that you identify your most compelling issue or issues, and choose to act. You have a part to play in ending animal suffering. Think about the 204 individuals in this book, who represent so many thousands and tens of thousands of other people. They would love you to join them.

We've learned about the cultural context for animals and *why* we respond to them. Yes, we love animals, but it is more than that. Animal advocates and activists have a vision of a compassionate world. It isn't just words to us; it is in our actions and how we live our lives. We are also receiving the rewards of the animals, who are safer, healthier, calmer, and able to live their species-appropriate lives as they should. I invite you to join the community of people who make a difference in the lives of animals. What part can you play in ending animal suffering?

APPENDIX: ORGANIZATIONS MENTIONED BY STUDY PARTICIPANTS

Alley Cat Allies (national headquarters in Maryland); https://www.alleycat.org/
American Sanctuary Association (Nevada); http://asaanimalsanctuaries.org
American Society for the Prevention of Cruelty to Animals (national headquarters in New York City); https://www.aspca.org/
Animal Advocates of Arizona (Arizona); http://www.meetup.com/animal-advocates-of-az/
The Animal Care League (Illinois); http://www.animalcareleague.org/
Animal Defense League of Arizona (Arizona); http://www.adlaz.org/
Animal Guardian Network (Arizona); http://animalguardiannework.org
Animal Justice Project (United Kingdom); https://www.facebook.com/animaljusticeproject
Animal Life Rescue (North Carolina); https://www.facebook.com/AnimalLifeInc/
Animal Place (California); http://animalplace.org/
Animal Rescue Inc. (Maryland); https://animalrescueinc.org/
Animal Rights Hawai'i (Hawai'i); https://www.facebook.com/pages/Animal-Rights-Hawaii/
Arizona Chihuahua Rescue (Arizona); http://azchihuahuarescue.org/
Arizona Cactus Corgi Rescue (Arizona); http://azcactuscorgirescue.com/

Best Friends (Utah); http://bestfriends.org
Blackhat Humane Society (Colorado); http://www.blackhathumanesociety.org/

Cat Crusaders (Florida); https://www.tampacatcrusaders.org/
Cat Haven (Louisiana); https://cathaven.org/
Catspan (Canada); http://catspan.com/index.html
CJ Acres Animal Rescue Farm (Florida); http://cjacres.org
Cochise Canine Rescue (Arizona); http://cochisecaninerescue.org
Compassion and Responsibility for Animals (Philippines); https://www.facebook.com/CARA-Phil/
Compassion Over Killing (national headquarters in Washington, DC); http://cok.net
Compassionate Action for Animals (Minnesota); https://www.exploreveg.org/
Compassionate Living (California); http://socoveg.org
Cozy Cat Cottage (Ohio); http://cozycatcottage.org/

Desert Paws (Arizona); http://www.desertpawsrescue.org/

Direct Action Everywhere (national headquarters in California); http://directactioneverywhere.com

Eden Farmed Animal Sanctuary (Ireland); http://www.edenfarmanimalsanctuary.com

Fargo Moorhead Vegetarians and Vegans (North Dakota); http://www.meetup.com/fm-veg/
Farm Sanctuary (Watkins Glen, New York, with several other sanctuary locations); http://www.farmsanctuary.org
Feral Cat Coalition of Oregon (Oregon); http://www.feralcats.com/
Foundation for Homeless Cats (Arizona); http://www.thefoundationforhomelesscats.org/
Free from Harm (national headquarters in Chicago, Illinois); http://freefromharm.org
Freeze Don't Shoot (national); https://www.facebook.com/FreezeDon'tShoot/
Friends for Seals (Canada); http://www.friendsforseals.org
Full Circle Farm Sanctuary (North Carolina); http://fullcirclefarmsanctuary.org
Furbaby Rescue of NC (North Carolina); http://www.furbabyrescuenc.org/
Furever Friends Rescue (Arizona); http://fureverfriendsrescue.org

Go Vegan World (Ireland); http://goveganworld.com
Golden Bone Rescue & Rehab Inc. (Arizona); http://www.dogadoptionrescue.com

Help A Dog Smile (Arizona); http://helpadogsmile.org
HART (Homeless Animal Rescue Team) (Arizona); http://www.hart-az.org
Humane League (national headquarters in Philadelphia); www.thehumaneleague.com
Humane Society of Southern Arizona (Arizona); http://hssaz.org
Humane Society of the United States (national headquarters in Washington, DC); http://humanesociety.org

In Defense of Animals (national headquarters in California); http://www.idausa.org
Ironwood Pig Sanctuary (Arizona); http://www.ironwoodpigs.org

Jewish Veg (headquarters in Pennsylvania); http://www.jewishveg.com

Kerulos Center (Oregon); http://kerulos.org
Kiss for Kittens (South Carolina); https://www.facebook.com/pages/Kiss-for-Kittens/
KitsnKats (South Carolina); https://www.facebook.com/kitsnkats

Leaps & Bounds Rabbit Rescue (California); http://leapsandboundsrabbitrescue.cfsites.org
Let the Animals Live (Israel); http://www.letlive.org.il/eng
Little Rascals Rescue (Arizona); http://www.littlerascalsrescue.com/
Lost Our Home Pet Rescue (Arizona); http://www.lostourhome.org
Lulu's Rescue (Pennsylvania); https://www.facebook.com/pages/Lulus-Rescue/

Maricopa County Animal Care and Control (Arizona); http//www.maricopa.gov/pets/
Mildcats at Arizona State University (Arizona); http://mildcatsatasu.org
Mercy for Animals (national headquarters in California); http://mercyforanimals.org

No Kill Pima County (Arizona); http://www.nokillpimacounty.org

Our Hen House (New York); http://www.ourhenhouse.org

Peaceful Fields Sanctuary (Virginia); https://peacefulfieldssanctuary.org/

People for the Ethical Treatment of Animals (PETA) (international; U.S. headquarters in Virginia); http://peta.org
Physicians Committee for Responsible Medicine (national headquarters in Washington, DC); http://www.pcrm.org/
The Pig Preserve (Tennessee); http://thepigpreserve.org
Pima Paws for Life (Arizona); http://www.pimapawsforlife.org/home.html
Poplar Spring Animal Sanctuary (Maryland); http://www.animalsanctuary.org

Rabbit Advocacy Network (international); http://www.rabbitadvocacynetwork.org/

San Francisco Vegetarian Society (California); http://www.sfvs.org/
Sanctuary at Haafsville (Pennsylvania); http://www.thesanctuarypa.org/
Save Our Strays (Louisiana); http://www.sosrescuebr.org/
Save Our Strays (Mississippi); http://www.saveourstraysms.com/
Save the Cats Arizona (Arizona); http://www.savethecatsaz.org
Sea Shepherd Conservation Society (international; U.S. headquarters in Virginia); http://www.seashepherd.org
Small Angels Rescue (Maryland); http://www.smallangelsrescue.org/
St. Martin's Animal Rescue (Oregon); http://www.stmartinsanimalrescue.org/
Stray Cats About Town (Canada); http://oscatr.ca/

Tailless Cat Rescue (North Carolina); http://www.taillesscatrescue.com/
Triangle Chance For All (North Carolina); http://trianglechanceforall.org
Tucson's Cause for Canines (Arizona); http://www.tucsonscauseforcanines.org/

United Poultry Concerns (national headquarters in Virginia); http://www.upc-online.org

Vegan Haven (Washington); http://veganhaven.org/
Vegan Outreach (international; U.S. headquarters in California); http://veganoutreach.org/
Vegetarian Resource Group (Maryland); http://www.vrg.org
Viva! (United Kingdom); http://www.viva.org.uk/

Wee Paws Animal Sanctuary (Nevada); https://www.facebook.com/WeePawsAnimalSanctuary/
Wildhorse Ranch Rescue (Arizona); http://www.wildhorseranchrescue.com
Wildlife Haven Rehabilitation Center (Manitoba, Canada); http://wildlifehaven.ca/
Wildlife Rehab of Greenville (South Carolina); http://www.wildlife-rehab.com/
Wolf Patrol (Michigan); https://wolfpatrol.org/

NOTES

INTRODUCTION

1. "Pets by the Numbers," The Humane Society of the United States, accessed 6/30/16, http://www.humanesociety.org/issues/pet_overpopulation/facts/pet_ownership_statistics.html

2. "Pet Industry Market Size & Ownership Statistics," American Pet Products Association, accessed 6/30/16, http://americanpetproducts.org/press_industrytrends.asp

3. "Get the Facts: Ten Fast Facts about Exotic 'Pets,'" Born Free USA, accessed 7/4/16, http://www.bornfreeusa.org/facts.php?p=439&more=1.

4. "Animal Tracker—Year 8," Humane Research Council, accessed 7/5/16, https://faunalytics.org/wp-content/uploads/2015/06/Animal-Tracker-Year-8-Topline-Report-Final.pdf.

5. "Animal Tracker—Year 8."

6. Rebecca Riffkin, "In U.S., More Say Animals Should Have Same Rights as People," accessed 8/17/15, http://www.gallup.com/poll/183275/say-animals-rights-people.aspx.

7. "Fewer Americans View Animal Testing as Morally Acceptable," National Anti-Vivisection Society, accessed 7/5/16, http://www.navs.org/gallup_2016/.

8. "How Does Judaism Say We Should Treat Animals?" Jewish Veg, accessed 7/5/16, http://jewishveg.org/faq-how-does-judaism-say-we-should-treat-animals.

9. Gypsy Wulff and Fran Chambers, eds., *Turning Points in Compassion* (Australia: SpiritWings Humane Education Inc., 2015), 53.

10. Donny Moss, "Cecil Lives On: Connecting the Dots Between One Lion and Billions of Suffering Animals," *Their Turn*, July 31, 2015, accessed 8/4/15, http://www.alternet.org/environment/i-am-cecil-connecting-dots-between-one-lion-and-billions-suffering-animals.

11. Go Vegan World, accessed 6/29/16, http://www.GoVeganWorld.com.

12. Seann Lenihann, "Stop Dogfighting by Addressing Supply Side Economics," *Animal People*, November 20, 2013, accessed 9/1/14, http://newspaper.animalpeopleforum.org/2013/10/01/stop-dogfighting-by-addressing-supply-side-economics/.

13. "Pets in Vehicles," American Veterinary Medical Foundation, accessed 6/3/16, https://www.avma.org/public/PetCare/Pages/pets-in-vehicles.aspx.

14. Damian Carrington, "Millions of Animal 'Trophies' Exported Across Borders," *Guardian UK*, June 14, 2016, accessed 6/15/16, http://readersupportednews.org/news-section2/318-66/37454-millions-of-animal-trophies-exported-across-borders.

15. "Global Luggage and Leather Goods Industry 2014-2019: Trends, Profits and Forecast Analysis," *Research and Markets*, accessed 6/29/16, http://researchandmarkets.com/reports/2965421/global-luggage-and leather-goods-industry-2014.

16. Richard A. Oppenlander, *Comfortably Unaware* (New York: Beaufort Books, 2012), 12; and John Dear, "The Only Diet for a Peacemaker Is a Vegetarian Diet," *National Catholic Reporter*, July 12, 2008, accessed July 12, 2008, http://www.alternet.org/story/91237.

17. Lorraine Chow, "Alec Baldwin and Candice Bergen Want You to Know Something Horrible About McDonald's Chicken," AlterNet, October 5, 2016, accessed 10/4/16, http://www.alternet.org/food/alec-baldwin-and-candice-bergen-want-you-know-something-horrible-about-mcdonalds-chicken-video?akid=14723.1893310.5WYhme&rd=1&src=newsletter1064810&t=12.

18. Tom Philpott, "We Have Terrible News for Anyone Who Eats Chicken," *Mother Jones*, June 22, 2016, accessed 6/22/16, http://motherjones.com/environment/2016/06/salmonella-chicken-usda-supermarket-inspection-flawed.

19. Michael Robinson, "3.2 Million Animals Killed by Federal Wildlife-Destruction Program in 2015," Center for Biological Diversity, June 24, 2016, accessed 6/24/16, http://readersupportednews.org/news-section2/318-66/37628-32-million-animals-killed-by-federal-wildlife-destruction-program-in-2015.

20. Oppenlander, *Comfortably Unaware*, 51

21. "About Animal Testing," Humane Society International, accessed 10/3/16, http://www.hsi.org/campaigns/end_animal_testing/qa/about.html.

22. Homeless Animal Rescue Team, accessed 10/21/15, http://www.hart-az. org.

23. "Fur Trade Facts," Last Chance for Animals, accessed 7/3/16, http:// www.lcanimal.org/index.php/campaigns/fur/fur-trade-facts.

24. Keith Dane, "Op-Ed: How to Stop the Cruelest Horse Show on Earth," The Humane Society of the United States, November 5, 2014, accessed 11/8/ 14, http://www.alternet.org/op-ed-how-stop-cruelest-horse-show-earth.

25. Wayne Pacelle, "Texas Law Banning Finning Goes into Effect in the Heat of Shark Week," *A Humane Nation*, accessed 7/1/16, http://blog. humanesociety.org/wayne/2016/07/texas-law-banning-finning-goes-effect-during-shark-week.html.

26. Karen Davis, "Perdue's Chickens: Could Their Lives Be Made Less Miserable?" *United Poultry Concerns*, accessed 7/5/16, http://www.upc-online. org/broiler/160705perdues_chickens_misery.html.

27. Melanie Joy, *Why We Love Dogs, Eat Pigs, and Wear Cows* (San Francisco, CA: Conari Press, 2011), 14.

28. Oppenlander, *Comfortably Unaware*, 11.

29. Mary P. Brewster and Cassandra L. Reyes, eds., *Animal Cruelty: A Multidisciplinary Approach to Understanding* (Durham, NC: Carolina Academic Press, 2013), 349.

I. WHO WE ARE

1. "Feral Cat Health Analysis: Living Healthy Lives Outdoors," Alley Cat Allies, accessed 7/30/15,http://www.alleycat.org/resources/feral-cat-health-analysis-living-healthy-lives-outdoors/.

2. "Feral Cat Health Analysis: Living Healthy Lives Outdoors."

3. "Feral Cat Health Analysis: Living Healthy Lives Outdoors."

4. "Managing Community Cats: A Guide for Municipal Leaders" (Washington, DC: The Humane Society of the United States, 2014), 4, accessed 7/30/ 15, https://www.animalsheltering.org/page/managing-community-cats-guide-municipal-leaders.

5. "Managing Community Cats," 10.

6. Karyen Chu and Wendy M. Anderson, "U.S. Public Opinion on Humane Treatment of Stray Cats," Law & Policy Brief (September 2007, Bethesda, MD: Alley Cat Allies), accessed 7/30/15, http://www.alleycat.org/resources/public-opinion-on-humane-treatment-of-cats/, 1.

7. "U.S. Public Opinion on Humane Treatment of Stray Cats," 2.

8. "Community Cat Care," Alley Cat Allies, accessed 10/11/16, http://www. alleycat.org/community-cat-care-category/cat-care/kittens/socializing-kittens/.

9. "Community Cat Care."

10. The Foundation for Homeless Cats, accessed 6/29/15, http://www.thefoundationforhomelesscats.org,

11. Alley Cat Allies, accessed 7/30/15, http://www.alleycat.org.

12. The Foundation for Homeless Cats, accessed 10/10/16, http://www.thefoundationforhomelesscats.org.

13. "FAQS," The Foundation for Homeless Cats, accessed 6/29/16, http://www.thefoundationforhomelesscats.org/faqs.

14. "Managing Community Cats," 12.

15. "About Us," The Foundation for Homeless Cats, accessed 6/29/16, http://www.thefoundationforhomelesscats.org/about/.

2. PATHS TO ACTION

1. "More Than 150 Billion Animals Slaughtered Every Year," Animals Deserve Absolute Protection Today and Tomorrow, accessed 12/7/16, http://www.adaptt.org/killcounter.html, and "Factory Farms, A Well-Fed World," accessed 12/7/16, http://awfw.org/factory-farms/.

2. "Taking Ag-Gag to Court," Animal Legal Defense Fund, accessed 10/17/16, http://aldf.org/cases-campaigns/features/taking-ag-gag-to-court/.

3. "ASPCA Research Shows Americans Overwhelmingly Support Investigations to Expose Animal Abuse on Industrial Farms," American Society for the Prevention of Cruelty to Animals, accessed 8/16/16, http://www.aspca.org/about-us/press-releases/aspca-research-shows-americans-overwhelmingly-support-investigations-expose.

4. This information is widely available, but relies heavily on www.upc-online.org. Unless otherwise noted, the information in this section on chickens and turkeys is from this website.

5. Anna Roth, "What You Need to Know about the Corporate Shift to Cage-Free Eggs," January 28, 2016, accessed 1/30/16, http://civileats.com/2016/01/28/what-you-need-to-know-about-the-corporate-shift-to-cage-free-eggs/.

6. Gregory Barber, "Are Cage-Free Eggs All They're Cracked Up to Be?" *Mother Jones*, February 10, 2016, accessed 2/11/16, http://www.motherjones.com/blue-marble/2016/02/corporations-are-going-cage-free-whats-next-hens.

7. Free from Harm, accessed 10/17/16, http://www.freefromharm.org.

8. United Poultry Concerns, accessed 10/17/16, http://www.upc-online.org.

9. The Pig Preserve, accessed 10/18/16, http://www.thepigpreserve.org.

10. David Jackson and Gary Marx, "Whipped, Kicked, Beaten: Illinois Workers Describe Abuse of Hogs," *Chicago Tribune*, August 4, 2016, accessed 8/8/16, http://www.chicagotribune.com/news/watchdog/pork/ct-pig-farms-abuse-met-20160802-story.html.

11. "Iowa Investigation: Hawkeye Sow Centers (Hormel Supplier)," Compassion Over Killing, accessed 10/18/16, http://cok.net/inv/hormel/iowa-pigs/.

12. "Iowa Investigation: Hawkeye Sow Centers (Hormel Supplier)"

13. "New COK Exposé: High-Speed Slaughter Hell at Hormel, Makers of SPAM," Compassion Over Killing, accessed 10/18/16, http://cok.net/inv/hormel/

14. "New COK Exposé: High-Speed Slaughter Hell at Hormel, Makers of SPAM."

15. Arelis R. Hernandez, Angela Fritz, and Chris Mooney, "Factory Farming Practices Under Scrutiny Again in North Carolina after Disastrous Hurricane Floods," *Washington Post*, October 16, 2016, accessed 10/18/16, https://www.washingtonpost.com/news/capital-weather-gang/wp/2016/10/16/factory-farming-practices-are-under-scrutiny-again-in-n-c-after-disastrous-hurricane-floods/.

16. The Pig Preserve, accessed 10/18/16, http://www.thepigpreserve.org.

17. Ironwood Pig Sanctuary, accessed 10/18/16, http://www.ironwoodpigsanctuary.org.

18. Tara Lohan, "Got Milk? A Disturbing Look at the Dairy Industry," AlterNet, January 26, 2010, accessed 1/26/10, http://www.alternet.org/story/145378/.

19. "Got Milk? A Disturbing Look at the Dairy Industry."

20. "Cattle Raised for Dairy and Meat Production," Farm Sanctuary, accessed 10/17/16, https://www.farmsanctuary.org/learn/factory-farming/dairy/.

21. "Cattle Raised for Dairy and Meat Production."

3. WHAT WE DO

1. "Puppy Mills: Facts and Figures," The Humane Society of the United States, accessed 10/21/16, http://www.humanesociety.org/assets/pdfs/pets/puppy_mills/puppy-mills-facts-and-figures.pdf.

2. Kim Kavin, *The Dog Merchants: Inside the Big Business of Breeders, Pet Stores, and Rescuers* (New York: Pegasus Books, 2016), 140.

3. Kavin, *The Dog Merchants*, 141.

4. "Pets by the Numbers," The Humane Society of the United States, accessed 6/30/16, http://www.humanesociety.org/issues/pet_overpopulation/facts/pet_ownership_statistics.html.

5. Kavin, *The Dog Merchants*, 142.

6. Robin Dorman, "Invented Fear and Injustice We Wrongly Place on Pit Bulls," In Defense of Animals, October 30, 2016, accessed 10/30/16, http://www.onegreenplanet.org/animalsandnature/invented-fear-and-injustice-we-wrongly-place-on-pit-bulls/.

7. "Spaying and Neutering: A Solution for Suffering," PETA, accessed 8/1/16, http://www.peta.org/issues/companion-animal-issues/companion-animals-factsheets/spaying-neutering-solution-suffering/.

8. "Spaying and Neutering: A Solution for Suffering."

9. "Overpopulation Facts," Spay-Neuter Assistance Program, accessed 8/5/16, http://snapus.org/spay-neuter-facts/overpopulation-facts.html.

10. Heather Moore, "A Record-Setting Year for PETA's Mobile Spay/Neuter Clinics!," accessed 1/23/16, http://www.peta.org/blog/a-record-setting-year-for-petas-mobile-spayneuter-clinics/.

11. "Health Benefits," Spay-Neuter Assistance Program, accessed 8/5/16, http://www.snapus.org/spay-neuter-facts/spay-neuter-health-benefits.html, and "Why You Should Spay/Neuter Your Pet," The Humane Society of the United States, accessed 8/5/16, http://www.humanesociety.org/issues/pet_overpopulation/facts/why_spay_neuter.html.

12. "Why You Should Spay/Neuter Your Pet."

13. "Why You Should Spay/Neuter Your Pet."

14. "Why You Should Spay/Neuter Your Pet."

15. "Bunny Care," Tranquility Trail Animal Sanctuary, accessed 8/7/16, http://www.tranquilitytrail.org/RabbitCare.html.

16. "Defining No Kill," No Kill Advocacy Center, accessed 8/1/16, http://www.nokilladvocacycenter.org/defining-no-kill.html.

17. "No-Kill: Best Friends Is the Leader of the Movement," Best Friends, accessed 7/28/16, http://bestfriends.org/our-work/no-kill-initiatives/.

18. "The Deadly Consequences of 'No-Kill' Policies," PETA, accessed 7/11/16, http://www.peta.org/features/deadly-consequences-no-kill-policies/.

19. "No-Kill: Best Friends Is the Leader of the Movement."

20. No-Kill Los Angeles, accessed 10/26/16, http://nkla.org/.

21. Kim Wilson, "What It Takes to Be a No-Kill Shelter," *Humanely Speaking*, Summer 2015, 12.

22. To read about each step in depth, see Nathan J. Winograd, "Revisiting the No Kill Equation," accessed 10/26/16, http://www.nathanwinograd.com/?p=1832.

23. Arianna Pittman, "All You Need to Know about the No-Kill Movement to Help Save Animals in Your Local Shelter," September 9, 2016, accessed 9/19/16, http://www.onegreenplanet.org/animalsandAnature/how-no-kill-movement-is-saving-animals-in-shelter/.

4. IDENTIFIED TOP ISSUES

1. "Shelter Intake & Surrender," ASPCA, accessed 8/13/16, http://www. aspca.org/animal-homelessness/shelter-intake-and-surrender/.

2. American Humane, accessed 8/13/16, http://www.americanhumane.org.

3. "Animal Shelter & Rescues for Pet Adoption," Petfinder, accessed 8/15/ 16,http://www.petfinder.com/animal-shelters-and-rescues

4. "Shelter Intake & Surrender."

5. Wayne Pacelle, "New HSUS Initiative Poised to Keep More Animals in Homes and Out of Shelters," accessed 8/13/16, http://blog.humanesociety.org/ wayne/2015/09/pets-are-welcome-hsus.html.

6. "Pets by the Numbers," The Humane Society of the United States, accessed 7/3/16, http://www.humanesociety.org/issues/pet_overpopulation/ facts/pet_ownership_statistics.html.

7. "Annual Report FY2015," Maricopa County Animal Care and Control, accessed 8/13/16, http://www.maricopa.gov/pets/pdf/annualreports/ annualreport_12212015.pdf.

8. "Our Impact in 2015," PetSmart Charities, accessed 8/15/16, https:// www.petsmartcharities.org/our-impact.

9. "The Petco Foundation," Petco, accessed 8/15/16, http://www.petco. com/petco-foundation.

10. TIME staff, "Wildlife Populations Have Dropped by Almost 60% in 40 years, WWF Says," *TIME*, October 27, 2016, accessed 10/27/16, http://time. com/4547132/wildlife-population-decline-wwf/.

11. Lucy Pasha-Robinson, "Hundreds of Animal Species 'Being Consumed to Extinction,'" October 19, 2016, accessed 10/20/16, http://www.independent. co.uk/environment/nature/hundreds-animal-species-consumed-extinction-a7369421.html.

12. Elizabeth Pennisi, "People are Hunting Primates, Bats, and Other Mammals to Extinction," October 18, 2016, accessed 10/22/16, http://www. sciencemag.org/news/2016/10/people-are-hunting-primates-bats-and-other-mammals-extinction.

13. Philimon Bulawayo and Mike Saburi, "Zimbabwean Charged over Killing of Cecil the Lion," *Reuters*, July 29, 2015, accessed 11/2/16, http://www. msn.com/en-us/news/world/zimbabwean-charged-over-killing-of-cecil-the-lion/ar-AAdE6n2.

14. Wayne Pacelle, "Breaking News: U.S. Says 'No Way' to Trophy Imports from South African Canned Lion Hunts," October 21, 2016, accessed 10/21/ 16, http://blog.humanesociety.org/wayne/2016/10/u-s-says-no-trophy-imports-south-african-canned-lion-hunts.html

15. "Breaking News: U.S. Says 'No Way' to Trophy Imports from South African Canned Lion Hunts."

16. Lena Masri, "Want to Hunt Exotic African Animals? Just Go to Texas," *Reuters*, August 25, 2015, accessed 8/28/15, http://readersupportednews.org/opinion2/277-75/32057-want-to-hunt-exotic-african-animals-just-go-to-texas.

17. Wayne Pacelle, "Pedals' Slaying Creates Momentum in New Jersey to Ban Bear Trophy Hunting," October 19, 2016, accessed 10/19/16, http://blog.humanesociety.org/wayne/2016/10/pedals-slaying-creates-momentum-new-jersey-ban-bear-trophy-hunting.html.

18. "Victims of Vanity II: Five Years Later, Cruel Indifference Continues," Born Free USA, accessed 11/2/16, http://www.bornfreeusa.org/victimsofvanity2.

19. Beckie Elgin, "Sustainable Sabotage: Activists Use New Tactics to Thwart Animal Trophy Hunters," *Earth Island Journal*, January 4, 2016, accessed 1/5/16, http://www.alternet.org/comments/environment/sustainable-sabotage-animal-activists-use-new-tactics-thwart-trophy-hunters.

20. Wayne Pacelle, "In Wake Of Zanesville Tragedy, Five States Still Have No Rules on Private Ownership of Dangerous Animals," October 20, 2016, accessed 10/20/16, http://blog.humanesociety.org/wayne/2016/10/wake-zanesville-tragedy-five-states-still-no-rules-private-ownership-dangerous-animals.html.

21. Kate Dylewsky, "Downloading Cruelty: An Investigation into the Online Sales of Exotic Pets in the US," (Washington, DC: Born Free USA, 2016), 19.

22. "Downloading Cruelty." 1

23. "Downloading Cruelty," 7.

24. "Downloading Cruelty," 13, 15.

25. Aisling Maria Cronin, "6 Reasons Why I No Longer Visit Zoos, Marine Parks, or Any Other Facility that Displays Animals," October 28, 2016, accessed 10/28/16, http://www.onegreenplanet.org/animalsandnature/why-i-no-longer-visit-marine-parks-or-zoos/.

26. "6 Reasons Why I No Longer Visit Zoos, Marine Parks, or Any Other Facility that Displays Animals."

27. Madison Montgomery, 9/25/16, "Breaking News: Research Suggests that Zoos Do NOT 'Educate or Empower' Children," accessed 11/21/16, http://www.onegreenplanet.org/news/research-suggests-that-zoos-do-not-educate-or-empower-children/.

28. "6 Reasons Why I No Longer Visit Zoos, Marine Parks, or Any Other Facility that Displays Animals."

29. Margi Prideaux, "Zoos Are the Problem, Not the Solution, to Animal Conservation," *Open Democracy*, June 30, 2016, accessed 7/8/16, http://www.alternet.org/zoos-are-problem-not-solution-animal-conservation.

30. Veronica Chavez, "Hydrated Through Tubes and Fed Medicated Fish: The Horrible Life of Dolphins Captured in Taiji," November 1, 2016, accessed 11/1/16, http://www.onegreenplanet.org/news/horrible-life-for-taiji-dolphins/.

31. David Kirby, "What Freedom Could Look Like for SeaWorld's Killer Whales," *TakePart*, June 18, 2016, accessed 6/20/16, http://www.ecowatch.com/what-freedom-could-look-like-for-seaworlds-killer-whales-1891174888.html.

32. "What Freedom Could Look Like for SeaWorld's Killer Whales."

5. SOCIAL JUSTICE CONNECTIONS

1. Elizabeth Buff, "Should Animal Abuse Be Considered a Violent Crime," November 11, 2016, accessed 9/11/16, http://www.onegreenplanet.org/animalsandnature/should-animal-abuse-be-considered-a-violent-crime/.

2. Nadia Prupis, *Common Dreams*, "FBI to Track Animal Abuse Like Homicide—But Which Animals?" January 8, 2016, accessed 1/10/16, http://www.commondreams.org/news/2016/01/08/fbi-track-animal-abuse-homicide-which-animals.

3. The Humane Society of the United States, "Clark, Ros-Lehtinen Bill Protects Domestic Violence Victims and Pets," March 5, 2015, accessed 12/1/15, http://www.humanesociety.org/news/press_releases/2015/03/domestic-violence-and-pets-030515.html?credit=web_id95800657.

4. Wayne Pacelle, "Breaking News: Key Lawmakers Propose Federal Anti-Cruelty Measure," May 13, 2015, accessed 8/22/16, http://blog.humanesociety.org/wayne/2015/05/congress-introduces-pact-act.html.

5. Evelyn Nieves, "Zeroing in on Sociopaths: Feds Finally Make Animal Cruelty a Top-Tier Felony," AlterNet, October 10, 2014, accessed 10/19/14, http://www.alternet.org/feds-finally-make-animal-cruelty-group-felony.

6. Karen Becker, "Why Is the Federal Government Killing Millions of Animals Every Year?" October 14, 2014, accessed 8/20/16, http://healthypets.mercola.com/sites/healthypets/archive/2014/10/14/usda-wildlife-services.aspx.

7. "Why Is the Federal Government Killing Millions of Animals Every Year?"

8. The Humane Society of the United States, "Wildlife Disservice," accessed 8/20/16, http://www.humanesociety.org/issues/lethal_wildlife_management/facts/usda-wildlife-services-inefficient-and-inhumane.html.

9. Dan Flores, "Stop Killing Coyotes," *New York Times*, August 11, 2016, accessed 8/12/16, http://www.nytimes.com/2016/08/11/opinion/stop-killing-coyotes.html?_r=0.

10. Bethany Cotton, "Landmark Settlement Reins in Rogue Federal Wildlife Killing Program," October 10, 2016, accessed 10/26/16, http://www.wildearthguardians.org/site/News2?page=NewsArticle&id=12723&news_iv_ctrl=-1#.WATr5pMrKGQhttp://www.wildearthguardians.org/site/News2?page=NewsArticle&id=12723&news_iv_ctrl=-1.

11. American Wild Horse Preservation, accessed 8/22/16, http://www.wildhorsepreservation.org.

12. American Wild Horse Preservation, "FAQ," accessed 8/22/16, http://www.wildhorsepreservation.org/faq.

13. Anissa Putois, "Why Wild Horses Are Being Pitted Against Cows and Will Likely Not Survive as a Result," July 15, 2016, accessed 7/15/16, http://www.onegreenplanet.org/environment/why-wild-horses-are-being-pitted-against-cows/.

14. Evelyn Nieves, "5 Horrific Ways People Mistreat Animals," AlterNet, February 4, 2015, accessed 2/7/15, http://www.alternet.org/5-horrific-ways-people-mistreat-animals.

15. The Humane Society of the United States, "The Facts about Horse Slaughter," accessed 6/30/16, http://www.humanesociety.org/issues/horse_slaughter/facts/facts_horse_slaughter.html.

16. American Wild Horse Preservation, "AWHPC Poll Results," accessed 8/22/16, http://www.wildhorsepreservation.org/media/awhpc-poll-results.

17. American Veterinary Medical Association, "Soring in Horses FAQ," February 15, 2012, accessed 11/14/16, https://www.avma.org/KB/Resources/FAQs/Pages/Soring-in-Horses.aspx.

18. "Soring in Horses FAQ."

19. Wayne Pacelle, "Obama Should Put a Ribbon on Anti-Soring Rule Before Inauguration Day," accessed 11/15/16, http://blog.humanesociety.org/wayne/2016/11/obama-put-ribbon-anti-soring-rule-inauguration-day.html.

20. Animal Legal Defense Fund, "Animal Fighting Facts," accessed 8/20/16, http://aldf.org/resources/laws-cases/animal-fighting-facts/.

21. American Society for the Prevention of Cruelty in Animals, "A Closer Look at Dog Fighting," accessed 11/14/16, http://www.aspca.org/animal-cruelty/dog-fighting/closer-look-dog-fighting.

22. Animal Legal Defense Fund, "Animal Fighting Case Study: Michael Vick," accessed 11/16/16, http://aldf.org/resources/laws-cases/animal-fighting-case-study-michael-vick/.

23. "Animal Fighting Case Study: Michael Vick"

24. Best Friends, "The Brave, Beautiful Dogs Out of Bad Newz Kennel," accessed 11/17/16, http://bestfriends.org/sanctuary/explore-sanctuary/dogtown/vicktory-dogs.

25. American Society for the Prevention of Cruelty to Animals, "Cockfighting," accessed 11/14/16, http://www.aspca.org/animal-cruelty/other-animal-issues/cockfighting and The Humane Society of the United States, "Cockfighting Fact Sheet," accessed 11/14/16, http://www.humanesociety.org/issues/cockfighting/facts/cockfighting_fact_sheet.html.

26. The Humane Society of the United States, "Authorities Bust Major Cockfighting Pit in Alabama," August 4, 2016, accessed 8/23/16, http://www.humanesociety.org/news/press_releases/2016/08/alabama-cockfighting-bust-080416.html.

27. "Animal Fighting Facts"

28. Kerry Sheridan, "Circus Elephants' Retirement Home Promises Pampered Life," May 2, 2016, accessed 8/20/16, http://phys.org/news/2016-05-circus-elephants-home-pampered-life.html.

29. "Animals Have No Business in Show Business!" PETA's Augustus Club, No. 3, Issue 73, 2016, 1.

30. Wayne Pacelle, "Animals Fall by the Wayside at Roadside Zoos," December 4, 2013, accessed 11/19/16, http://blog.humanesociety.org/wayne/2013/12/animals-fall-by-the-wayside-at-roadside-zoos.html.

31. Wayne Pacelle, "HSUS Undercover Investigations at Roadside Zoos in Virginia, Oklahoma Reveal Severe Abuse," January 22, 2015, accessed 11/19/16, http://blog.humanesociety.org/wayne/2015/01/roadside-zoos-investigation.html.

32. Wayne Pacelle, "Puppy Mill Dogs Rescued in Big Sky Country," August 10, 2016, accessed 8/23/16, http://blog.humanesociety.org/wayne/2016/08/puppy-mill-dogs-rescued-big-sky-country.html.

33. "8 Reasons Why Horse-Drawn Carriages Are Just Plain Wrong," accessed 8/23/16, http://www.petakids.com/save-animals/horse-drawn-carriages/?utm_campaign=0816%20horse%20drawn%20carriages%20promo%20EA&utm_source=PETA%20Kids%20E-Mail&utm_medium=E-News.

34. Animal Legal Defense Fund, "Animal Hoarding Facts," accessed 8/23/16, http://aldf.org/resources/when-you-witness-animal-cruelty/animal-hoarding-facts/.

35. American Society for the Prevention of Cruelty to Animals, "A Closer Look at Animal Hoarding," accessed 8/23/16, http://www.aspca.org/animal-cruelty/animal-hoarding/closer-look-animal-hoarding.

36. Karen Becker, "This Routine Procedure Could Soon Become a Criminal Animal Cruelty Offense," July 19, 2016, accessed 7/19/16, http://healthypets.mercola.com/sites/healthypets/archive/2016/07/19/new-york-to-ban-cat-declawing.aspx.

6. PERSONAL IMPACTS

1. American Anti-Vivisection Society, "Project Animal Welfare Act: An Act for All," accessed 8/31/16, http://aavs.org/our-work/campaigns/birds-mice-rats/.

2. Alla Katsnelson, "A Conversation with Amy Clippinger," *ACS Cent. Sci.* 2 (2016): 432, accessed July 12, 2016, DOI: 10.1021/acscentsci.6b00186.

3. Wayne Pacelle, "Breaking News: Fur Flies with New HSUS Exposé of Retailers Selling Real Fur as Fake," August 9, 2016, accessed 8/9/16, http://blog.humanesociety.org/wayne/2016/08/breaking-news-fur-flies-new-hsus-expose-retailers-selling-real-fur-fake.html.

4. *MarketWatch*, "This Chart Proves Americans Love Their Meat," December 1, 2016, accessed 9/6/16, http://www.marketwatch.com/story/this-chart-proves-americans-love-their-meat-2016-08-15.

5. Jenny Luna, "Americans Are Gorging Themselves on Cheap Meat," *Mother Jones*, March 30, 2016, accessed 6/13/16, http://www.motherjones.com/environment/2016/03/us-increase-meat-consumption-europe-less-meat-sustainability.

6. Joe Loria, "Study: Number of Vegans in Britain up 360 Percent!" May 18, 2016, accessed 6/1/16, http://www.mfablog.org/study-number-of-vegans-in-britain-up-360.

7. The Food Revolution Network, "Chinese Government Announces: Time to Cut Meat Consumption by 50 Percent," July 13, 2016, accessed 8/3/16, https://foodrevolution.org/blog/food-and-health/china-plan-reduce-meat-consumption/.

8. *Vegetarian Times*, "Vegetarianism in America," accessed 9/6/16, http://www.vegetariantimes.com/article/vegetarianism-in-america/.

9. "Vegetarianism in America."

10. Frank Newport, "In U.S., 5% Consider Themselves Vegetarians," July 26, 2012, accessed 9/6/16,http://www.gallup.com/poll/156215/Consider-Themselves-Vegetarians.aspx.

11. The VRG Blog Editor, "How Many Adults Are Vegan in the U.S.?" December 5, 2011, accessed 5/14/15, http://www.vrg.org/blog/2011/12/05/how-many-adults-are-vegan-in-the-u-s/.

12. The Vegetarian Resource Group Blog Editor, "How Often Do Americans Eat Vegetarian Meals? And How Many Adults in the U.S. Are Vegetarian?" May 18, 2012, accessed 7/14/15, http://www.vrg.org/blog/2012/05/18/how-often-do-americans-eat-vegetarian-meals-and-how-many-adults-in-the-u-s-are-vegetarian/.

13. Hannah Sentenac, "Exclusive: Research Suggests 36 Percent of Americans Open to Plant-Based Eating," *Latest Vegan News*, May 27, 2015,

accessed 9/3/16, http://latestvegannews.com/research-suggests-36-of-americans-open-to-plant-based-eating/#.

14. Hal Herzog, "84% of Vegetarians and Vegans Return to Meat. Why?" December 2, 2014, accessed 7/4/16, https://www.psychologytoday.com/blog/animals-and-us/201412/84-vegetarians-and-vegans-return-meat-why.

15. Ginny Messina, "Preventing Ex-Vegans: Why Feeling 'Normal' Matters," The Vegan r.d., July 21, 2015, accessed 7/22/15, http://www.theveganrd.com/2015/07/preventing-ex-vegans-why-feeling-normal-matters.html.

16. See http://www.americanhumanescam.com/, accessed 9/11/16, for a Mercy for Animals undercover investigation at Foster Farms, "American Humane Certified."

17. Merritt Clifton, "Courting Hen & Egg Producers Leads Animal Charities into Deep @#$%," June 24, 2015, accessed 7/1/15, http://www.animals24-7.org/2015/06/24/courting-hen-egg-producers-leads-animal-charities-into-deep/.

18. Leslee Goodman, "Advocating for the Souls of Animals," The MOON Magazine, accessed 5/26/15, http://moonmagazine.org/advocating-souls-animals-interview-gay-bradshaw-2015-01-03/.

19. "Exclusive: Research Suggests 36 Percent of Americans Open to Plant-Based Eating"

20. Hannah Sentenac, "Vegan Meat Now Available in Over 23,000 Stores Nationwide," *Latest Vegan News*, June 21, 2016, accessed 9/3/16, http://latestvegannews.com/vegan-meat-available-23000-stores-nationwide/#.

21. Hannah Sentenac, "Plant-Based Food Named a Top Trend for 2016," *Latest Vegan News*, December 31, 2015, accessed 9/11/16, http://latestvegannews.com/plant-based-food-named-top-trend-2016/.

22. Specialty Food Association, "Meatless-Meat Industry Gains Ground, Market Share," May 13, 2015, accessed 9/11/16, https://www.specialtyfood.com/news/article/meatless-meat-industry-prepares-growth/.

23. Sarah Von Alt, "Wow! More Than Half of Americans Plan to Eat More Vegan Foods," April 27, 2016, accessed 9/11/16, http://www.mfablog.org/wow-more-than-half-of-americans-plan-to-eat.

24. Taco Bell, "How to Eat Vegetarian and Meatless at Taco Bell," accessed 9/11/16, https://tacobell.com/feed/how-to-eat-veggie.

25. Animal Place, "21 Reasons to Adopt a Veg-Friendly Menu Policy," accessed 11/29/16, http://www.foodforthoughtcampaign.org/21-reasons.html.

26. Hannah Sentenac, "Vegan Google Searches Climb 32% from 2014 to 2015," *Latest Vegan News*, January 20, 2016, accessed 9/11/16, http://latestvegannews.com/vegan-google-searches-climb-32-2014-2015/.

27. The *Vegan Street* Blog, "10 Questions: Vegan Rockstar Edition with Ginny Kisch Messina," February 4, 2015, accessed 2/12/15, http://

veganfeministagitator.blogspot.com/2015/02/10-questions-vegan-rockstar-edition.html.

28. Jared Piazza and Steve Loughnan, "When Meat Gets Personal, Animals' Minds Matter Less: Motivated Use of Intelligence Information in Judgments of Moral Standing," *Social Psychological and Personality Science* (2016): 1-8, accessed July 22, 2016, doi: 10.1177/1948550616660159

29. Jared Piazza, Matthew B. Ruby, Steve Loughnan, Mischel Luong, Juliana Kulik, Hanne M. Watkins, and Mirra Seigerman. "Rationalizing Meat Consumption. The 4Ns," *Appetite* 91 (2015): 114-128, accessed 6/20/16, doi: 10.1016/j.appet.2015.04.011.

30. "Rationalizing Meat Consumption. The 4Ns."

31. To see the photos used and questions asked, go to Nick Cooney, "Report: Which Farm Animal Photos Are Most Likely to Inspire People to Eat Vegan?" January 25, 2015, accessed 11/17/15, http://www.humaneleaguelabs.org/blog/2015-01-25-which-farm-animal-photos-inspire-vegan-eating/.

32. Nick Cooney, "Report: Is Animal Cruelty or Abolitionist Messaging More Effective?" September 20, 2015, accessed 11/17/15, http://www.humaneleaguelabs.org/blog/2015-09-20-animal-cruelty-or-purity-messaging-more-effective/.

33. Nick Cooney, "Report: Which Request Creates the Most Diet Change?" November 4, 2015, accessed 11/17/15, http://www.humaneleaguelabs.org/blog/2015-09-20-which-request-creates-most-diet-change/.

34. Casey Taft, "Psychology and Long-Term Goals in Vegan Advocacy," June 26, 2016, accessed 7/21/16, http://freefromharm.org/animal-advocacy/casy-taft-book-excerpt.

35. Lori Amos, "Joaquin Phoenix on Huge New Animal Justice Campaign: 'Now More than Ever, the World Needs to Hear this Message,'" AlterNet, August 19, 2016, accessed 8/19/16, http://www.alternet.org/food/be-fair-be-vegan-most-ambitious-animal-justice-campaign-ever-launched-new-york.

7. OUR GOALS

1. Gary L. Francione, "The Abolitionist Approach to Animal Rights and Veganism as the Moral Baseline," in *Turning Points in Compassion*, eds. Gypsy Wulff and Fran Chambers. (Australia: SpiritWings Humane Education Inc., 2015), 151.

2. Kate Good, "We Can Save the Planet with Plant-based Food . . . Find Out How," September 16, 2016, accessed 9/16/16, http://www.onegreenplanet.org/news/we-can-save-the-planet-with-plant-based-food/.

3. George Monbiot, "Pregnant Silence," November 19, 2015, accessed 11/23/15, http://www.monbiot.com/2015/11/19/pregnant-silence.

4. "Pregnant Silence."

5. Richard A. Oppenlander, *Comfortably Unaware* (New York: Beaufort Books, 2012), 52

6. Reynard Loki, "The 3 Most Environmentally Damaging Habits You Might Be Able to Change," AlterNet, April 14, 2016, accessed 4/14/16, http://www.alternet.org/environment/3-most-environmentally-damaging-habits-you-might-be-able-change, and http://cowspiracy.com/facts, accessed 7/20/16.

7. *Comfortably Unaware*, 41

8. *Cowspiracy: The Sustainability Secret*, "The Facts," accessed 7/20/16, http://cowspiracy.com/facts.

9. Mercy for Animals, *Planet Earth*, accessed 9/29/16, https://www.youtube.com/watch?v=9seoBrcbxYA.

10. Environmental Working Group, "Wasted Food Is a Major Source of Emissions," accessed 9/29/16, http://www.ewg.org/meateatersguide/a-meat-eaters-guide-to-climate-change-health-what-you-eat-matters/wasted-food-is-a-major-source-of-emissions/.

11. "The Facts."

12. *Comfortably Unaware*, 51.

13. "The Facts."

14. "The Facts."

15. *Comfortably Unaware*, 27.

16. "The Facts."

17. *Comfortably Unaware*, 28.

18. *Comfortably Unaware*, 28.

19. "The Facts."

20. One Green Planet, "Deforestation in the Amazon Is Up by 29 Percent and Our Appetite for Meat is Largely to Blame," December 1, 2016, accessed 12/1/16, http://www.onegreenplanet.org/news/deforestation-in-the-amazon-is-up-cattle-ranching/.

21. Anissa Putois, "These Aren't Clouds, They're 300 Football Fields Worth of Flames—Caused by Our Snacks," June 7, 2016, accessed 10/13/16, http://www.onegreenplanet.org/environment/palm-oil-is-causing-football-fields-worth-of-flames/.

22. Food and Agriculture Organization of the United Nations, "Major Cuts of Greenhouse Gas Emissions from Livestock within Reach," accessed 9/29/16, http://www.fao.org/news/story/en/item/197608/icode/.

23. Environmental Working Group, "Climate and Environmental Impacts," accessed 9/29/16, http://www.ewg.org/meateatersguide/a-meat-eaters-guide-

to-climate-change-health-what-you-eat-matters/climate-and-environmental-impacts/.

24. "Climate and Environmental Impacts."

25. Rick Stafford, "How Overfishing and Shark-finning Could Increase the Pace of Climate Change," *The Conversation*, October 27, 2016, accessed 11/5/16, https://theconversation.com/how-overfishing-and-shark-finning-could-increase-the-pace-of-climate-change-67664.

26. *Comfortably Unaware*, 54

27. "Pregnant Silence"

28. Arelis R. Hernandez, Angela Fritz, and Chris Mooney, "Factory Farming Practices Are under Scrutiny Again in N.C. after Disastrous Hurricane Floods," *Washington Post*, October 17, 2016, accessed 10/18/16, https://www.washingtonpost.com/news/capital-weather-gang/wp/2016/10/16/factory-farming-practices-are-under-scrutiny-again-in-n-c-after-disastrous-hurricane-floods/?utm_term=.d46815df28e9.

29. Georgina Gustin, "Factory Farms Get Bigger, Pollution Grows, but Regulators Don't Even Know Where They Are," *InsideClimate News*, October 21, 2016, accessed 10/21/16, https://insideclimatenews.org/news/19102016/cafo-epa-regulations-factory-farms-get-bigger-pollution-grows-environmental-impact-methane'

30. *Comfortably Unaware*, 54

31. Claire Groden, "Report: Plastic Pollution in the Ocean Is Reaching Crisis Levels," *Fortune*, October 1, 2015, accessed 12/5/16, http://fortune.com/2015/10/01/ocean-plastic-pollution/.

32. Feeding America, "Food Waste in America," accessed 12/5/16, http://www.feedingamerica.org/about-us/how-we-work/securing-meals/reducing-food-waste.html.

33. Chris Hedges. "Chris Hedges: I've Gone Vegan to Help Try to Save the Planet," *Truthdig*, November 10, 2014, accessed 12/1/14, http://www.alternet.org/environment/chris-hedges-ive-gone-vegan-help-try-save-planet.

CONCLUDING COMMENTS

1. Beth Levine, "Open Letter to Organizations that Research and Promote Empathy and Compassion," November 10, 2015, accessed 12/14/16, http://www.bethlevineblog.com/blog/2015/9/9/open-letter-to-organizations-that-research-and-promote-empathy-and-compassion.

2. Lindsay Patton, "Why We Need 'Crazy' Cat People," October 8, 2016, accessed 10/9/16, http://www.onegreenplanet.org/animalsandnature/why-we-need-crazy-cat-people/.

3. Rob Nixon, "Future Footprints," review of *The Human Age*, by Diane Ackerman, *New York Times* Sunday Book Review, September 5, 2014, https://www.nytimes.com/2014/09/07/books/review/the-human-age-by-diane-ackerman.html?_r=0.

4. Gene Baur, "Beyond Harambe: Why Our Opinion About Animals in Zoos Desperately Needs to Evolve," Farm Sanctuary, June 29, 2016, accessed 6/29/16, http://www.onegreenplanet.org/animalsandnature/beyond-harambe-why-zoos-need-to-evolve/.

5. Maureen Nandini Mitra, "Serious Question: Should Humans Extend Personhood to Animals?" *Earth Island Journal*, December 5, 2016, accessed 12/10/14, http://www.alternet.org/environment/serious-question-should-humans-extend-personhood-animals.

6. "Serious Question: Should Humans Extend Personhood to Animals?"

7. "Serious Question: Should Humans Extend Personhood to Animals?"

8. "Serious Question: Should Humans Extend Personhood to Animals?"

9. "Serious Question: Should Humans Extend Personhood to Animals?"

10. Lauren Choplin, "Interview with Kevin Schneider re: Tommy, Kiko, Hercules & Leo," June 15, 2016, accessed 7/3/16, http://www.nonhumanrightsproject.org/2016/06/15/interview-with-kevin-schneider-re-tommy-kiko-hercules-leo/.

11. "The Success of Nonviolent Civil Resistance: Erica Chenoweth at TEDxBoulder," accessed 12/13/16, https://www.youtube.com/watch?v=YJSehRlU34w.

12. Wayne Pacelle, *The Humane Economy* (New York: HarperCollins, 2016)

13. Netherlands National Committee for the Protection of Animals Used for Scientific Purposes, "Opinion Provided by NCad as to How the Netherlands Can Become a Pioneer in No-Animal Research," December 15, 2016, accessed 12/22/16, https://english.ncadierproevenbeleid.nl/latest/news/16/12/15/ncad-opinion-transition-to-non-animal-research.

14. Martha Rosenberg & Ronnie Cummins, "Time to Drive Factory Farmed Food Off the Market," Organic Consumers Association, October 3, 2016, accessed 10/6/16, http://www.alternet.org/food/end-factory-farmed-food.

15. Georgina Gustin, "New Project Aims to Lure People Away from Meat, to a Climate-Healthier Diet," *InsideClimate News*, December 22, 2016, accessed 12/23/16, https://insideclimatenews.org/news/22122016/meat-consumption-diet-plants-climate-change.

16. Andrea Gunn, "Effective Activism: How to Create Big Change for Animals in Our Everyday Lives," accessed 12/13/16, http://plantpuresummit.com/speaker-andrea-gunn.

17. American Society for the Prevention of Cruelty to Animals, "Animal Cruelty," accessed 11/14/16, http://www.aspca.org/animal-cruelty/other-animal-issues/greyhound-racing.

18. "Animal Cruelty: Greyhound Racing"

19. Jaime Mishkin, "Arizona Ends Greyhound Racing—Now Hundreds of Dogs are Looking for Forever Homes," May 10, 2016, accessed 12/7/16, http://www.onegreenplanet.org/news/arizona-ends-greyhound-racing/.

BIBLIOGRAPHY

"8 Reasons Why Horse-Drawn Carriages Are Just Plain Wrong." Accessed 8/23/16. http://www.petakids.com/save-animals/horse-drawn-carriages/?utm_campaign=0816%20horse%20drawn%20carriages%20promo%20EA&utm_source=PETA%20Kids%20E-Mail&utm_medium=E-News.

A Well-Fed World. "Factory Farms." Accessed 12/7/16. http://awfw.org/factory-farms/.

Alley Cat Allies. "Feral Cat Health Analysis: Living Healthy Lives Outdoors." Accessed 7/30/15. http://alleycat.org/resources/feral-cat-health-analysis-living-healthy-lives-outdoors/.

Alley Cat Allies. "U.S. Public Opinion on Humane Treatment of Stray Cats." Accessed 7/30/15. http://www.alleycat.org/resources/public-opinion-on-humane-treatment-of-cats/.

Alley Cat Allies. "Community Cat Care." Accessed 10/11/16. https://www.alleycat.org/community-cat-care/kitten-socialization-how-to/.

American Anti-Vivisection Society. "Project Animal Welfare Act: An Act for All." Accessed 8/31/16. http://aavs.org/our-work/campaigns/birds-mice-rats/.

American Humane. Accessed 8/13/16, http://www.americanhumane.org.

American Pet Products Association. "Pet Industry Market Size & Ownership Statistics." Accessed 6/30/16. http://americanpetproducts.org/press_industrytrends.asp.

American Society for the Prevention of Cruelty to Animals. "ASPCA Research Shows Americans Overwhelmingly Support Investigations to Expose Animal Abuse on Industrial Farms." Accessed 8/16/16. http://www.aspca.org/about-us/press-releases/aspca-research-shows-americans-overwhelmingly-support-investigations-expose.

American Society for the Prevention of Cruelty to Animals. "Shelter Intake & Surrender." Accessed 8/13/16. http://www.aspca.org/animal-homelessness/shelter-intake-and-surrender/.

American Society for the Prevention of Cruelty in Animals. "A Closer Look at Dog Fighting." Accessed 11/14/16. http://www.aspca.org/animal-cruelty/dog-fighting/closer-look-dog-fighting.

American Society for the Prevention of Cruelty to Animals. "Cockfighting." Accessed 11/14/16. http://www.aspca.org/animal-cruelty/other-animal-issues/cockfighting.

American Society for the Prevention of Cruelty to Animals. "Animal Hoarding." Accessed 8/23/16. http://www.aspca.org/animal-cruelty/animal-hoarding/closer-look-animal-hoarding.

American Society for the Prevention of Cruelty to Animals. "A Closer Look at Animal Cruelty: Greyhound Racing." Accessed 11/14/16. http://www.aspca.org/animal-cruelty/other-animal-issues/greyhound-racing.

American Veterinary Medical Association. "Soring in Horses FAQ," February 15, 2012. Accessed 11/14/16. https://www.avma.org/KB/Resources/FAQs/Pages/Soring-in-Horses.aspx.

American Veterinary Medical Foundation. "Pets in Vehicles." Accessed 6/3/16. https://www. avma.org/public/PetCare/Pages/pets-in-vehicles.aspx.

American Wild Horse Preservation. "Home." Accessed 8/22/16. http://www. wildhorsepreservation.org.

American Wild Horse Preservation. "FAQ." Accessed 8/22/16. http:// www.wildhorsepreservation.org/faq.

American Wild Horse Preservation. "AWHPC Poll Results." Accessed 8/22/16. http:// www.wildhorsepreservation.org/media/awhpc-poll-results.

Amos, Lori. "Joaquin Phoenix on Huge New Animal Justice Campaign: 'Now More Than Ever, the World Needs to Hear This Message.'" *AlterNet*, August 19, 2016. Accessed 8/ 19/16. http://www.alternet.org/food/be-fair-be-vegan-most-ambitious-animal-justice-campaign-ever-launched-new-york.

Animal Legal Defense Fund. "Taking Ag-Gag to Court." Accessed 10/17/16. http://aldf.org/ cases-campaigns/features/taking-ag-gag-to-court/.

Animal Legal Defense Fund. "Animal Fighting Case Study: Michael Vick." Accessed 11/16/ 16. http://aldf.org/resources/laws-cases/animal-fighting-case-study-michael-vick/.

Animal Legal Defense Fund. "Animal Fighting Facts." Accessed 8/20/16. http://aldf.org/ resources/laws-cases/animal-fighting-facts/.

Animal Legal Defense Fund. "Animal Hoarding Facts." Accessed 8/23/16, http://aldf.org/ resources/when-you-witness-animal-cruelty/animal-hoarding-facts/.

Animal Place. "21 Reasons to Adopt a Veg-Friendly Menu Policy." Accessed 11/29/16. http:// www.foodforthoughtcampaign.org/21-reasons.html.

Animals Deserve Absolute Protection Today and Tomorrow. "More than 150 Billion Animals Slaughtered Every Year." Accessed 12/7/16. http://www.adaptt.org/killcounter.html.

"Animals Have No Business in Show Business!" PETA's Augustus Club, No. 3, Issue 73, 2016.

Barber, Gregory. "Are Cage-Free Eggs All They're Cracked Up to Be?" *Mother Jones*. February 10, 2016. Accessed 2/11/16. http://www.motherjones.com/blue-marble/2016/02/ corporations-are-going-cage-free-whats-next-hens.

Baur, Gene. "Beyond Harambe: Why Our Opinion About Animals in Zoos Desperately Needs to Evolve." Farm Sanctuary. June 29, 2016. Accessed 6/29/16. http://www. onegreenplanet.org/animalsandnature/beyond-harambe-why-zoos-need-to-evolve/.

Becker, Karen. "Why Is the Federal Government Killing Millions of Animals Every Year?" October 14, 2014. Accessed 8/20/16. http://healthypets.mercola.com/sites/healthypets/ archive/2014/10/14/usda-wildlife-services.aspx.

Becker, Karen. "This Routine Procedure Could Soon Become a Criminal Animal Cruelty Offense." July 19, 2016. Accessed 7/19/16. http://healthypets.mercola.com/sites/ healthypets/archive/2016/07/19/new-york-to-ban-cat-declawing.aspx.

Best Friends. "No-Kill: Best Friends Is the Leader of the Movement." Accessed 7/28/16. http://bestfriends.org/our-work/no-kill-initiatives/.

Best Friends. "The Brave, Beautiful Dogs Out of Bad Newz Kennel." Accessed 11/17/16. http://bestfriends.org/sanctuary/explore-sanctuary/dogtown/vicktory-dogs.

Born Free USA. "Get the Facts: Ten Fast Facts about Exotic 'Pets'." Accessed 7/4/16. http:// www.bornfreeusa.org/facts.php?p=439&more=1.

Born Free USA. Victims of Vanity II: Five Years Later, Cruel Indifference Continues." Accessed 11/2/16. http://www.bornfreeusa.org/victimsofvanity2.

Brewster, Mary P. and Cassandra L. Reyes, eds. *Animal Cruelty: A Multidisciplinary Approach to Understanding*, Durham, NC: Carolina Academic Press, 2013.

Buff, Elizabeth. "Should Animal Abuse Be Considered a Violent Crime?" November 11, 2016. Accessed 9/11/16. http://www.onegreenplanet.org/animalsandnature/should-animal-abuse-be-considered-a-violent-crime/.

Bulawayo, Philimon, and Mike Saburi. "Zimbabwean Charged over Killing of Cecil the Lion." *Reuters*. July 29, 2015. Accessed 11/2/16. http://www.msn.com/en-us/news/world/ zimbabwean-charged-over-killing-of-cecil-the-lion/ar-AAdE6n2.

Carrington, Damian. "Millions of Animal 'Trophies' Exported Across Borders." *Guardian UK.* June 14, 2016. Accessed 6/15/16. http://readersupportednews.org/news-section2/318-66/37454-millions-of-animal-trophies-exported-across-borders.

Chavez, Veronica. "Hydrated through Tubes and Fed Medicated Fish: The Horrible Life of Dolphins Captured in Taiji." November 1, 2016. Accessed 11/1/16. http://www.onegreenplanet.org/news/horrible-life-for-taiji-dolphins/.

Choplin, Lauren. "Interview with Kevin Schneider re: Tommy, Kiko, Hercules & Leo." June 15, 2016. Accessed 7/3/16. http://www.nonhumanrightsproject.org/2016/06/15/interview-with-kevin-schneider-re-tommy-kiko-hercules-leo/.

Chow, Lorraine. "Alec Baldwin and Candice Bergen Want You to Know Something Horrible About McDonald's Chicken." AlterNet. October 5, 2016. Accessed 10/4/16. http://www.alternet.org/food/alec-baldwin-and-candice-bergen-want-you-know-something-horrible-about-mcdonalds-chicken-video?akid=14723.1893310.5WYhme&rd=1&src=newsletter1064810&t=12.

Chu, Karyen, and Anderson, Wendy M. (September 2007). "U.S. Public Opinion on Humane Treatment of Stray Cats." Law & Policy Brief (Bethesda, MD: Alley Cat Allies). Accessed 10/11/16. http://www.alleycat.org/resources/public-opinion-on-humane-treatment-of-cats/.

Clifton, Merritt. "Courting Hen & Egg Producers Leads Animal Charities into Deep @#$%." June 24, 2015. Accessed 7/1/15. http://www.animals24-7.org/2015/06/24/courting-hen-egg-producers-leads-animal-charities-into-deep/.

Compassion Over Killing. "Iowa Investigation: Hawkeye Sow Centers (Hormel Supplier)." Accessed 10/18/16. http://cok.net/inv/iowa-pigs/.

Compassion Over Killing. "New COK Exposé: High-Speed Slaughter Hell at Hormel, Makers of SPAM." Accessed 10/18/16. http://cok.net/inv/hormel/.

Cotton, Bethany. "Landmark Settlement Reins in Rogue Federal Wildlife Killing Program." October 10, 2016. Accessed 10/26/16. http://www.wildearthguardians.org/site/News2?page=NewsArticle&id=12723&news_iv_ctrl=-1#.WATr5pMrKGQhttp://www.wildearthguardians.org/site/News2?page=NewsArticle&id=12723&news_iv_ctrl=-1.

Cronin, Aisling Maria. "6 Reasons Why I No Longer Visit Zoos, Marine Parks, or Any Other Facility That Displays Animals." October 28, 2016. Accessed 10/28/16. http://www.onegreenplanet.org/animalsandnature/why-i-no-longer-visit-marine-parks-or-zoos/.

Dane, Keith. "Op-Ed: How to Stop the Cruelest Horse Show on Earth." The Humane Society of the United States, November 5, 2014. Accessed 11/8/14. http://www.alternet.org/op-ed-how-stop-cruelest-horse-show-earth.

Davis, Karen. "Perdue's Chickens: Could Their Lives Be Made Less Miserable?" *United Poultry Concerns.* Accessed 7/5/16. http://www.upc-online.org/broiler/160705perdues_chickens_misery.html.

Dear, John. "The Only Diet for a Peacemaker Is a Vegetarian Diet." *National Catholic Reporter*, July 12, 2008. Accessed July 12, 2008. http://www.alternet.org/story/91237.

Dorman, Robin. "Invented Fear and Injustice We Wrongly Place on Pit Bulls." In Defense of Animals, October 30, 2016. Accessed 10/30/16. http://www.onegreenplanet.org/animalsandnature/invented-fear-and-injustice-we-wrongly-place-on-pit-bulls/.

Dylewsky, Kate. "Downloading Cruelty: An Investigation into the Online Sales of Exotic Pets in the U.S." Washington, DC: Born Free USA, 2016.

Elgin, Beckie. "Sustainable Sabotage: Activists Use New Tactics to Thwart Animal Trophy Hunters." *Earth Island Journal*, January 4, 2016. Accessed 1/5/16. http://www.alternet.org/comments/environment/sustainable-sabotage-animal-activists-use-new-tactics-thwart-trophy-hunters.

Environmental Working Group. "Wasted Food Is a Major Source of Emissions." Accessed 9/29/16. http://www.ewg.org/meateatersguide/a-meat-eaters-guide-to-climate-change-health-what-you-eat-matters/wasted-food-is-a-major-source-of-emissions/.

Environmental Working Group. "Climate and Environmental Impacts." Accessed 9/29/16. http://www.ewg.org/meateatersguide/a-meat-eaters-guide-to-climate-change-health-what-you-eat-matters/climate-and-environmental-impacts/.

Farm Sanctuary. "Cattle Raised for Dairy and Meat Production." Accessed 10/17/16. http://
    www.farmsanctuary.org/learn/factory-farming/dairy/.
Feeding America. "Food Waste in America." Accessed 12/5/16. http://www.feedingamerica.
    org/about-us/how-we-work/securing-meals/reducing-food-waste.html.
Flores, Dan. "Stop Killing Coyotes." *New York Times*. August 11, 2016. Accessed 8/12/16.
    http://www.nytimes.com/2016/08/11/opinion/stop-killing-coyotes.html?_r=0.
Food and Agriculture Organization of the United Nations. "Major Cuts of Greenhouse Gas
    Emissions from Livestock within Reach." Accessed 9/29/16. http://www.fao.org/news/
    story/en/item/197608/icode/.
Foundation   for   Homeless   Cats.   "About   Us."   Accessed   6/29/16.   http://
    www.thefoundationforhomelesscats.org/about/.
Foundation   for   Homeless   Cats.   "FAQS."   Accessed   6/29/16.   http://
    www.thefoundationforhomelesscats.org/faqs.
Francione, Gary L. "The Abolitionist Approach to Animal Rights and Veganism as the Moral
    Baseline." *Turning Points in Compassion*, edited by Gypsy Wulff and Fran Chambers,
    146–153. Australia: SpiritWings Humane Education Inc., 2015.
Free from Harm. Accessed 10/17/16. http://www.freefromharm.org.
Good, Kate. "We Can Save the Planet with Plant-based Food . . . Find Out How." Septem-
    ber 16, 2016. Accessed 9/16/16.
Goodman, Leslee. "Advocating for the Souls of Animals." *The MOON Magazine*. Accessed 5/
    26/15. http://moonmagazine.org/advocating-souls-animals-interview-gay-bradshaw-2015-
    01-03/.
Go Vegan World. Accessed 6/29/16. http://www.GoVeganWorld.com.
Groden, Claire. "Report: Plastic Pollution in the Ocean Is Reaching Crisis Levels." *Fortune*,
    October   1,   2015.   Accessed   12/5/16.   http://fortune.com/2015/10/01/ocean-plastic-
    pollution/.
Gunn, Andrea. "Effective Activism: How to Create Big Change for Animals in Our Everyday
    Lives." Accessed 12/13/16. http://plantpuresummit.com/speaker-andrea-gunn.
Gustin, Georgina. "Factory Farms Get Bigger, Pollution Grows, but Regulators Don't Even
    Know Where They Are." *InsideClimate News*, October 21, 2016. Accessed 10/21/16.
    https://insideclimatenews.org/news/19102016/cafo-epa-regulations-factory-farms-get-
    bigger-pollution-grows-environmental-impact-methane.
Gustin, Georgina. "New Project Aims to Lure People Away from Meat, to a Climate-
    Healthier Diet." *InsideClimate News*. December 22, 2016. Accessed 12/23/16. https://
    insideclimatenews.org/news/22122016/meat-consumption-diet-plants-climate-change.
Hedges, Chris. "Chris Hedges: I've Gone Vegan to Help Try to Save the Planet." *Truthdig*,
    November 10, 2014. Accessed 12/1/14. http://www.alternet.org/environment/chris-
    hedges-ive-gone-vegan-help-try-save-planet.
Hernandez, Arelis R., Angela Fritz, and Chris Mooney. "Factory Farming Practices Under
    Scrutiny Again in North Carolina after Disastrous Hurricane Floods." *Washington Post*,
    October 16, 2016. Accessed 10/18/16. https://www.washingtonpost.com/news/capital-
    weather-gang/wp/2016/10/16/factory-farming-practices-are-under-scrutiny-again-in-n-c-
    after-disastrous-hurricane-floods/.
Homeless Animal Rescue Team. Accessed 10/21/15. http://www.hart-az.org.
Humane Research Council. "Animal Tracker—Year 8." Accessed 7/5/16. https://faunalytics.
    org/wp-content/uploads/2015/06/Animal-Tracker-Year-8-Topline-Report-Final.pdf.
Humane Society International. "About Animal Testing." Accessed 10/3/16. http://www.hsi.
    org/campaigns/end_animal_testing/qa/about.html.
Humane Society of the United States. "Pets by the Numbers." Accessed 6/30/16. http://www.
    humanesociety.org/issues/pet_overpopulation/facts/pet_ownership_statistics.html.
Humane Society of the United States. "Puppy Mills: Facts and Figures." Accessed 10/21/16.
    http://www.humanesociety.org/assets/pdfs/pets/puppy_mills/puppy-mills-facts-and-fig-
    ures.pdf.
Humane Society of the United States, "Why You Should Spay/Neuter Your Pet." Accessed 8/
    5/16.   http://www.humanesociety.org/issues/pet_overpopulation/facts/why_spay_neuter.
    html.

Humane Society of the United States. "Clark, Ros-Lehtinen Bill Protects Domestic Violence Victims and Pets." March 5, 2015. Accessed 12/1/15. http://www.humanesociety.org/news/press_releases/2015/03/domestic-violence-and-pets-030515.html?credit=web_id95800657.

Humane Society of the United States. "Wildlife Disservice." Accessed 8/20/16. http://www.humanesociety.org/issues/lethal_wildlife_management/facts/usda-wildlife-services-inefficient-and-inhumane.html.

Humane Society of the United States. "The Facts About Horse Slaughter." Accessed 6/30/16. http://www.humanesociety.org/issues/horse_slaughter/facts/facts_horse_slaughter.html.

Humane Society of the United States. "Cockfighting Fact Sheet." Accessed 11/14/16. http://www.humanesociety.org/issues/cockfighting/facts/cockfighting_fact_sheet.html.

Humane Society of the United States. "Authorities Bust Major Cockfighting Pit in Alabama." August 4, 2016. Accessed 8/23/16. http://www.humanesociety.org/news/press_releases/2016/08/alabama-cockfighting-bust-080416.html.

Ironwood Pig Sanctuary. Accessed 10/18/16. http://www.ironwoodpigsanctuary.org.

Jackson, David, and Gary Marx. "Whipped, Kicked, Beaten: Illinois Workers Describe Abuse of Hogs." *Chicago Tribune*, August 4, 2016. Accessed 8/8/16. http://www.chicagotribune.com/news/watchdog/pork/ct-pig-farms-abuse-met-20160802-story.html.

Jewish Veg. "How Does Judaism Say We Should Treat Animals?" Accessed 7/5/16. http://jewishveg.org/faq-how-does-judaism-say-we-should-treat-animals.

Joy, Melanie. *Why We Love Dogs, Eat Pigs, and Wear Cows.* San Francisco, CA: Conari Press, 2011.

Katsnelson, Alla. "A Conversation with Amy Clippinger." *ACS Cent. Sci.* 2 (2016): 432–433. Accessed July 12, 2016. DOI: 10.1021/acscentsci.6b00186.

Kavin, Kim. *The Dog Merchants: Inside the Big Business of Breeders, Pet Stores, and Rescuers.* New York: Pegasus Books, 2016.

Kirby, David. "What Freedom Could Look Like for SeaWorld's Killer Whales." *TakePart*, June 18, 2016. Accessed 6/20/16. http://www.ecowatch.com/what-freedom-could-look-like-for-seaworlds-killer-whales-1891174888.html.

Last Chance for Animals. "Fur Trade Facts." Accessed 7/3/16. http://www.lcanimal.org/index.php/campaigns/fur/fur-trade-facts.

Lenihann, Seann. "Stop Dogfighting by Addressing Supply Side Economics." *Animal People.* November 20, 2013. Accessed 9/1/14. http://newspaper.animalpeopleforum.org/2013/10/01/stop-dogfighting-by-addressing-supply-side-economics/.

Lohan, Tara. "Got Milk? A Disturbing Look at the Dairy Industry." AlterNet, January 26, 2010. Accessed 1/26/10. http://www.alternet.org/story/145378/.

Loki, Reynard. "The 3 Most Environmentally Damaging Habits You Might Be Able to Change." AlterNet. April 14, 2016. Accessed 4/14/16. http://www.alternet.org/environment/3-most-environmentally-damaging-habits-you-might-be-able-change.

Luna, Jenny. "Americans Are Gorging Themselves on Cheap Meat." *Mother Jones.* March 30, 2016. Accessed 6/13/16. http://www.motherjones.com/environment/2016/03/us-increase-meat-consumption-europe-less-meat-sustainability.

Maricopa County Animal Care and Control. "Annual Report FY2015." Accessed 8/13/16. http://www.maricopa.gov/pets/pdf/annualreports/annualreport_12212015.pdf.

MarketWatch. "This Chart Proves Americans Love Their Meat." December 1, 2016. Accessed 9/6/16. http://www.marketwatch.com/story/this-chart-proves-americans-love-their-meat-2016-08-15.

Masri, Lena. "Want to Hunt Exotic African Animals? Just Go to Texas." *Reuters.* August 25, 2015. Accessed 8/28/15. http://readersupportednews.org/opinion2/277-75/32057-want-to-hunt-exotic-african-animals-just-go-to-texas.

Mercy for Animals. *Planet Earth.* Accessed 9/29/16. https://www.youtube.com/watch?v=9seoBrcbxYA.

Mishkin, Jaime. "Arizona Ends Greyhound Racing—Now Hundreds of Dogs Are Looking for Forever Homes." May 10, 2016. Accessed 12/7/16. http://www.onegreenplanet.org/news/arizona-ends-greyhound-racing/.

Mitra, Maureen Nandini. "Serious Question: Should Humans Extend Personhood to Animals?" *Earth Island Journal*. December 5, 2016. Accessed 12/10/14. http://www.alternet. org/environment/serious-question-should-humans-extend-personhood-animals.

Monbiot, George. "Pregnant Silence." November 19, 2015. Accessed 11/23/15. http://www. monbiot.com/2015/11/19/pregnant-silence.

Moore, Heather. "A Record-Setting Year for PETA's Mobile Spay/Neuter Clinics!" Accessed 1/23/16. http://www.peta.org/blog/a-record-setting-year-for-petas-mobile-spayneuter-clinics/.

Moss, Donny. "Cecil Lives On: Connecting the Dots Between One Lion and Billions of Suffering Animals." *Their Turn*. July 31, 2015. Accessed 8/4/15. http://www.alternet.org/ environment/i-am-cecil-connecting-dots-between-one-lion-and-billions-suffering-animals.

National Anti-Vivisection Society. "Fewer Americans View Animal Testing as Morally Acceptable." Accessed 7/5/16. http://www.navs.org/gallup_2016/.

Netherlands National Committee for the Protection of Animals Used for Scientific Purposes. "Opinion Provided by NCad as to How the Netherlands Can Become a Pioneer in No-Animal Research." December 15, 2016. Accessed 12/22/16. https://english.ncadierproevenbeleid.nl/latest/news/16/12/15/ncad-opinion-transition-to-non-animal-research.

Newport, Frank. "In U.S., 5 Percent Consider Themselves Vegetarians." July 26, 2012. Accessed 9/6/16. http://www.gallup.com/poll/156215/Consider-Themselves-Vegetarians. aspx.

Nieves, Evelyn. "Zeroing In on Sociopaths: Feds Finally Make Animal Cruelty a Top-Tier Felony." AlterNet. October 10, 2014. Accessed 10/19/14. http://www.alternet.org/feds-finally-make-animal-cruelty-group-felony.

Nieves, Evelyn. "5 Horrific Ways People Mistreat Animals." AlterNet. February 4, 2015. Accessed 2/7/15. http://www.alternet.org/5-horrific-ways-people-mistreat-animals.

Nixon, Rob. "Future Footprints." Review of *The Human Age*, by Diane Ackerman. *New York Times*, September 5, 2014. https://www.nytimes.com/2014/09/07/books/review/the-human-age-by-diane-ackerman.html?_r=0.

No Kill Advocacy Center. "Defining No Kill." Accessed 8/1/16. http:// www.nokilladvocacycenter.org/defining-no-kill.html.

No-Kill Los Angeles. Accessed 10/26/16. http://nkla.org/.

One Green Planet. "Deforestation in the Amazon Is Up by 29 Percent and Our Appetite for Meat Is Largely to Blame." December 1, 2016. Accessed 12/1/16. http://www. onegreenplanet.org/news/deforestation-in-the-amazon-is-up-cattle-ranching/.

Oppenlander, Richard A. *Comfortably Unaware*. New York: Beaufort Books, 2012.

Pacelle, Wayne. *The Humane Economy*. New York: HarperCollins, 2016.

Pasha-Robinson, Lucy. "Hundreds of Animal Species 'Being Consumed to Extinction.'" October 19, 2016. Accessed 10/20/16. http://www.independent.co.uk/environment/nature/hundreds-animal-species-consumed-extinction-a7369421.html.

Patton, Lindsay. "Why We Need 'Crazy' Cat People." October 8, 2016. Accessed 10/9/16. http://www.onegreenplanet.org/animalsandnature/why-we-need-crazy-cat-people/.

Pennisi, Elizabeth. "People Are Hunting Primates, Bats, and Other Mammals to Extinction." October 18, 2016. Accessed 10/22/16. http://www.sciencemag.org/news/2016/10/people-are-hunting-primates-bats-and-other-mammals-extinction.

People for the Ethical Treatment of Animals (PETA). "Spaying and Neutering: A Solution for Suffering." Accessed 8/1/16. http://www.peta.org/issues/companion-animal-issues/companion-animals-factsheets/spaying-neutering-solution-suffering/.

People for the Ethical Treatment of Animals (PETA). "The Deadly Consequences of 'No-Kill' Policies." Accessed 7/11/16. http://www.peta.org/features/deadly-consequences-no-kill-policies/.

Petco. "The Petco Foundation." Accessed 8/15/16. http://www.petco.com/petco-foundation.

Petfinder. "Animal Shelter & Rescues for Pet Adoption." Accessed 8/15/16. http://www. petfinder.com/animal-shelters-and-rescues.

PetSmart Charities. "Our Impact in 2015." Accessed 8/15/16. https://www.petsmartcharities. org/our-impact.

Philpott, Tom. "We Have Terrible News for Anyone Who Eats Chicken." *Mother Jones*. June 22, 2016. Accessed 6/22/16. http://motherjones.com/environment/2016/06/salmonella-chicken-usda-supermarket-inspection-flawed.

Piazza, Jared, and Steve Loughnan. "When Meat Gets Personal, Animals' Minds Matter Less: Motivated Use of Intelligence Information in Judgments of Moral Standing." *Social Psychological and Personality Science* (2016): 1–8. Accessed July 22, 2016. doi: 10.1177/ 1948550616660159.

Piazza, Jared, Matthew B. Ruby, Steve Loughnan, Mischel Luong, Juliana Kulik, Hanne M. Watkins, and Mirra Seigerman. "Rationalizing Meat Consumption. The 4Ns." *Appetite* 91: 114–128. Accessed 6/20/16. doi: 10.1016/j.appet.2015.04.011.

The Pig Preserve. Accessed 10/18/16. http://www.thepigpreserve.org.

Pittman, Arianna. "All You Need to Know About the No-Kill Movement to Help Save Animals in Your Local Shelter." September 9, 2016. Accessed 9/19/16. http://www. onegreenplanet.org/animalsandnature/how-no-kill-movement-is-saving-animals-in-shelter/.

Prideaux, Margi. "Zoos Are the Problem, Not the Solution, to Animal Conservation." *Open Democracy*. June 30, 2016. Accessed 7/8/16, http://www.alternet.org/zoos-are-problem-not-solution-animal-conservation.

Prupis, Nadia. "FBI to Track Animal Abuse Like Homicide—But Which Animals?" *Common Dreams*. January 8, 2016. Accessed 1/10/16. http://www.commondreams.org/news/2016/ 01/08/fbi-track-animal-abuse-homicide-which-animals.

Putois, Anissa. "Why Wild Horses Are Being Pitted Against Cows and Will Likely Not Survive as a Result." July 15, 2016. Accessed 7/15/16. http://www.onegreenplanet.org/ environment/why-wild-horses-are-being-pitted-against-cows/.

Putois, Anissa. "These Aren't Clouds, They're 300 Football Fields Worth of Flames Caused by Our Snacks." June 7, 2016. Accessed 10/13/16. http://www.onegreenplanet.org/ environment/palm-oil-is-causing-football-fields-worth-of-flames/.

Research and Markets. "Global Luggage and Leather Goods Industry 2014-2019: Trends, Profits, and Forecast Analysis." Accessed 6/29/16. http://researchandmarkets.com/reports/ 2965421/global-luggage-and-leather-goods-industry-2014.

Riffkin, Rebecca. "In U.S., More Say Animals Should Have Same Rights as People." Accessed 8/17/15. http://www.gallup.com/poll/183275/say-animals-rights-people.aspx.

Robinson, Michael. "3.2 Million Animals Killed by Federal Wildlife-Destruction Program in 2015." Center for Biological Diversity. June 24, 2016. Accessed 6/24/16. http:// readersupportednews.org/news-section2/318-66/37628-32-million-animals-killed-by-federal-wildlife-destruction-program-in-2015.

Rosenberg, Martha, and Ronnie Cummins. "Time to Drive Factory Farmed Food Off the Market." *Organic Consumers Association*. October 3, 2016. Accessed 10/6/16. http:// www.alternet.org/food/end-factory-farmed-food.

Roth, Anna. "What You Need to Know About the Corporate Shift to Cage-Free Eggs." January 28, 2016. Accessed 1/30/16. http://civileats.com/2016/01/28/what-you-need-to-know-about-the-corporate-shift-to-cage-free-eggs/.

Sentenac, Hannah. "Exclusive: Research Suggests 36 Percent of Americans Open to Plant-Based Eating." *Latest Vegan News*. May 27, 2015. Accessed 9/3/16. http:// latestvegannews.com/research-suggests-36-of-americans-open-to-plant-based-eating/#.

Sentenac, Hannah. "Vegan Meat Now Available in over 23,000 Stores Nationwide." *Latest Vegan News*, June 21, 2016. Accessed 9/3/16. http://latestvegannews.com/vegan-meat-available-23000-stores-nationwide/#.

Sentenac, Hannah. "Plant-Based Food Named a Top Trend for 2016." December 31, 2015. Accessed 9/11/16. http://latestvegannews.com/plant-based-food-named-top-trend-2016/.

Sentenac, Hannah. "Vegan Google Searches Climb 32 Percent from 2014 to 2015." *Latest Vegan >News*. January 20, 2016. Accessed 9/11/16. http://latestvegannews.com/vegan-google-searches-climb-32-2014-2015/.

Sheridan, Kerry. "Circus Elephants' Retirement Home Promises Pampered Life," May 2, 2016. Accessed 8/20/16. http://phys.org/news/2016-05-circus-elephants-home-pampered-life.html.

Spay-Neuter Assistance Program. "Overpopulation Facts." Accessed 8/5/16. http://snapus.org/spay-neuter-facts/overpopulation-facts.html.

Spay-Neuter Assistance Program. "Health Benefits." Accessed 8/5/16. http://www.snapus.org/spay-neuter-facts/spay-neuter-health-benefits.html.

Specialty Food Association. "Meatless-Meat Industry Gains Ground, Market Share." May 13, 2015. Accessed 9/11/16. https://www.specialtyfood.com/news/article/meatless-meat-industry-prepares-growth/.

Stafford, Rick. "How Overfishing and Shark-finning Could Increase the Pace of Climate Change." *The Conversation.* October 27, 2016. Accessed 11/5/16. https://theconversation.com/how-overfishing-and-shark-finning-could-increase-the-pace-of-climate-change-67664.

Taco Bell. "How to Eat Vegetarian and Meatless at Taco Bell." Accessed 9/11/16. https://tacobell.com/feed/how-to-eat-veggie.

Taft, Casey T. *Motivational Methods for Vegan Advocacy.* Danvers, MA: Vegan Publishers, 2016.

Taft, Casey. "Psychology and Long-Term Goals in Vegan Advocacy." June 26, 2016. Accessed 7/21/16. http://freefromharm.org/animal-advocacy/casey-taft-book-excerpt.

TIME staff. "Wildlife Populations Have Dropped by Almost 60 percent in Forty Years, WWF Says." *TIME.* October 27, 2016. Accessed 10/27/16. http://time.com/4547132/wildlife-population-decline-wwf/.

Tranquility Trail Animal Sanctuary. "Bunny Care." Accessed 8/7/16. http://www.tranquilitytrail.org/RabbitCare.html.

United Poultry Concerns. Accessed 10/17/16. http://www.upc-online.org.

Vegetarian Times. "Vegetarianism in America." Accessed 9/6/16. http://www.vegetariantimes.com/article/vegetarianism-in-america/.

Wilson, Kim. "What It Takes to Be a No-Kill Shelter." *Humanely Speaking.* (Summer 2015).

Winograd, Nathan J. "Revisiting the No Kill Equation." Accessed 10/26/16. http://www.nathanwinograd.com/?p=1832.

Wulff, Gypsy, and Fran Chambers, eds. *Turning Points in Compassion.* Australia: Spirit-Wings Humane Education Inc., 2015.

INDEX

ABOUT THE AUTHOR

Lori B. Girshick, PhD, is a retired sociology professor. She has dedicated her life to working for social justice and ending inequalities. She is author of several books, including *Soledad Women: Wives of Prisoners Speak Out*; *No Safe Haven: Stories of Women in Prison*; *Woman-to-Woman Sexual Violence: Does She Call It Rape?*; and *Transgender Voices: Beyond Women and Men*. Girshick, also an animal rights activist for over thirty years, volunteers for animal rights/protection organizations, including Wildhorse Ranch Rescue, Fearless Kitty Rescue, Factory Farming Awareness Coalition, Vegan Outreach, and Homeless Animal Rescue Team (HART).